My Europe

By the same Author

Memoirs of a British Agent (1932)
Retreat from Glory (1934)
Return to Malaya (1936)
My Scottish Youth (1937)
Guns or Butter (1938)
Comes the Reckoning (1947)
The Marines were There (1950)
Scotch (1951)

With Dropmore Press

My Rod My Comfort (1949)
Jan Masaryk: A Personal Memoir (1951)

Sir Robert Bruce Lockhart

My Europe

PUTNAM

42 Great Russell Street

LONDON

First published 1952

Printed in Great Britain by
Wyman & Sons, Limited, London, Fakenham and Reading

Contents

I

RUSSIAN POSTSCRIPT

II

RETREAT FROM PRAGUE

Contents

III

HOPES AND FEARS IN THE WEST

My Europe

BOOK I

RUSSIAN POSTSCRIPT

"It is not possible for all things to be well unless all men are good, which I think will not be for these many years."

THOMAS MORE. 1516.

Chapter I

MOSCOW BEFORE THE WARS

"Other nations have endured oppression; the Russian nation loved it and loves it still."
MARQUIS DE CUSTINE. Moscow, August 8, 1839.

RUSSIA has been the dominant influence in my life. Try as I will, I cannot escape from it. I was twenty-four when, as a junior Vice-Consul, I first went to Moscow at the end of 1911. In October, 1918, I was expelled from the country under the escort of a Bolshevik praetorian guard and, later, was tried in my absence and condemned to death. Since then I have not been back, and nowadays, whenever I am introduced on a public platform, the chairman rarely fails to point out that in September 1918, I was imprisoned in the Kremlin and that, when I was in danger of my life, the British Government arrested Maxim Litvinov, then the Bolshevik representative in London, and eventually succeeded in exchanging him for me. On these occasions my friends point out that His Majesty's Government made a bad bargain. Usually I smile sheepishly, but inwardly I feel an acute embarrassment and sometimes a sense of guilt.

Russia was the scene of my youthful rise and fall, and even today she haunts me like an unfaithful mistress whom I cannot discard. The experience has affected my subsequent career, my character, and my attitude to life. It has given me confidence and fears, disgust and tolerance, an unrealised desire to forget, and a constantly recurring and at times almost uncontrollable longing to return. Even today my strongest feeling is affection for that country, with its wide horizons and boundless fields of corn shimmering into a golden infinity, and for its people, unrivalled in attractiveness as individuals and, in the mass, cruel beyond Western imagination. I still follow diligently the pattern of Russia's political development.

I quote reams of Russian poetry learnt by heart in those early days and I read everything Russian that I can buy. After thirty-three years of absence I can visualise the Moscow scene as if I were present. I do not lack entirely the canniness of the Scot, but I am still affected by the Russian passion for extremes to the point of sometimes accepting as a reproach my own adherence to the less exacting middle way.

This Russian passion for extremes ranges from energy to laziness, from violence to submissive indifference, and from selfless generosity and an infinite capacity for sacrifice to almost incredible egotism and ingratitude. To some extent at least, these characteristics spring from the influence of climate on temperament. As Kliuchevsky, the fairest and most eminent of all Russian historians, wrote: "There is no people in Europe more capable of a tremendous effort for a short space of time than the Great Russian, but there is also no people less accustomed to regular, sustained, unceasing labour than this same Great Russian."

In spite of the convulsions which the country has undergone, these characteristics have not changed substantially. They explain why throughout their long history the Russians have so often been ruled by foreigners. Nevertheless, it is his readiness at certain indeterminable moments to sacrifice everything for a single idea, or even a whim like gambling, which makes the Russian so attractive a companion and so intractable a negotiator.

My Russian life divides itself neatly into three sections: the two-and-a-half years before the First World War; the war years and the first revolution; and the year 1918 when I was head of the first British Mission to the Bolshevik Government. When I arrived in Moscow in January 1912, I knew even less of the country and its people than the average British subject of my age. I remembered, as a small boy, my father telling me a thrilling story of a Russian landowner who, pursued in his sleigh by a pack of wolves, threw himself to them and by this self-sacrifice gained time for his daughter to escape. At school I had read the novels of Wishaw and Seton Merriman and a little later I was entranced by Harry de Windt's *Through Savage Europe*. All three authors portrayed Russia as a land of mystery and intrigue in which abounded secret agents, beautiful spies, and fierce bearded Cossacks, armed with leaded whips called "nagaikas". I gained the impression that almost anything could happen to the innocent new arrival, from sharing a twin-berth sleeper with a fascinating blonde to losing his passport and finding himself in Siberia. Soon after my arrival the sturdy Lancashiremen who formed the nucleus of the British colony in Moscow told me that these yarns bore no relation to the realities of Russian life. Disillusioned, I accepted their advice and made up my mind to form my own impressions.

When I think back today, I realise that we erred seriously in regarding Seton Merriman as a mere spinner of dreams. Few foreigners have written so prophetically of Russia as this studious and shy Scot, who changed his name to Merriman in order to prevent his stern father from knowing that his son was engaged in writing novels instead of studying shipping. Already in the eighteen-nineties Merriman foresaw the revolution, predicted a Terror worse than France had ever experienced, and foretold accurately both the defensive strength of a country in which there is always room to retreat and the latent power in the Russian people for national aggrandisement. His *The Sowers* and *Barlasch of the Guard* contain many shrewd observations on the Russian character and the Russian way of life. "In this country," he wrote, in *The Sowers*, "the less you find, the less you see, the less you understand, the simpler is your existence." It is a precept which ninety per cent of the people of Soviet Russia have learnt to follow through bitter experience. Incidentally *The Sowers* was published in 1896 and went through thirty-one editions.

As I soon discovered, the truth was that in Tsarist Russia there were two forms of existence. As long as one kept rigidly aloof from politics and never even discussed them, life was free, and there were no restrictions to pleasure and indulgence except the limits of one's purse. On the other hand, the bulk of the intelligentsia was politically minded and opposed to the régime. Its sympathies ranged from Western Liberalism to the extreme forms of revolutionary Socialism. The secret police, never wholly free from corruption, kept a detailed record of these political malcontents and watched them with variable vigilance. When I arrived in Moscow in January 1912, Lenin was presiding over a Bolshevik Conference in Prague. Stalin, who had recently completed a term of imprisonment, was living under police supervision in Vologda. Except to the secret police and a small circle of revolutionary Marxists, he was completely unknown, and until the Bolshevik revolution I never heard him mentioned either by his real name of Djugashvilli or as Stalin, Koba, or the other baker's dozen of aliases with which he had already cloaked his identity.

For purposes of police supervision the population of Tsarist Russia was divided into four classes: Dvorianin (nobleman), Kupets (merchant), Mieschanin (artisan) and Krestianin (peasant). Every Russian had to carry a passport, and every passport-holder was registered under one or other of the four categories. Apart from the titled aristocracy, the classification of "dvorianin" was acquired automatically by promotion to high rank in the civil and military services and became hereditary. To quote only one example, Lenin's father attained the rank of Inspector-General in the Ministry of Education and automatically acquired "nobility". In this manner Lenin's own passport bore the classification of "dvorianin".

In Moscow, then the commercial capital of Russia, members of the titled aristocracy were few in number and kept severely to themselves. Officialdom was represented by the Prefect, in my time always a General, by the Governor of the Moscow province, and by the General Officer Commanding the Moscow Military District. Wealth and luxury were provided by the rich manufacturers and merchants who had a monopoly of the important post of Mayor of Moscow. The intelligentsia formed a society of its own, although its members, drawn from the professional and intellectual classes, were registered on their passports under one of the four official classifications. Far below came the illiterate masses forming nearly seventy-five per cent of the whole population.

Tsarist Moscow, less beautiful in its architecture, but in the warmth of its heart more endearing than St. Petersburg, was a vast village sprawling round a city, half modern and half medieval, the centre of which was the Kremlin. It was a town of churches and factories. The dazzling blue and gold cupolas of the churches were Byzantine; the chimneys of the factories were English. More, I imagine, by a happy accident than by design the Moscow river divided the church area of the Kremlin from the factory district. I fell in love with the town at once. I liked the gay colour of the churches, the richness of their interiors with the glittering altar gates, the golden crowns of the priests and the enchanting names of the ikons. One ikon in a little church built in the wall of the Kremlin was called "Our Lady of Unexpected Joy". I visited it often and it inspired one of the first sketches that I ever wrote. This ikon has a special place in my heart, for in September 1918, when I was a prisoner in the Kremlin and in the unpleasant vacuum between life and death, I prayed before it on my daily walk, while my Lettish guards stood by in silent contempt.

Most of all I liked the snow-roads and the silence of the winter traffic which, apart from the trams and a few motor-cars, moved entirely on horse-sleighs. The passenger sleighs were built for two but were so tiny that to avoid falling out one had to hold one's companion firmly by the waist. Most of the horses were good, and, if well-paid, the Moscow drivers, genial bearded fellows for the most part and often humorous philosophers, were always ready to race. Hiring was a matter of bargaining which most foreigners found irksome. I enjoyed it. When I wanted a sleigh, I signalled from the pavement and walked ahead. A driver drove up alongside. "Theatre Place—forty copecks," I would say and continue walking. "Ech, master, eighty copecks," the driver would reply and keep pace with me. Finally we would agree on sixty copecks, and with a ten copeck tip at the end the driver would be all smiles. Best of all were the winter nights when the sky was ablaze with stars and the frost, sharp as a razor, set one's cheeks tingling and made the snow beneath the horse's shoes sparkle like diamonds. In July and August Moscow was an inferno of heat. In winter it was a fairy-land of romance and adventure, and I was young with wild Celtic blood in my veins.

On the other hand, I could not help being startled by the glaring contrasts between wealth and poverty. The poor were with one always; especially in the streets which were full of wretchedly clad beggars and vodka-addicts who had become sub-human. Judged even by American standards, the wealth was great. It sprang from

the Russian industrial revolution which, starting much later than
the English prototype, brought large fortunes to its pioneers. In
particular, Moscow had become the centre of a flourishing textile
industry. The early Russian manufacturers were mostly of peasant
origin and wore the long Russian boots which are familiar to the
world today in the photographs of Stalin. These served as purses
in which the new rich stuffed their rouble notes. From this period
dates the reign of Baron Knop, the Russo-German millionaire, who
by importing English machinery and Lancashire technicians did
more to foster the Russian textile industry than any other man.
When I first came to Moscow, there was a popular jingle which ran:

"There is no church without its pope,
No factory without its Knop."

The men of Lancashire prospered. From manager to the heads
of the various technical departments, they ran the factories while
the sons and grandsons of the Russian magnates built themselves
palatial mansions, travelled abroad, had their wives painted by
leading artists and patronised literature and music. It was a Moscow
textile king who first discovered Chaliapin, then a young man hauling
a barge on the Volga, and gave him his chance to prove himself
as a singer in a Moscow opera house financed by Moscow manufacturers. Two other magnates had world-famous collections of
the French Impressionists. Nearly all were boundless in their hospitality, but manufacturer entertained manufacturer and only on
rare occasions stepped out of his merchant class to give an official
banquet. Few of the Moscow merchants and manufacturers spoke
English. Most of them and all the senior officials spoke French, but
in a business city German was by far the best-known foreign language. The German Consulate-General was easily the most imposing of the foreign Consular offices and the German Consul-
General was the only Consular officer who gave and received
hospitality on a large scale.

In this respect Consular officers of other countries held a humble
position with little or no personal contact with their own embassies,
and of the Great Powers Britain alone had no Consulate-General.

Indeed, Major Montgomery Grove, my first chief, was the first career Consul ever to be appointed to a post which, opened as a Vice-Consulate in 1889, had been held until 1901 by a local British merchant called Arthur Medhurst.

Grove was a tactful and kind chief with a sound knowledge of Russian, but, like most British Consuls in those days, he suffered from three handicaps: a rich and prosperous British colony, a salary and office allowance barely sufficient to support his own existence, let alone permit the services of a clerk, and an unfortunate legacy from his predecessor. During the Boer War Medhurst had been the victim of an unpleasant incident. At an official party at which the Grand Duke Serge and the Grand Duchess Elizabeth were present a young Russian officer sitting opposite Medhurst raised his glass and proposed a toast to "the gallant Boers". The remark was not made demonstratively, and only a few people could have heard it, but, rightly or wrongly, Medhurst left the table and went home.

The incident caused much gossip and some ill-feeling. The Grand Duchess Elizabeth, a grand-daughter of Queen Victoria, took drastic measures against the young Russian officer. The Foreign Office defended Medhurst by keeping him at his post until the gossip had died down, but decided that in future Moscow must have a Consul *de carrière*. Incidentally, the Grand Duke Serge was assassinated in Moscow during the abortive revolution of 1905–06. The Grand Duchess Elizabeth became a nun and devoted her life to good works until she was murdered by the Bolsheviks.

By tact and goodwill Grove improved our relations with the Russian officials with whom he became very popular. He was, however, in no position to compete in hospitality with the merchant princes and, preferring not to accept what he could not return, he lived a life of comparative seclusion.

Several times a year I put on uniform and attended Te Deums on the birthdays and name-days of the leading members of the Imperial Family and *Panikhidi* or memorial services for the decease of Imperial personages. From a seat in a window of the British Club I watched the Imperial procession when the Tsar rode to the Kremlin for the centenary anniversary of Borodino in 1912. It was a magnificent pageant, but the preparations for it were tedious

and affected even the British Consulate.   For weeks before the procession the police had pestered us with inquiries regarding the
reliability of almost every British subject who lived anywhere within
a mile of the Emperor's route.

Such occasions were rare: for the most part I was left to my
own devices with ample free time to satisfy my thirst for knowledge.
As a Vice-Consul I was not overworked.   I had most afternoons
and all my evenings to myself, and in the Moscow of 1912 there
was much to attract the curiosity of a young man.   There was far
more intellectual freedom in Tsarist Russia than in the Soviet
Union of today.   All the political parties had their own newspapers which, within certain limits, were free to criticize.   True,
there was a pre-publication censorship.   Objectionable articles or
paragraphs were "caviared", that is, smeared over with a caviare-
coloured paste.   It was not very effective, for the public soon learnt
or guessed what had been obliterated.   There was little restriction
of movement.   Prostitutes paraded the cafés and the streets.   In
front of the National Hotel deformed beggars thrust pornographic
postcards under your nose and followed you with persistent appeals
until in order to be rid of them you flung a "poltinik" (equivalent
of a shilling) at them.   In the evening there was the ballet or the
opera and the best drama in the world, and when the theatres
closed down the night haunts opened; garish, expensive palaces in
which every artiste was a lady of easy virtue and which stretched
in a long succession far out into the Petrovsky Park so that at the
end of a prolonged carousal the weary reveller could drive home
in a fast sleigh and let the keen frosty air restore him for his morning's
work.   Half Moscow lived by night.   The rich drank champagne
and concluded their best business deals in "Yar" or "Strelna" to the
seductive accompaniment of the gypsy singers.   For the wretched
poor there were low and lousy "Kabaks", foul hovels where a man
could drink himself stupid on vodka, a government monopoly
product which sold at a price of one shilling a bottle for the dearer
variety and sixpence a bottle for the cheaper and, in my opinion,
better sort.   The dearer bottle bore a blue label; the cheaper a
red one!

A night-out in Moscow did not appeal to all foreigners.   That redoubtable warrior General Carton de Wiart found it the most boring entertainment in the world and told me once that, as far as he could see, the average Russian's idea of perfect bliss was to sit up all night in a cabaret, drink gallons of champagne, listen to the dreariest wailing of so-called gypsies, gaze all night into the eyes of the pretty girl who made him spend his money, and then at six o'clock in the morning reach the height of his voluptuous melancholy when he saw her go off with another man. General Carton de Wiart, however, is a Polonophile. On the other hand, Maurice Baring loved gypsy music with all the passion of a poet and always prepared for the dangers of the night by attaching a label with his address to the collar of his fur coat. The precaution was wise. A night with the gypsies was a formidable test, for the exit from a stiflingly hot room into thirty degrees of frost was liable to upset even the strongest head.

Of course there was some truth in Carton de Wiart's criticism, but in this controversy I was on the side of Maurice Baring and the gypsy angels who, incidentally, always behaved with a decorum rarely observed in other Russian society. I went back more often than I should. Indeed, I realise today that I might have fallen dangerously to this curiously seductive combination of plaintive minor melody and sweet champagne which ruined so many of my Russian friends. Three influences, however, reasserted my Scottish caution: lack of money, a chance invitation to play football for a team of Russian workers, and my entry into the Ertel family. My salary as a Vice-Consul was £350 per annum. In my first week in Moscow I saw a young Russian friend, the son of a rich manufacturer, spend more than this sum on one gypsy party.

My football brought me into early touch with the cotton operatives of the large Vikul Morozov factory and provided both entertainment and useful experience. On my first night in Moscow I met Harry Charnock, the leading member of a Lancashire family long prominent in the Russian textile industry. As the managing director of the Vikul Morozov factory, Harry was an ardent believer in the educational value of football for the Russian worker who previously had been accustomed to spend his Sundays in drinking vodka and talking politics, He persuaded me to play for his factory team.   Our home ground at Oriechovo-Zuyevo, a purely industrial town about forty miles from Moscow, was splendidly equipped, and at the league matches the workers turned up in their thousands to follow the fortunes of the factory team.   At this time the "Morozovtsi" were just about the best team in Russia, and one of my few possessions which have survived fire, blitz, and burglary is my gold medal for the Moscow League Championship of 1912.   The team was composed of six Russians, four Lancashire lads, and one Scot in myself, and the star performers were Billy Charnock, the youngest brother of the managing director, and a Russian half-back called Akimov.   The team spirit was excellent, and the enthusiasm and behaviour of the spectators would have been an object lesson to many British crowds.

Sooner or later Stalin will claim "soccer" football as a Russian invention, but the truth is that in Russia the game was started by Englishmen and as a workers' team the "Morozovtsi" were the forerunners of the famous Dynamos, although of course the football was of a lower standard.   Indeed, not long before the First World War a team of London students came to play a picked Moscow eleven and won more or less as they liked.   At least two of the students distinguished themselves in later life: J. H. Lockton as an amateur footballer and a county cricketer, and Godfrey Ince, now Sir Godfrey, and Under-Secretary of the Ministry of Labour, as a civil servant.   It has always been Harry Charnock's conviction that, if football had been started in all Russian factories a quarter of a century sooner, the course of Russian history might have run differently.   It is not so wild a claim as it sounds.   By 1914 the Tsar had appointed a Minister of Sport, the first, I think, in history. Unfortunately, like everything else in a country where "seichas" (at once) meant—and probably still means—tomorrow and "zavtra" (tomorrow) meant never, the appointment came too late.

Apart from the Lancashiremen and other English firms connected with industry, Moscow, regarded rightly as the most Russian of cities, owed much of such modern luxury as it enjoyed to foreign enterprise.   The great confectioners of Moscow were French, and not even in France have I eaten such luscious cakes and chocolates. The three leading French firms, who also manufactured scents and soaps as a side line, ran elegant cafés in connexion with their business, and to these came the *élite* of Moscow, the wives of the rich merchants and the actresses and ballerinas, to discuss clothes or, more frequently perhaps, to gossip with their latest lover. The Germans, prominent in almost every aspect of the import business, monopolised the trade in music and musical instruments.

England and Scotland were represented more by quality than by quantity, but the quality was high and situated in the best part of the city. Adjacent to the Bolshoy Theatre was the great store of Muir and Mirrielees, the first and then only Harrods of Russia. On the Kuznetsky Most, the Bond Street of Moscow, was the shop of Shanks where at a price too high for me the finest luxury goods could be bought. Aylmer Maude, the biographer of Leo Tolstoy, once served in it until he married a Shanks. Greater than these, however, was the giant concern of William Miller & Co., whose activities ranged over the whole country. Begun as a partnership for the import of coal and herrings, it launched out later into local industry on a large scale. Although its headquarters were in St. Petersburg, it had in Moscow alone a great brewery, a factory for sweet mineral waters including a highly popular cranberry cordial, and the largest stearine works in the country. Among other products the stearine works supplied the faithful with the church candles which at Easter and, indeed, at all times they lit in great profusion.

In 1912 the chief shareholder of William Miller was the late W. M. Cazalet, father of the two well-known sportsmen Victor and Peter Cazalet, and of Mrs. Thelma Cazalet-Keir, the former member of Parliament and ardent advocate of equal pay for women. At that time W. M. Cazalet must have been a millionaire several times over. Even after the revolution, which ruined all the foreign enterprises in Russia, he remained a rich man with a lovely house at Fairlawne in Kent, and a racing stable which produced several winners. W. M. Cazalet's children were brought up in England, but Victor, whom I knew well and who was killed during the war in an aeroplane accident at Gibraltar, had visited Russia and spoke some Russian. There were also poorer relatives living in Moscow right up to the revolution.

The two-and-a-half-years before the First World War were the freest from care in my Russian existence. Too young and too unsophisticated to pre-occupy my mind with forebodings of war and revolution, I entered readily into the attractions of a life which, even after my experiences in Malaya and a voyage round the world, seems to me more exotic than that of the East and more enchanting than that of the New World. With much that was both good and bad, this life has now gone for ever, and with every month the number of foreigners who shared it grows fewer.

Chapter II

PRELUDE TO REVOLUTION

*"Civil troubles, and the casting down of thrones, are
always forewarned by want and poverty striking the people."*
JOHN GALT.

My knowledge of Russia is built in large measure on the
year and a half which I spent as a boarder and a pupil
with the Ertel family. If I were to be of any use to my
chief, I had to learn to read, write and type Russian as soon as
possible, and Montgomery Grove recommended me to Madame
Ertel, the widow of Alexander Ertel, the well-known novelist and
friend of Leo Tolstoy. She had a large flat in a modern house
not far from the Kremlin, and here in January 1912, I transferred
my few belongings and soon found myself at home. My room
looked out across the main street on a church with an azure cupola,
and in the far distance I could see the smoke from the factory stacks
in the "Across the River" district where lived the proletarians
whose acquaintance I was to make when they became the dictators
of the new Soviet society.

Madame Ertel was an excellent teacher with a thorough knowledge of Russian literature and of Russian literary life. Not content
with giving me a daily lesson, she treated me as one of the family.
In this manner I made my first acquaintance with the intelligentsia
which I soon found to be the most interesting section of Moscow
social life. As my knowledge of Russian improved, I gradually
got to know a wide circle of writers, painters, musicians, actors,
doctors and university professors, all of whom were Liberals or
Socialists and ardent advocates of parliamentary democracy.

At this time the intellectuals were going through a period of
acute depression. The failure of the 1905–6 revolution in which
some had taken part, and with which all sympathised, had enabled

the Tsarist régime to take back most of the reforms which it had
granted under pressure, and, bitterly disillusioned, most members of
the intelligentsia were suffering from an inertia of despair which
was reflected in their art and literature. In both it was the period
of the so-called decadents. Idealism was under a cloud, and, convinced that without a foreign war, which could put arms into the
hands of the people, a successful revolution was out of the question,
the intelligentsia resigned itself to a long period of reactionary
government and took refuge in a gloomy introspection. The mood
of the times in best illustrated by a remark made several years earlier
by Chekhov: "In Nature an ugly grub becomes a ravishing butterfly; with men it's just the other way round: a ravishing butterfly
becomes an ugly grub."

As far as politics were concerned, the pessimism of the intellectuals was justified. For years they had made it their duty
to bring culture and education to the people in order to prepare
them for reform and parliamentary government. Their work
had nearly always been frustrated by an autocracy which still
followed the precept of Pobedonostsev, the civilian head of the
Orthodox Church: "The more illiterate the people, the easier it
is to govern them." From this maxim, then already a quarter of a
century old, successive Tsarist governments departed only when
expediency demanded, returning to it always as soon as they felt
strong enough and curbing the activities of the intellectuals by censorship or banishment. There were few of the great Russian writers
who had not suffered in this manner. Now reaction was again in
the saddle, and the people who formed seventy-five per cent of
the whole population of Russia remained illiterate. Their lot was
hard.

In 1912 I witnessed the cautious celebration of the fiftieth
anniversary of the liberation of the serfs. There were long articles
on land reform in all the newspapers, but no demonstrations in the
street. Land reform, a plank in the platform of all the opposition
parties, was urgently necessary. Since 1862 the peasants had
doubled in number and the land which had been given them at the
time of their liberation remained the same. The intelligentsia were
helpless. Lenin, although later eager enough to enlist the services

of those intellectuals who were prepared to accept Bolshevism without questioning, despised them for what he called their bourgeois mentality.

If bourgeois they were according to Marxist dogma, they bore no resemblance to the bourgeoisie of Western Europe. Excluded from active political life by an intolerant Government, their own tolerance in all other matters was astonishing. Intensely serious and brilliantly intellectual, they talked the night out in endless discussion. Their conversation ranged over all the arts, science and every aspect of human life. No subject was barred. Suicide and sex were discussed as impartially as the weather and the state of the crops. Gossip rarely fouled their talk. The only scandals were political scandals. Free and easy in their morals, they despised everything that resembled cant. Although they admired the political liberties, they disliked English hypocrisy and regarded Byron and Oscar Wilde as the greatest of geniuses who had been shamefully persecuted and under-estimated by the English. I remember vividly the withering contempt with which the gentle Stanislavsky referred to the withdrawal of Wilde's *The Importance of Being Earnest* from the St. James's Theatre in London on the night of Wilde's conviction. Indeed, because of his persecution the Russians gave to Wilde a far higher place in world literature than he merits. In the Moscow of 1912 his plays were performed regularly, and his works, admirably translated, were available in a twopenny edition. In 1951, perhaps for the same reason, he shared with Shakespeare the honour of being the only British dramatist whose plays were allowed by Stalin to be presented on the Moscow stage.

It would be wrong on my part if I were to give the impression that the intelligentsia were lugubrious or over-burdened with their own cares. They had their full share of Russian humour, laughed heartily at their own jokes, and delighted in clever witticisms, especially when the shafts were directed against the Government. The *Russkiya Viedomosti*, their favourite organ, was then the best written newspaper in the world, partly perhaps because its contributors were adepts at circumventing the censors by literary metaphors which were above their heads. Nor were these Russian intellectuals in any respect lean and hungry ascetics. On the contrary, most of them fed and drank lustily and in "Butter-Week", which corresponds to the Catholic Carnival, and at Easter they vied with one another in the number of rich, caviare-stuffed pancakes and glasses of vodka that they could consume.

One rare and admirable virtue they possessed in larger measure than any other race. In almost every family there was one lame dog who had fallen from better days into poverty, generally through gambling or reckless extravagance. He was always treated as a member of the family, never as an incubus. If ever I asked what so-and-so was doing, the reply was always the same. "Ech, dear Nikolai Nikolaievitch, he is so good and kind. When he had money, he helped so many people."

Indeed, their open-handed generosity came naturally to most Russians. When they had money, they shared it. When it was gone, they felt no shame in asking it from others. "Shirokaya natura", the Russians called it, and expansive nature is a feeble translation. As for the intelligentsia, their mental horizons were as wide as their attitude towards life, and both were refreshingly free from any taint of intellectual and social snobbishness. Because education was limited to the few, its standard was remarkably high and was reflected in the bookshops which, subject to the political censorship, contained only the best literature of all countries. To start with at any rate, universal education brings a levelling down and a glut of trashy sex and crime novels. In Tsarist Russia every subject, bar politics, could be and was treated in all the arts with brutal frankness, but sensationalism made no appeal, and the kind of poll, which in 1951 returned Dorothy Sayers, Hugh Walpole, and Leslie Charteris as the most widely read authors in the Manchester public library, would have been unthinkable in St. Petersburg and Moscow. The Russian intelligentsia had their faults. Some drank too heavily. Many were unconventional in their sex life. But with all, artistic merit came first.

I liked these charming intellectuals whose talk was so often above my own middle-brow intellect and who belied Pushkin's dictum that Russians were lazy and not inquisitive. Although their minds probed everything within the range of human imagination, their weaknesses were obvious. They had no use for compromise and, because they despised it, argument was merely a pleasant exercise which always ended inconclusively. They could organise a theatre, and, since they had no political gods to worship, their heroes were actors and novelists. But in the practical humdrum matters which make life run smoothly they were woefully weak. Mr. Churchill's famous exhortation of *Action Today* was a standard of efficiency which they would have admired from afar but could never have attained, and I always felt that, if the most brilliant of them had been appointed postmaster in a village sub-office, the stamp account would have been muddled by the end of the first week. Nevertheless, I doubt if in any other country there existed at that time so scintillating and so talented a society, and in retrospect I realise that it had a formative and lasting influence on my character and my whole outlook on life.

At the Ertels I heard much of a young captain called Wavell who had been Madame Ertel's star pupil and with whom I over-lapped for a fortnight. Quiet, reserved and very studious, he had learnt Russian with great thoroughness and had acquired by heart whole pages of Pushkin and other Russian poets. I suffered and benefited a little from his efficiency, for Madame Ertel continually emphasised the value of learning poetry by heart as an asset to mastering a foreign language, and stimulated me to follow the example of Wavell who had passed his examination for a military interpretership with the highest credit. He never lost his command of Russian or his interest in the Ertel family. Almost my last conversation with him was, when, during the Second World War, he telephoned to me to say he wished to see me. As he was then Viceroy-Designate of India, I suspected that he wished to discuss some problem of political warfare and, knowing nothing about India, I felt some trepidation. To my surprise all that he wanted was to talk about the Ertels. I told him that Madame Ertel had long been dead, but that her two daughters were in London and that the elder, Mrs. Natalie Duddington, had made a reputation for herself both as the collaborator of Constance Garnett and as a gifted translator of Russian novels in her own right. I gave him their address and, busy as he then was, he went to see them.

.   .   .   .   .

The year 1913 brought a great change to my life. Our Moscow
Consulate was raised to a Consulate-General, and we launched into
new offices complete with a trained Consular clerk and typists.
Clive Bayley, my new chief, was an excellent organiser and a stickler
for accurate and efficient work. Outside the office he had a jovial
presence, wore a monocle with great effect, and was a generous host
with a fund of apparently inexhaustible stories. He had a strong
sense of the importance of British prestige and was not afraid to
spend his own money on raising it. The leading Muscovites liked
the Bayley "cocktails" and dinners and responded generously to his
hospitality. I benefited greatly from the ripe experience of a man
who knew how to make friends, stood up fearlessly for his staff,
wrote as an equal to our Embassy, and allowed no one to take a
liberty with him. From him I learnt how a Consular office should
be run and through him I was able to extend my circle of Russian
acquaintances.

The advantages were to be helpful to me when the First World
War started. In all Russia it was welcomed with immense enthusiasm and supreme optimism. The mobilisation went smoothly.
The soldiers, cheered by vast crowds, sang cheerfully as they
marched to the troop-trains. A visitor from Mars would have
concluded that Russians were single-minded patriots united in
loyalty to the Tsar, their "Little Father," and many foreign
observers who came from nearer parts formed the same conclusion.
The early successes of the Russian armies fanned the initial enthusiasm and gave some verisimilitude to the British story of the
Russian steam-roller.

In the spring of 1915 a new responsibility fell upon me. Clive
Bayley fell ill and had to go to England for an operation. During
his convalescence he was appointed Consul-General in New York
and I was left in charge of the Moscow Consulate-General. This
change coincided with a crushing disaster to the Russian arms or
rather to the Russian armies, for lack of arms and shells were responsible for the failure. The Tsarist Government had tried to fight
a total war without enlisting the help of the political opposition,
and its whole supply organisation had broken down. The effect
on Moscow, which had become in a broad sense the patriotic capital

of Russia, was immediately noticeable. Anger took the place of enthusiasm.

One of my early tasks as Acting Consul-General was to write a report on the effect of the first year of the war on the morale of the people. I finished my reports on August 4, 1915. Warsaw fell on the same day. My report was pessimistic. Many of my Russian friends already felt that the war would end in revolution. I shared their view. At this time I began my periodical visits to St. Petersburg to see Sir George Buchanan, our ambassador, who gave me generous encouragement and sound advice. But Lady Buchanan and most of the Embassy staff regarded me as a gloomy pessimist.

At the beginning of the war I began to keep a diary, a habit which I have continued ever since. This first diary was kept spasmodically, but it contains some curious entries which throw a revealing light on the period and on my own character. Reading it today, I realise with a sense of shame my lack of experience, my instability, and my over-weening, not to say bumptious, self-confidence. I wrote and said exactly what I felt with a firm belief in my own prescience. I had no knowledge of diplomacy or of politics. Hitherto my interest had been concentrated on the Russian theatre. Now that the war had forced politics upon me, they absorbed my whole life and I expressed my views with the force and fearlessness which spring naturally from the cocksure confidence of youth. Inevitably I rubbed many people up the wrong way and made enemies. On the credit side this naïve little diary shows that I worked tremendously hard, did with a minimum of sleep, got to know the leading Liberals, Social-Revolutionaries and Mensheviks in Moscow, and still found time to visit the theatre, to augment my meagre official salary by writing short stories and sketches of Russian life, and to get into mischief in other ways. Today I think of my youthful energy with amazement and nostalgic regret.

Throughout the war the Russians always astonished me by the mercurial nature of their temperament which swayed violently from extreme optimism to the lowest pessimism. The worst example was the brilliant Lykiardopoulos, the Secretary of the Moscow Arts Theatre, and an ardent Anglophile.

Apart from being a talented journalist, he spoke half a dozen languages including modern Greek, and, when I was authorised to start a small propaganda bureau in Moscow, he became my assistant and, indeed, the sole member of my staff. Incidentally, this was my first introduction to propaganda, and the total expenses of my bureau amounted to less than £1000 a year. Before he joined me, "Lyki", as we called him, had been to Sweden and had come back with the conviction that Germany was invincible.

Later, when the Russian cause was already as good as lost, I sent him to Germany with a Greek passport. He returned with a devastating picture, supported by figures, of the economic distress of the German people and with the firm belief that the war would end with a revolution, not in Russia but in Germany. The slightest success sent his hopes soaring. A Russian defeat plunged him into despair. His attitude was typical of many Russians.

Of course there were exceptions, notably men like Michael Chelnokov, a former Vice-President of the Duma and then Mayor of Moscow. He was also head of the Union of Russian Cities which together with the Union of Zemstvos did splendid work in producing munitions when, at the insistence of the Grand Duke Nicholas, these public organisations were at last called upon to come to the rescue of the Ministry of War. Chelnokov, with whom I maintained the friendliest relations, was a solid type of Russian, sound in his judgment and calm and imperturbable in success or disaster. Throughout the war he kept me informed of all the details of the growing struggle between the democrats and the reactionaries. In a broad sense it was a conflict between Moscow and St. Petersburg. Moscow was patriotic and on the whole pro-English. It wanted a Russian victory which, it felt, could be attained only under a Government enjoying the full confidence of the people. St. Petersburg feared that a prolonged war would provoke a disastrous revolution and was therefore suspected of defeatism and pro-Germanism. It was also anti-English and was responsible for the story that England would fight to the last drop of Russian blood. The same story was given wide circulation by the Soviet Communists during the Second World War.

The conflict between the two cities was to continue until the first revolution. Although it did not take place until March, 1917, the fall of Warsaw on August 4, 1915, was its prelude. The Tsar's reaction to this disaster was to prorogue the Duma, dismiss the few popular Ministers, and to remove the not unpopular Grand Duke Nicholas from his post of Commander-in-Chief. By assuming the Supreme Command himself, the Tsar sealed his own fate.

The intervening eighteen months brought increasing military disaster, broken only by some minor successes, growing despair, and rapidly diminishing faith in victory. It was a period in which the Emperor was absent at Headquarters and Rasputin enjoyed untramelled domination over the superstitious and neurotic Empress; a period in which Moscow was overrun by refugees and wounded soldiers whose stories swelled the rising tide of pessimism; a period of mounting confusion and shortages of food; above all, a period in which rumour ran wild and created the atmosphere of discontent for which the subversive elements had waited.

Although most of the leading Bolsheviks were in exile or in Siberia, there were other malcontents who were ready enough to obey Lenin's order to turn the imperialist war into a civil war. Strikes in the factories became more frequent and more turbulent. The calling-up of reserves and new recruits provoked increasing hooliganism.

The only policy which ministers could devise for alleviating discontent was increasing ruthlessness. Recalcitrant strikers were shot down or ridden down. One evening I heard a great commotion and the sound of firing in the streets and at once rushed out to see what was happening. The disturbance was in the Tverskaia, now Gorki Street, and, when I got there, Cossacks and police had herded the crowd into the boulevard and side-streets. I mingled with the people who were now cowed and sullen. The trouble had started when the police tried to arrest a drunken soldier. Some students had sprung to the help of the soldier. A crowd gathered quickly, and the police, hard-pressed, lost their heads. The Cossacks were brought up, fired on the crowd, and killed five and wounded ten others. Several officers who drew their swords in defence of the soldier were arrested.

As there had been several strikes and demonstrations at this time

c

in protest against the dissolution of the Duma, I went to the Prefect to seek official information. General Klimovich dismissed my apprehensions with nonchalant assurance. Neither the strikes nor the demonstrations were serious. If repressive measures had been used at once, there would have been no trouble. His difficulty was the lethargy of the ministers. He hoped that the Duma would be recalled because it would allow the progressive *bloc* to talk and once they began to talk they were sure to quarrel among themselves. The progressives, he said with great confidence, had no guts.

In the minds of the prefects, the police, and, indeed, nearly all the high officials repression was the only cure for discontent On the other hand, apart from political offences, Russian justice was amazingly indifferent to other crimes, especially if the police or reliable officials were implicated. In Moscow in April 1916, there was an extraordinary case which roused the indignation even of the Russians. An assistant police commissioner in Warsaw fell in love with the wife of an officer who was serving at the front. When Warsaw fell, the police commissioner took the lady with him to Moscow and installed her in his own flat. In due course the officer came back to Moscow on leave and, already warned by friends of what was going on, went to the flat. Told by the maid that no one was at home, he pushed his way in and soon found the locked bedroom. The police commissioner then fired several shots through the door and killed the officer who was unarmed. Brought to trial on a charge of murder, he was acquitted.

The case did nothing to lessen the unpopularity of the police who, loathed at all times, were especially hated because none of them had been sent to the war.

Both at the front and in the rear there were patriots who saw what was wrong, did their best to put it right, and continued to pass resolutions demanding that no peace must be made until complete victory was achieved. Their efforts crumbled beneath the towering weakness of the supreme autocrat. Already in January 1916, General Alexeiev, the ablest and the wisest of the Russian Generals, had said to Chelnokov: "The Emperor's all right. The trouble is that he's surrounded by a bunch of bastards."

The Emperor was far from "all right". Doubtless, his intentions were good, but like many weak men he vacillated when he should have been strong and showed a stubborn obstinacy when he should have made concessions. Land reform would have won for him the continued support of the peasants who furnished ninety per cent of the rank and file of the Russian armies, but, like all other surrenders to liberty, land reform was against the interests of his entourage. Moreover, he was a pliable tool in the hands of the Empress who even before the military disasters of 1915 was known far and wide as "The German". Wholly unfitted to be an autocrat, yet unwilling to make a shameful peace, the Emperor carried on a war which became increasingly unpopular, and long before the final tragedy he had lost the loyalty and affection of the masses.

The rot began in the rear where "Down with the Government" and "Away with the War" became the popular cries not only of the factory workers but also of the peasants. In spite of its terrible losses, the front maintained its fighting spirit until it, too, was infected by the new recruits who brought strange tales of perfidy and corruption in high places. Before the end of 1916 it was clear to everyone who was in close contact with the people that Russia was moving rapidly towards a cataclysm. The artificial life of St. Petersburg denied these contacts not only to the reactionary politicians who pooh-poohed the possibility of a revolution but also to the Allied ambassadors whom diplomatic etiquette restrained from all but the most formal association with the progressive opposition.

When it came, the March revolution of 1917 took me by surprise, not because I had not expected it, but because it started in a desultory and typically Russian manner. It was not organised. The Tsar had once again dissolved the Duma. Simultaneously there had been bread-riots in St. Petersburg, and once again the police had fired on the crowd. On Monday, March 12, the workers came out into the streets. The Duma remained sitting in defiance of the Imperial *ukaz*. The troops joined the people. The autocracy collapsed like a house of cards. By spontaneous combustion the revolution had arrived.

The news spread like wildfire, and on the evening of Tuesday, March 13, Moscow followed St. Petersburg's example. Wednesday was a bitterly cold day even for Moscow, and I was glad of the warmth of the crowd as I pushed my way through the cheering masses into the Town Hall to ask for Chelnokov. No one knew where he was. The vast building was packed with workers who had spent the night there, and the heated rooms were heavy with the cloying smell of human sweat. I was well received by Rudnev, the head of the Revolutionary Committee, who assured me that there had been no bloodshed, that the troops had come over spontaneously, and that complete order prevailed. It was more or less true. The crowds in the streets were friendly and, on the whole, well-behaved. One fact, however, was abundantly clear. The Liberal progressives and the Socialists were both committed to the revolution, but the Social-Revolutionaries and the Mensheviks held the upper hand. It was soon evident that they meant to maintain it.

St. Petersburg was at once renamed Petrograd, and on the Thursday morning the new Government was appointed. The Moscow representation was strong and included Prince Lvov, the new Prime Minister. On paper it was a good Cabinet which pledged itself to continue the war until victory was won. Unfortunately, it had a rival in the Petrograd and Moscow Soviets which had been set up at once. The bourgeois were in the Government and the proletariat in the Soviets, and the fight for power began almost immediately. In three days Russia had passed from centuries of despotism to unrestricted freedom. Before the first week was passed Socialist and Bolshevik newspapers were on the streets, and the very first number of *Social-Democrat*, the Moscow organ of the Bolshevik Party, called for an immediate end to the war. The second carried a bitter attack on England. All over Russia the political prisoners, irrespective of their attitude towards the war were released at once. Stalin came hurrying back after five years of banishment in Siberia. At the request of the Russian Government a British ship conveyed Trotsky from Canada to Petrograd. Later, the German Government, eager to destroy the Russian will to fight, sent Lenin through Germany in the famous sealed wagon in order to spread his gospel of "All Power to the Soviets" and "Turn the Imperialist War into a Civil War."

In this welter of indigestible licence the Lvov Government resigned and was succeeded by a Cabinet headed by Alexander Kerensky, who at that moment was the darling of the people and the hope of the bourgeoisie. For six months he strove against ill-health and mounting opposition to stem the tide of anarchy, but his prospects were ruined from the start. Only on one condition could he have succeeded. Had he been allowed to make a separate peace, the Bolshevik revolution might never have taken place. To France and Britain who were then facing the pick of the German armies such a course of action was unthinkable, and strong allied pressure was put on Kerensky to continue the War. As a patriot and a man of honour he yielded to this persuasion and thereby committed political suicide.

One curious incident, which can now be safely related, illustrates the fundamental weakness of the Kerensky Government. In July 1917, the Bolsheviks made their first attempt to overthrow Kerensky. It failed, and Trotsky, always to the fore in action, was arrested. The Petrograd Chief of Police was then Kerensky's old friend, Rutenberg, who is better known to Englishmen for his subsequent work in the development of Palestine. Rutenberg was tough both by nature and in appearance. Eleven years previously he had been ordered by the Social-Revolutionary Party to get rid of the agent-provocateur, Father Gapon. He shot his man in a public lavatory. Now he wanted to have Trotsky shot, but the Government of free Russia refused. It had abolished the death sentence. More than once Rutenberg told me that the greatest regret of his life was not having taken the law into his own hands. He believed that, if he had done so, there would have been no Bolshevik revolution.

Looking back today, I realise how immense a part chance—and women—play in life. The March revolution had brought to the top ministers with most of whom I had been intimately acquainted. I also got on well with Kerensky whom I liked and for whom I interpreted in his conversations with our ambassador. I had been able to provide information which I assume was regarded as useful, for I had been informed officially some months before the revolution that I was to be left in charge of the Moscow Consulate-General until the end of the war.   Had I listened to the referee's whistle, I should doubtless have remained in Moscow until the end of the war and then gone home with our other diplomats and Consular officials.   Then I should have been transferred to some other part of the world and, if all had gone according to the rules, should now be a retired and respectable Consul-General.

Revolutions, however, are heady wine for young blood. I ignored the whistle and, because of an infatuation for a Russian lady, was sent home at the end of September 1917, nominally and officially for leave after strain from overwork, but, as between the ambassador and myself, more or less in disgrace.

Contrary to all the principles of moral rectitude, I was back in Russia within three months as head of the first British Mission to the Bolshevik Government.

Chapter III

THE MASTER-MIND OF LENIN

*"I know that it is impossible to consider as Lenin's equals
even the greatest people in his Party."*

MAXIM GORKI: *Days with Lenin.*

IN *Memoirs of a British Agent* I described my experiences with the
Bolsheviks in 1918 as fully as I dared without endangering the
safety of men and women then living. Today most of the
leading actors in this exciting drama are dead, and I can now explain
certain matters which have created misunderstandings both in this
country and in the Soviet Union.

First, I was not and never have been a member of what foreigners
call the British Intelligence Service. I was a permanent official,
although my mission in 1918 was only semi-official. The British
Government had not recognised the Bolshevik Government. On
the contrary, it had withdrawn our ambassador and all his staff. The
British Government, however, had thought it right to have a
liaison with the Bolsheviks who were bent on concluding a seperate
peace with Germany. Maxim Litvinov was then the most prominent Bolshevik in London. By granting to him a semi-official
status in London, the British Government were able to arrange
certain privileges, including the right to use cypher telegrams, for
me in Petrograd and Moscow. The telegrams which I received
from the Foreign Office were addressed "British Agent", this being
the title customarily given to British representatives in countries
which have not full diplomatic status. Hence the popular but in
many respects unfortunate title chosen for my book.

The Bolshevik leaders were fully aware of the nature of this
arrangement. From the moment of my arrival they received me
well, granted me more privileges than I had foreseen, and assured
me that I should enjoy full diplomatic immunity. At this time

they were nervously conscious of their own weakness, and I doubt if even Lenin himself expected that his régime would last longer than a few months. They therefore exaggerated my role and in their notes to me always addressed me as "British Diplomatic Representative". As they were then making a pretence of practising open diplomacy, the notes were published in the newspapers.

In varying degrees of intimacy I got to know nearly all the leaders from Lenin and Trotsky to Derjinski and Peters, respectively President and Vice-President of the Cheka. I had a special pass into Smolny, the Bolshevik headquarters in Petrograd. More than once I attended a meeting of the Central Executive Committee in the main restaurant of the Metropole Hotel in Moscow, where in Tsarist days I had taken part in entertainments of a very different kind, and on my journey from Petrograd to Moscow I travelled in Trotsky's troop train and dined with him before an audience of open-mouthed peasants in Liuban station. My daily work was mainly with Trotsky and with Chicherin, Karachan and Radek who, after Trotsky's appointment as Commissar for War, formed the Triumvirate of the Soviet Commissariat for Foreign Affairs.

My mission ended in a dismal failure. It was difficult from the start. The Bolsheviks were very afraid of the Germans whom they were in no position to resist. They were therefore eager for recognition by, and an understanding with, Great Britain and the United States. But, having won the supreme power by their promise of immediate peace, they had no illusions about their own fate if they plunged the country into war. Peace at almost any price was therefore an essential condition of Bolshevik survival. Only if the Germans had attempted to conquer the whole country would Lenin have agreed to accept the armed aid of France, Great Britain and the United States. Trotsky, who had refused to sign the Brest-Litovsk peace, might have fought, but for all his martial and administrative abilities he was not Lenin.

The French Government wanted intervention with or without Bolshevik consent, and at once. As an historian President Wilson was opposed in principle to intervention without consent. In the

British Cabinet opinions were divided. Intervention by agreement with the Bolsheviks was the ideal, but the service departments, eager to obtain some relief for the hard-pressed French and British armies in the West, were bent on restoring the Eastern front at almost any cost. My instructions from home were therefore vague, but they can be summarised in one sentence: Stimulate Bolshevik resistance to the Germans in every possible manner.

I was opposed to intervention without Bolshevik consent and, when I realised that consent would not be given except on Lenin's formula: "If we are attacked, we shall invite your aid," my opposition hardened. It was based on four main principles. The Bolsheviks had the power and were likely to retain it. The anti-Bolshevik forces were weak and both in Moscow and in Petrograd some of the bourgeois made no concealment of their hope that the Germans would take over the whole country and "restore order". The workers and peasants wanted peace, and, deserting in masses from the front, the Russian armies had already made it with their legs. An Eastern front could be restored only by sending large numbers of Allied troops, and a force of this magnitude could not be spared. Intervention without consent would incidentally drive the Bolsheviks into the arms of the Germans and could end only in disaster.

I therefore advocated giving material aid to the Bolshevik Government and accepting Lenin's formula of eventual intervention in the hope that the situation would develop in our favour. The Bolsheviks had no love for the Germans. It was better for us to leave it to the Germans to make mistakes than to commit a cardinal blunder ourselves.

My views were shared by Raymond Robins, the head of the American Red Cross Mission in Russia, who had direct access to President Wilson, and by Captain Jacques Sadoul, the personal representative of M. Albert Thomas, who had been a vigorous French Minister of Munitions. In our different ways we defended our attitude with what skill we could.

I still think that our advice was right, but I realise today that my method of giving it was deplorable. My telegrams, written and cyphered laboriously late at night after a strenuous day, were cheeky to the point of insolence. They irritated instead of convincing, and I made scores of powerful enemies. I received telegrams from my wife, Hugh Walpole, and other friends stating in unmistakable terms that I was ruining my career and advising me to come home at once. They did not disturb me at the time. I had the self-confidence and the ignorance of youth. Moreover, the telegrams strengthened my position in Moscow, for, as they came *en clair*, the Bolsheviks read them and drew their own conclusions, and for some months I stood high in their favour although I never enjoyed their trust. Even in those days they suspected every enemy, and then as now any non-Communist was regarded as an enemy. Almost every week agents-provocateurs visited me and sought to trap me. Sometimes they showed ingenuity and skill, but more often than not their methods were obvious. What worried me most was the fact that throughout the whole Russian Empire we had representatives at the headquarters of the various anti-Bolshevik forces. I knew of their existence, but was kept entirely in the dark about their activities. It was the roulette policy of the reckless gambler who puts a chip on every number in the hope of pulling off a big coup.

As it became clear that France and Britain were determined to go ahead with intervention without Bolshevik consent, our little trio of opposition broke up. Raymond Robins went back to the United States to intercede personally with President Wilson. Jacques Sadoul, who had long been at loggerheads with the French Government, became more and more bitter. As for myself, I was a permanent official and, when I knew that intervention was to take place, I accepted the policy.

When the Allies landed at Archangel on August 4, 1918, the news was at once announced in the Bolshevik newspapers. For several days there was considerable excitement. The anti-Bolsheviks, who imagined that the Allies had come in great force, were jubilant. The Bolsheviks were alarmed, and Karachan told me that they had made arrangements to blow up Petrograd and Moscow. They would never surrender and, if necessary, would go underground again. They might be wiped out, but at any rate they would have struck a brave blow for revolution and fired the world by their example. He showed no fear, but his agitation betrayed a certain lack of confidence. His attitude, I imagine, was more or less that of all his colleagues in the Government.

A few days later he was all smiles: "The intervention," he said cheerfully, "is not serious. You have landed only a tiny force." It was true. The intervention was not an intervention at all. It was a compromise between widely conflicting views at home. Officially its purpose was to protect the large British military stores lying at Archangel and to prevent them from falling into the hands of the Germans. Doubtless, too, it was designed to give aid to the anti-Bolshevik forces in Russia in the event of the Bolsheviks refusing to co-operate. Its only effect was to galvanise Bolshevik resistance, strengthen the revolutionary movement, and release a spate of propaganda against the French and British.

The intervention placed all British citizens in Russia in an impossible situation. Although the Bolsheviks did not declare war on the Allies, they opposed the interventionists with such military force as they could collect. Sporadic fighting was going on in many parts of Russia, and, whether by accident or design, the Allies found themselves in the position of siding with the counter-revolutionary elements in an increasingly active civil war. Moreover, all exits from Russia were now held either by the Germans or by the Allies. The British in Moscow and Petrograd were trapped, and, although I did not foresee what was to happen, I felt instinctively that we were the victims of the intervention and that at the best we should be retained as hostages.

Exactly four weeks after the landing at Archangel, Uritsky, the head of the Petrograd Cheka, was shot dead by a young officer. The same evening a fanatical young Jewess called Kaplan fired two shots point-blank at Lenin as he stepped off the platform at Michelsen's factory in Moscow. In the early hours of the next morning I was arrested and accused of organising a fantastic plot to overthrow the Bolsheviks by a series of murders. If the plot ever existed, I certainly had no part in it, although I do not deny that both assassins were probably encouraged by the mere fact of the intervention and by the exaggerated hopes which it raised.

Had Lenin died, I should not be alive today. Fortunately, he recovered. Luckily, too, for me, the Allies were winning the war and Germany's defeat was already certain. After an unpleasant week at Loubianka II, which was the Headquarters of the Cheka, I was transferred to more comfortable confinement in the Kremlin. A month later, I was exchanged for Litvinov whom the British Government had arrested as a reprisal for my incarceration. As for the so-called plot I feel sure today that the Bolsheviks were determined, for the purpose of propaganda, to fix the responsibility for the assassinations firmly on the Allies. It was the first example of a technique which they have developed in a high degree in relation not only to foreigners but also to their own deviationists. I should also point out that the attempt on Lenin's life provoked the first mass executions of innocent victims. The young officer and Kaplan, with whom I was confronted in prison for several hours during the night, were executed almost immediately. At the same time seven hundred notabilities were shot in the hope of deterring further violence against the régime. In this respect the attempt on Lenin's life marked the beginning of the Red Terror on a large scale.

Today two impressions, formed in 1918, stand out in my mind above all others: the pre-eminence of Lenin as a revolutionary leader and the failure of the outside world to realise the significance of the Bolshevik revolution. It was not only the foreign statesmen who under-estimated the prospects of Bolshevik survival in a vast, illiterate country which had suffered over-whelming defeat in war and which, in social progress, was three hundred years behind the nations of Western Europe. There were few Russians outside the Bolshevik Party who did not believe that Bolshevism was a temporary and evanescent phase of military defeat. There were many who welcomed the fall of Kerensky, because they were convinced that the Bolshevik régime would not last six weeks.

But for Lenin their forecast might have proved correct. The Bolshevik revolution was made by a small band of professional revolutionaries, most of whom had spent their lives in exile. Their dogma was unknown and unintelligible to the masses. Their only asset was their fanaticism which gave them courage in a country in which morale had sunk to the lowest depths of apathy and despair. The workers wanted peace and bread, the peasants peace and land; and on the promise of bread, land and immediate peace Lenin made his revolution.

True, it brought civil war instead of peace. For a long time it produced little bread, and the promise of land to the peasants was an opportunistic departure from Marxist theory and was sub-sequently broken. But the policy served its immediate purpose. To the masses who had never understood the war against Germany, civil war was intelligible and inviting. The peasants, frustrated by the slowness of the Kerensky Government in implementing its scheme of agricultural reform, eagerly accepted Lenin's invitation to seize the land and scuttled from the armies to stake their claims. By the chaos which the policy created deliberately, the Bolsheviks were able to seize power with a minimum of effort and of armed strength. Eight months of ultra-democratic government, for which the Russian people were unripe, had been sufficient to restore a dictatorship, different in class and character but maintained by the same methods by which Russia had always been ruled. It had been established by the resolute will of a realist who knew exactly what he wanted when his compatriots were bogged in theory or wallowing in the inertia of despair.

Easy as the Bolshevik conquest had been, the prospect of con-solidating it was complicated and uninviting. Many historians hold the view that the hour creates the man, and certainly the hour favoured Lenin. He himself, however, had always counted on it. In a sense he was almost a stranger in his own country. "I know very little of Russia," he said to Gorki. "Simbirsk, Kazan, Peters-burg, exile in Siberia and that is nearly all." But he had devoted his whole life to the study of revolution and already in Switzerland in 1915 had seen in the war which he had long predicted the oppor-tunity of putting to the practical test his formulated policy of turning the imperialist war into a civil war. When his chance came, he did more than take it. He never allowed it to slip from his grasp.

As a close eye-witness of the period, I am convinced that no one else but Lenin could have steered the Bolshevik Party through all

the immense difficulties of 1918: the threat of German occupation
of Petrograd and Moscow, the antagonistic pressure of the Allies,
the stupendous task of feeding a starving population throughout the
civil war. He benefited from the mistakes of his enemies whose
greatest blunder perhaps was under-estimation of the man himself.
He had as his chief lieutenant an exceptionally able man of action in
Trotsky. But without his own calm judgment, his indomitable
power of will, and his supreme self-confidence his colleagues would
have committed many blunders, and the régime might easily have
collapsed.

His mastery over them was complete. It was achieved entirely
by a mental superiority of which they and he himself were fully
conscious. Indeed, mental superiority was his only vanity. He
felt that he alone saw clearly while his colleagues groped and,
although he allowed others to argue, he had an unshakable belief
in the rectitude of his own judgment. He was the man who
decided, and his decisions were never questioned.

He made a deep impression on me from the moment when I first
saw him, and today, with riper knowledge, I find little to alter in
the appreciation of him which I wrote at the time for the Foreign
Office and which I summarised in *Memoirs of a British Agent*. Apart
from his large dome-shaped forehead and his slightly Mongolian
eyes there was nothing impressive about his personal appearance.
He cared nothing for finery of any sort. His clothes hung loosely
about his stocky figure and his tie was nearly always awry. His
favourite attitude both in private and on the public platform was
standing with his head back and his thumbs comfortably fixed in
the arm-holes of his waistcoat. Except in the severest frosts a
workman's cap was his usual headgear. Imperturbable in temperament, he had been a cheerful exile, fond of shooting and fishing in
Siberia and hiking and cycling in Switzerland. He had a keen and
sometimes caustic sense of humour and was human enough to be
irritated when he lost a game of chess. His tastes in the arts were
those of the ordinary man. He preferred the Russian classics to the
modern Soviet literature and mistrusted Mayakovsky, the revolutionary futurist poet. He had an ear for classical music, especially
Beethoven, but with rare exceptions the theatre bored him.

By 1917, however, he had put away what he considered childish things in order to devote his whole time and dynamic energy to the fulfilment of his life's task.

Such was his concentration that he could work in the noisiest din, and I myself saw him writing notes with the greatest unconcern on scraps of cheap paper in the middle of the rowdiest Congress of Soviets in the history of the Soviet Union. He hated all the trappings and pomp with which other dictators have surrounded themselves and was, in 1918 at least, always accessible to his own people. Although, like all Communists, he considered that the end justified all means including deliberate deception, he was astonishingly frank with the few foreigners whom he saw, thereby affording a striking contrast with the present rulers of the Soviet Union. As far as I can remember, he was rarely wrong in his appreciation of the future. Nor was he ever rude or intemperate in conversation. Cruel and ruthless he undoubtedly was, but his cruelty was impersonal and in his mind justified by the needs of the cause. I do not think that he ever pursued a personal vengeance. I know that in 1918 he spared many intellectuals who today would have been liquidated without trace.

On the other hand, he was ruthless with regard to the general line of his policy and if, in his opinion, the success of that policy had depended on a Herodian massacre of the innocents he would have ordered it not only without fear, but also without the slightest trace of compunction. Doubtless, he would have found many to excuse him, for the idea that man is humane is an illusion. In the Tretyakov Gallery in Moscow there used to hang and probably still hang the pictures of Verestchagin, the painter of battles and of skulls massed in pyramids by savage conquerors like Gengis Khan and Timurlane. Their artistic merit is not great, but in the peaceful days before the First World War they were a very popular attraction to foreign tourists.

Time alone will determine the extent of Lenin's success or his failure, but to deny to him the quality of greatness, as was done at the time of his death by many newspapers, seems today foolish prejudice. Bertrand Russell, no lover of Communism, ranks him as the only man in public life that he could regard as equal to

Gladstone in personal impressiveness. Writing after Lenin's death, at a time when Stalin already held supreme power, Gorki made the following significant comment: "I know that it is impossible to consider as Lenin's equals even the greatest people in the Party." I agree with this verdict. In no aspect of greatness can either Trotsky or Stalin be compared with Lenin. On the evidence of my own eyes and ears I can say without fear of contradiction that in 1918, which even Stalin refers to as the heroic year of Bolshevism, Lenin was the only Bolshevik who enjoyed the wide-spread favour of the masses. In my opinion they liked him for two reasons. He spoke to them as one of themselves. They felt instinctively that his burning faith in his own ability to create a better life for them was free from all personal ambition.

I have often been asked what Lenin would have thought of the results of his revolution if he had been alive today. Would he have been delighted with the political and economic developments which have taken place since his death or would he have regarded his life's work as a failure? It is a foolish question because any answer must be purely speculative and has therefore no significance. Personally, I think that he would have gloried in the advance of Russian science, the conversion of Russia from a backward agricultural nation to a modern industrialised state, the giant strides made in education and in the elimination of illiteracy, and the spectacular triumphs of Russian engineering. Here were the fruits of the material progress for which he had striven and which conformed with the Marxist interpretation of historical inevitability. Moreover, the progress had been achieved by Russians whom he regarded as the most talented of all peoples. Had he not predicted that, given the education and the proper training, they would make Russia the foremost country of the world within twenty-five years?

He would also have accepted the *Kolkhozi*, the extinction of the peasant, and the working of the land by robot labour gangs, for he himself had initiated the policy and would have regarded its development as a logical consequence of his own interpretation of Marxist dogma. Nor would he have opposed the militant advances of Communism, for this, too, was in his scheme of things.

Nevertheless, he would have found much to criticise and much that would have shocked him: the glaring inequalities which have been created by the emergence of a new privileged class, the growth of the secret police into an *imperium in imperio*, the deliberate falsification of history for the glorification of individuals, the subjugation of small nations, the prolongation of the terror, and the reversion to distinctive ranks, gaudy uniforms, and methods of government which he had always associated with the worst aspects of Tsarist rule. He had always disliked and feared the growth of a professional and power-conscious bureaucracy. The terror he had envisaged as a temporary measure necessitated by the civil war. The purges and the slave camps would have shocked him, and he would have resisted to the utmost the liquidation of the men with whom he had made the revolution. As a Marxist he had envisaged the withering of the state. He would not have rejoiced to find it larger, more powerful, and more exacting than it had been. Assuredly, too, he would have bitterly resented the cruelty that he would have found. For all his own ruthlessness his ideal had always been to eliminate the need for force, and by nature he was neither cruel nor haunted by the suspicion which breeds cruelty. He was fond of children, and only a year or two before his death said: "They will have happier lives than we had. They will not experience much that we lived through. There will not be so much cruelty in their lives."

He would have found more in the Soviet Union of today.

These, however, are idle speculations. The fact remains that Lenin promised liberty to the masses, meant to bestow it, and died without settling the question of his successor. In the abstract, liberty is the hardest of all words to define. In the free countries more and more restrictions are introduced to preserve it. Negatively, every human being knows instinctively that the presence of millions, mostly Socialist and Communist deviationists, in slave-camps masquerading as "corrective labour institutions" is not liberty.

Lenin is still a symbol—a misused symbol—in the Soviet Union of today. Too popular to be ignored, he lives as a kind of Communist mummy whose name is used to justify all that has happened in Russia since his death. And this, I am convinced, he would have resented most of all.

D

Chapter IV

MIXED COMPANY

"Now by two-headed Janus
Nature hath formed strange fellows in her time."

THE Soviet leaders of 1917 and 1918 were different in character and, above all, in personal appearance from the well-groomed ministers and heavily medalled generals of the Stalin epoch. Today the régime has a traditional Tsarist respect for rank and protocol and is confident that time is on its side. In 1917 and 1918 such was the speed of events that neither day nor night was long enough to keep pace with it. The leaders slept in their clothes and went unshaven for days. They worked on kitchen-tables, shrieked orders by telephone, and lived in a litter of paper. The corridors of Smolny, the first headquarters, were crowded with deputations of workers and peasants, all of whom had to be received. The Red Guard, then all-powerful in the big cities, was a rabble composed of sailors, ragged soldiers, and workers whose only sign of rank was a red brassard on the arm. There were no epaulettes for generals and no means of distinguishing an officer from a soldier.

This indifference to dress and the general untidiness continued long after the transfer of the Government to Moscow, and I remember well my first meeting with the gaunt and ascetic Derjinski, the first head of the Cheka. He was dressed in a buttoned-up tunic, long loose trousers, and a pair of carpet-slippers. I was assured that he wore them always in his office. Today, M. Beria, the clean-shaven, bespectacled head of the all-powerful M.V.D., looks like a natty, respectable foreign lawyer. Of the Commissars of the 1917–18 period only Trotsky and Karachan had any thought for their personal appearance, and they alone had manicured nails.

All the Commissars looked and undoubtedly were tired, but their red-rimmed eyes burnt with enthusiasm. As far as I could judge, there was complete equality among them and no dragooning of their supporters. Indeed, from the point of view of efficiency they wasted valuable time in arguing with one another and in attending meetings. Nor did I ever notice any signs of the suspicion which now poisons the atmosphere of the Stalin régime. There were minor jealousies, but in 1917 and 1918 no member of the Government or of the Petrograd and Moscow Soviets felt any personal danger or harboured a thought that the revolution would devour its own children. Yet today, of the thirty-two members of the Central Committee which made the October revolution, only Stalin survives. Some died a natural death. Several committed suicide. The others were "liquidated", the one new word which the Bolshevik revolution has given to all languages.

Until June 1918, when the policy of the Allies became clearly hostile to the Bolshevik régime, it never entered my mind that I ran any personal risk. True, the streets were dangerous at night, for marauders and so-called anarchists lurked at dark corners in wait for unwary victims. The banks were closed, and food, clothes and money were worth life itself to men who, as Baudelaire wrote, saw no future except "*pour vivre quelques mois et vêtir leurs maîtresses.*" Hold-ups were therefore frequent, and on one wintry evening Uritsky, the first head of the Petrograd Cheka, was taken from his sleigh on his way from Smolny to the centre of the city, stripped of everything he had, and then left stark-naked to continue his journey.

These nocturnal dangers, however, counted for little in the excitement of a life which brought me into close touch with the men whose names today belong to history, but which were then almost unknown to the outside world. Because the issue of the war was still in doubt, they were eager to maintain contact with the Allies, and, as opponents of intervention, people like Robins, Sadoul and myself were well received. I had a free pass from Trotsky to go anywhere I liked, had his private telephone number —in those days a most valuable privilege—and called him always by his Christian name and patronymic of "Lev Davidovitch". Chicherin, Karachan, Radek and Peters I saw frequently, and both Radek and Karachan came in casually on several occasions to see me and drink a whisky, smoke a cigar or a pipe of English tobacco and gossip freely about the course of events and about their colleagues.

These five represented a typical cross-section of the men of 1918. Trotsky was a South Russian Jew and Radek a Polish Jew. Karachan was an Armenian and Peters a Lett. The only pure Russian was Chicherin who belonged to a noble family and had begun his career as a Tsarist diplomat. Chicherin died in Moscow in solitary senility. The others perished in the Stalin purges. Now that they are dead I can add by way of epitaphs some personal details which when they were alive I had to omit, for their own safety, from *Memoirs of a British Agent*.

Trotsky I never saw again after 1918, although in the winter of 1936 I had an opportunity of visiting him when he was on the point of being expelled from Norway. Being unwilling to embroil myself again in Bolshevik politics, I let the chance go by default, a sin of omission which I should never have committed in my youth. Perhaps it was just as well, for in September 1937, my friend, John Wheeler-Bennett, spent two days with Trotsky in his fortified villa of Diego Rivera in Coyoacan, a suburb of Mexico City, in order to consult him on several points in connexion with the history of the Brest-Litovsk Treaty which John was then writing. In the course of their conversation John introduced my name. The temperamental Trotsky frowned. "Lockhart!" he said. "I do not want to hear his name. He betrayed me over the Czechoslovak Legions." This assertion is untrue.

One of my main tasks in 1918 had been to obtain from Trotsky a free exit from Russia for the Czechoslovak Legionaries who, after the Brest-Litovsk Treaty, wished to go to the Western Front. After long negotiations Trotsky gave his word, and the Legionaries set out on their long trek to the west via Siberia. At Krasnoyarsk fighting broke out between them and the Bolsheviks, and even today no one knows for certain whether the clash was instigated by the French officers who were with the Legionaries or by the local Bolshevik authorities. I do not think that Moscow was to blame, and I certainly had no hand in the fracas. Admittedly, it caused a rift in my relations with Trotsky which up to then had been amicable.

My crime, however, in the eyes of the present Soviet régime is my alleged participation in the so-called Lockhart plot soon after the Allied landing. Today in the official history of Soviet diplomacy I am accused of having "conspired with the traitor Trotsky against the Soviet state." At that time and indeed until Lenin's death Trotsky was the popular and powerful Commissar for War.

Karel Radek, the most confiding, the most impish, and in agility of mind and pen the most brilliant of the Bolsheviks, looked more like a bandit than an intellectual and was on good terms with all the foreign anti-interventionists and therefore with myself. Regarded by his Party colleagues as a highly privileged court jester to Lenin, he was an ardent smoker with a pipe nearly as large as himself and a keen taste for the special tobacco of the Royal Navy. The prospect of a tin—and I had a good supply—brought him regularly to my rooms, and in return I received full payment in his racy conversation. In the early months of 1918 he was violently and, I think, genuinely anti-German and was bitterly opposed to the Brest-Litovsk Treaty. When it was signed, he thought the end had come. "My God," he exclaimed, "if we'd had any other race but Russians behind us in the struggle we'd have upset the world."

Radek, too, I never saw again. During the last war when I was in friendly relations with various members of the Soviet Embassy in London and could discuss almost any matter with them with considerable frankness, I asked several of them individually what had happened to Radek. The answer was always the same: embarrassment and dead silence. At his trial he was accused with several other prominent Bolsheviks of being a Trotskyist and "a Fascist agent". Such was his insolence during the proceedings that when he was taken from the court-room a man sitting next to Alexei Tolstoy, the great Bolshevik writer, whispered in admiration: "Devil and not man." Alone of the accused, Radek was not condemned to be shot, but was never seen again in public. The last mention of his fate that I have found is in Gustav Herling's *A World Apart* in which the author recounts how he heard of an important prisoner being beaten up in the same prison-camp as his own. The prisoner was said to be Radek, but no indication or date of his death has ever been published.

With Lev Michaelovitch Karachan I was more fortunate. Tall, good-looking and well-dressed, he had always been extraordinarily frank and courteous in his dealings with me. On the day when the Allies landed at Archangel, he made a personal appeal to me. If the British came to Moscow, the Bolsheviks would retire to the Urals and carry on the struggle. He would go with them, but his wife would have to remain behind. Would I take her under my protection? Of course I gave my word. It stood me in good stead when a month later I was arrested, for he came to see me in prison several times and by his friendliness did much to alleviate my personal anxiety. Nor did he disguise his knowledge that the accusations against me were false. He justified them with the comment: "Your Government is supporting the war against the revolution. Every kind of irregularity has been committed by Allied agents in this country. You have become the symbol of these irregularities. In a clash between two world forces the individual has to suffer." When he came to say good-bye to me on the day of my release, I felt that I had at least one friend among the Bolsheviks.

I was not mistaken. On July 1, 1935, I was called to the telephone in London by M. Maisky, the Soviet ambassador. "There is an old friend here who wishes to speak to you," he said and passed the receiver. The old friend was Karachan. I invited him to luncheon on the following day at Boulestin's, and he asked if he might bring his wife.

The next day I was a minute late and was told that my guests were already seated. I peeped round the corner to be sure of recognising them. Karachan I spotted at once, but the wife was not the one whom I had known in Moscow. She was, in fact, Semenova, the famous ballerina, who, Alexei Tolstoy told me, was a greater dancer than even Pavlova.

Karachan, who was then Soviet ambassador to Turkey, had changed little. His hair was now tinged with grey, but his good looks and his youthful appearance remained. I congratulated him on his figure. He told me proudly that he kept fit by playing tennis with members of the British Embassy. One of them, as I discovered later, was Bob Dixon, now Sir Pierson Dixon, the right hand of Mr. Eden in the Foreign Office. In spite of his obvious enthusiasm for tennis Karachan surprised me when he told me that he was spending his leave in London in order to see the Wimbledon tournament. In 1918 there had been no time for tennis or for any sport.

Soon, however, we were talking of old days, and in two hours he told me more gossip about what was going on inside the Soviet Union than I had learnt in the eighteen years of my absence. *Memoirs of a British Agent*, he said, had been a very fair picture of the events of 1918. There had been, however, great changes since my time. Lenin's death had made an immense difference and there had been factions in the Party. Many of my old acquaintances were out of favour. Trotsky had lost his battle and was in exile. Zinoviev, whom he described as a loathsome creature, was in disgrace. Karel Radek was still the brilliant leader-writer, but had lost all his influence. He had once admired Trotsky, and that was enough or rather too much for Stalin. Peters, too, was out of favour. In spite of these inner dissensions, there had been great progress, and, thanks to Litvinov, relations with the West were improving. Nazi Germany was the enemy, and we all should be on our guard.

He plied me with questions about English politics. What sort of a man was Baldwin? Why was Churchill, who seemed to understand the situation best, kept in the background?

I was amazed by the new Karachan. I might have been talking to a Western diplomat or, indeed, to any cultured man of the world who took an interest in foreign affairs. His talk was excellent: a mixture of politics, reminiscences and good stories. One story, in particular, still pleases me. Pavlov, the great Russian physicist, who was then still alive and in high favour because of the glory which he shed on Soviet science, was deeply religious. When Stalin saw him crossing himself, he would say: "There he goes again—a slave to his reflexes."

Karachan himself was brimful of self-confidence. Obviously he had no inkling of the purges that were to come so soon, and, knowing him as I did, I could swear that he had no sense of any danger to himself. He had talked with casual indifference of his colleagues who were already out of favour, speaking neither for nor against them and never even hinting at their subsequent fate.

Later, I took him to the House of Commons. It was a dull debate in a half-empty House. But even if there had been fireworks or oratory, Karachan would not have been impressed. He was eager to get to Wimbledon, and kept looking at his watch. We left in half an hour, and I put him into a taxi and said good-bye. His last words were: "*Au revoir* in Moscow."

Two years later he was dead, a victim of Stalin's suspicion and vengeance. I cannot say for certain whether this mundane and attractive Communist was guilty or innocent. Conspiracy was foreign to his nature, and I think it more probable that his carelessness and exuberance of speech led to his denunciation by a secret informer eager to curry favour or by some envious rival who coveted his post.

I cannot claim Vassili Georgevitch Chicherin as exactly a friend, although I had more dealings with him than with any other Bolshevik. As a former professional diplomat who spoke French, English and German with punctilious accuracy, he was invaluable to the Soviet Government in its early days through his knowledge of procedure and his skill in drafting official notes. With his redrimmed eyes, sandy-coloured moustache and pointed beard, and drooping shoulders, he looked half-starved and over-worked, and in very truth he was both. When he embraced Socialism, he sacrificed all his possessions and lived only for his work.

In negotiation he gave nothing away, listened quizzically, and never took a decision without consulting Lenin whom he worshipped with a dog-like devotion. Only when he spoke of Lenin did he seem human. At all other times he was an automaton who toiled at his desk until the early hours of the morning. He lived in a single room in a wretched lodging-house near his office and gave most of the food which he received to an old professional prostitute who lived in the next room. When the March Revolution broke out in Russia he was living in exile in London and became at once Secretary of the Organisation for the Return of

Political Emigrés. He was arrested by the British authorities and incarcerated in Brixton prison. There he remained until November, 1917, when he was allowed to return to Russia. The Bolsheviks have their little vanities. Today their official *Encyclopaedia* states that Chicherin was exchanged for Sir George Buchanan, the then British ambassador to Russia.

During the whole period of my relations with Chicherin he wore the same horrible yellow tweed suit in which in 1917 he had travelled from his English prison to Russia. The coat, covered with stains, hung about him like a sack. The trousers, baggy and bulging at the knees, had long lost all semblance of shape. The suit, I felt, was no advertisement for English tailoring.

Incidentally, it inspired Karel Radek to his most successful practical joke. As the Soviet Government consolidated its position and began to have relations with other governments, some of the Communists hinted to Chicherin that he might dress more appropriately for the reception of foreign ambassadors. Little as he liked the British, Chicherin was not to be separated from his English suit. After consulting Lenin, Radek, therefore, collected a new morning-coat, waistcoat and striped trousers complete with white shirt, stiff collar, tie, and patent leather shoes and, stealing into Chicherin's room when he was asleep, laid the new outfit on a chair and carried off the old yellow suit. Then he rushed back to the Kremlin, telephoned to Chicherin and told him that Lenin wanted to see him at once. There was a long interval, but at last a very sheepish-looking Chicherin made his appearance in his new clothes and was received with warm congratulations. That was the end of the yellow suit.

Chicherin's own end was more tragic. In 1929 I established an indirect contact with him when I was in Berlin and met Madame Siemens, the daughter of Helmholz, the forerunner of Herz and Marconi. We talked about Russia, and she told me that she had made friends with Chicherin in a most curious manner. Being very fond of music, she used to have summer concerts at her villa in Wannsee. Near by was a sanitorium, and whenever she had a quartet to play she noticed that a bent old man used to creep near the garden wall so that he could hear. She invited him to come in and listen, and he came regularly not into the house, but to a chair underneath the open windows. It was Chicherin. He was, she discovered, a brilliant musician and so emotional that the tears came into his eyes when he listened. He was then undergoing treatment for advanced diabetes.

I was amazed. I had never heard him mention music. Karachan, however, confirmed the story when I saw him in London and gave me the last picture of his former colleague. Chicherin was then still alive and living by himself in solitary seclusion in the Arbat. He was suffering not only from diabetes but from mental breakdown. He had written an account of his work as Foreign Commissar for the *Soviet Encyclopædia*. Now he kept his door on a chain, and saw no one except one or two old comrades like Karachan himself. By day he was in another world, but at night he became almost normal, played the piano and talked of Lenin and of Mozart, but mostly of Mozart. He died in 1936.

In *Memoirs of a British Agent* I have described the character and strange behaviour of Jan Peters, the vice-President of the Cheka and my gaoler and chief inquisitor during the period of my imprisonment in the Loubianka and in the Kremlin. I have told how, impressed by the courage of Moura, the heroine of my Russian life, he was fascinated by our romance, and allowed her to communicate with me daily in short notes written in Russian and censored by Peters himself. I have them still. I have related how he brought her to see me, told me my career was finished, and urged me to stay with her and make a new life in the Soviet Union; how, when I refused, he wondered at my weakness; and how, when he came to tell me that I was to be exchanged for Litvinov, he had given me a signed photograph of himself and had handed me sheepishly a letter for his English wife.

The story has a strange sequel. Peters, then just thirty-two, was a Lett who had been a fanatical revolutionary since the age of fifteen. He had suffered imprisonment under the Tsarist régime, and his short, stubby fingers still bore marks of the torture he had undergone from his gaolers. He had then gone to England, found employment in the transport firm of Gerhardt & Hey in London,

MIXED COMPANY   49

and had married an English girl. When the revolution broke out, he went back to Russia, leaving his wife and young daughter behind him.

When I was sent to England in October 1918, I delivered the letter, and after a long delay Mrs. Peters was allowed to go to Russia to join her husband. On arriving in Moscow, she found that Peters had married again. Eventually she obtained employment as cook to Anna Louise Strong, an American Communist who for some years edited the *Moscow News* in English. In 1950, when Communist hatred of the Americans was reaching its apogee, Anna Louise Strong was denounced as a spy and expelled from the country. I do not know whether Mrs. Peters is alive or not. In due course her daughter Mary became the chief telephonist at the British Embassy in Moscow where she served for many years until in 1948 she was kidnapped by the secret police. As she was in the unfortunate position of being a British subject in Britain, but a Soviet subject in the Soviet Union, all attempts by the British Government to communicate with her, let alone to secure her freedom, have been fruitless.

Peters himself fell out of favour long before the last war, presumably as a suspected supporter of Trotsky, and disappeared during the great purges of the late 'thirties. I have no knowledge of the time and place of his death.

As Karachan had told me, there had been great changes since my time.

Two facts are perhaps worth recording. Of the leading Bolsheviks who organised the October revolution only Lenin was over forty. In stature nearly all were small. Although described by Hugh Walpole in his *The Secret City* as "a bearded tall fellow who argued very hotly with the *izvozchik* about his fare", Lenin was not more than five feet eight, nor would he have queried the driver's price. One or two, like Karachan, were tall and, if they did not justify Bacon's aphorism that exceeding tall men have ever very empty heads, they were not among the foremost in ability. Even among the Bolsheviks Karachan's nickname, coined by Radek, was "The Donkey of Classical Beauty."

The foreign officials who were closest to the tumultuous events of 1917 and 1918 have passed from the scene or are old men living in retirement. In their time they enjoyed an intimacy with the revolutionary leaders which today must seem strange to the isolated diplomatic corps of Moscow. By far the most independent in position and the most striking in character was Raymond Robins, the head of the American Red Cross Mission. His whole attitude to life had been crystallised by one incident. As a young man he had gone to the Yukon to seek gold. After months of searching he found it, marked out his claim, and set out for the nearest camp in order to register it. No sooner had he started than a blinding blizzard obscured the whole landscape. He had no companion and no compass, and with death staring him in the face he sat down to wait. After two hours the sky cleared as by a miracle. The snow, however, had covered all his tracks, and he was still helpless. Then in the changing sky he saw a white crucifix shining clearly before him. Without hesitation he made his way towards it, and it brought him straight to the camp.

This experience gave him his religion, riches, and a profound sympathy with the under-dog. For some years he devoted his life to slum-work in Chicago. Then he met Theodore Roosevelt, conceived an admiration for him, and became his right-hand in the "Bull-Moose's" campaign for the American Presidency in 1912. Robins had a passion for hero-worship, and, when the Bolshevik revolution broke out, he was the first of the Allied officials to establish relations with the Bolshevik régime. In this manner he met Lenin, liked him, and became not only a violent opponent of intervention but also a convinced advocate of recognition of the Soviet Government.

He was no sycophant. For three months I saw him daily and can testify to his resoluteness. We lived in the same hotel and, while I played poker with his staff at night, Robins read his Bible and gathered fresh strength for an assault on Lenin or on his own Embassy, for he was fearless in his approach to both. He was the only foreigner to whom Lenin was always accessible and the only person, I imagine, who never minced his words to him. He had considerable influence with Lenin and was indirectly responsible for the destruction of the Anarchists who were then making life unendurable for everyone in Moscow.

Here are the facts. On April 10, 1918, Robins' motor-car was stolen while he was inside the main post office. In high dudgeon he went to complain to Chicherin. The meek and gentle Chicherin condoled but could not help. "Mine was pinched last week," he said pathetically. Off went Robins, now like an Indian chief on the warpath, to see Trotsky who could offer only a more vigorous sympathy than that of Chicherin. Trotsky, too, had had a car stolen by the Anarchists. By this time Robins was really angry, and in such moods there was no stopping him. He must see Lenin. He was received at once. Told by Robins that, if he could not deal with a bunch of bandits, his Government was "bust", Lenin gave his orders. At 3 a.m. on April 12 the Bolsheviks carried out a simultaneous attack with armoured cars on the twenty-six headquarters of the Anarchists who, taken completely by surprise, were driven out of the fine houses which they had occupied and were forced to give up their machine-guns, rifles, ammunition and loot. The attack was Trotsky's first great operation as Commissar for War. Later in the day Derjinski gave Robins and me a car and, with Peters as our guide, we were driven round the scenes of the victory. The sight was grim. Typical of the times was the fact that Peters and our Cheka chauffeur wore exactly the same clothes as the dead bandits: breeches and belted brown-leather jackets with side-pockets in which a revolver or a Browning could be held ready to fire.

Robins was on much better terms with Lenin than he was with the American Embassy which disliked both his policy and his methods. Robins was quite impenitent and, when he saw that he could make no headway in Russia, went back to the United States to enlist such Congressional support for his policy as he could command.

He had to wait a long time for his triumph, but when it came it was in full measure. Early in the first presidency of Franklin Roosevelt the Government of the United States accorded full recognition to the Soviet Union, and to celebrate the occasion a dinner, attended by nearly 2000 people, was given to Litvinov in the Waldorf-Astoria Hotel in New York. It was Robins' evening.

He made the big speech and named one by one the Americans who had fought for recognition.

Inevitably his enthusiasm for his policy made many Americans suspect him of being a Communist. This, I am sure, he was not. At the time—and his time was before Stalin's purges—he believed that the revolution was a step forward for Russia and, like most Americans, he fought hard for his own way. I saw him in New York in February 1934, at a small luncheon-party at the Century Club. He was in his best form and, denying the charge of Communist sympathies, described himself as a petty capitalist with a religious complex and a realistic outlook on Russian affairs.

Long retired from public life, he now lives in Florida where he owns a large orange plantation. He is still mentally alert, but a fall from one of his orange trees has lamed him so severely that he cannot get about except in a wheel-chair.

Robins, who spoke no Russian, owed much of his success with the Bolsheviks to his Russo-American assistant, Alex Gumberg, a highly intelligent and quick-witted young man with a keen sense of humour, great political prescience, and a thorough knowledge of the mentality of both Communists and American capitalists. He had a brother who was a Commissar. With these advantages, which he used to the full, he was of great help to both Robins and myself. Not only was his information nearly always reliable, but his judgment of the constantly changing situation was excellent. The Bolsheviks, I am sure, would have been glad to use his services, but, although his sympathies were then with the Left, he had no wish to change life in the United States for the risks of Soviet Russia.

He was a good friend to me both in the Soviet Union and in the United States which I visited in 1934 and 1939. By 1939 his brother had been "liquidated" and Alex himself had become a cynic as far as Russia was concerned. Still interested in politics, he was deeply involved in high finance for which he had a real flair and on which he was consulted by firms like Morgans and the Atlas Company. Affluent and hospitable, he was a striking example of what the American melting-pot can do for a poor Eastern European emigré. Had he remained in Russia, he would probably have shared his brother's fate. In the United States he died in his bed.

In their relations with the Bolshevik Government in 1918 the French were at a disadvantage compared with the Americans and British, partly because the attitude of the French Government and of the French ambassador was violently hostile to the régime and partly because Jacques Sadoul, the chief French liaison with the Bolsheviks, was a member of the French Military Mission and therefore under military discipline. Sadoul, whom I knew well, was a successful French lawyer who had begun his career as a junior to Labori, the famous defender of Dreyfus, and had then gone into politics as a Socialist. When the war came, he became an officer, and Albert Thomas sent him to Russia.

A convinced Marxist, Sadoul was soon on good terms with Trotsky from whom he obtained some useful concessions which Noulens, the French ambassador, refused contemptuously to accept. When, later, Noulens withdrew from him the right to communicate with Albert Thomas by cypher telegram, then the only means of communication with the outside world, Sadoul became more and more embittered, and I was not astonished when on his return to France he joined the French Communist Party. In addition to Sadoul, there were two other members of the French Military Mission, René Marchand and the gentle and charming Pierre Pascal, who, irritated by the irascible Noulens, sided with the Communists. Both were eventually disillusioned, and Pierre Pascal is now Professor of Russian at the Sorbonne. In those days, at least, some ambassadors and generals made more converts to Communism than the best professional Communist missionaries.

As for my own tiny Mission, we were only three in number when, after the departure of the members of the British Embassy, we set out with Trotsky from a deserted Petrograd to Moscow on March 16, 1918. Today I am the only survivor. Will Hicks, my chief assistant and most loyal friend, died in Berlin in 1930. Denis Garstin, a young officer and a confirmed opponent of intervention, was taken away from me early in July by the War Office and sent to Archangel where he was killed a few weeks later by the people with whom he had worked so hard for an understanding.

My own journey home was unpleasant, and in the ship the

King's Messenger attacked me in front of all the passengers and declared loudly that I was entirely responsible for the Bolsheviks remaining in power.

By first opposing the intervention and then, as a dutiful official, accepting the contrary policy of the British Government, I had fallen between two stools if, indeed, such an acrobatic feat is possible. By the interventionists I was regarded as a romantic and foolish young man who had delayed and spoilt their plans. The anti-interventionists saw in me a chicken-hearted official who had put his career before his principles. By many of my middle-class friends who had no inside knowledge of what had been happening I was praised to my face as a gallant secret service agent who had done all the desperate deeds of which he had been accused. And this was the hardest cut of all. Nor did the story of my romance with Moura help. Long before my return it had gone the round of the gossips in numerous versions of which the most popular was that I had been bewitched by a beautiful Bolshevik spy.

At the time I was unhappy, and the experience cost me much of my youthful self-confidence. But today the pin-pricks have long been forgotten, and, although I sometimes wonder how far the course of history might have been changed if there had been no intervention, I see myself now as a tiny cork thrown by chance —yes, and by good luck—into a maelstrom which in the name of material progress has engulfed millions of lives.

The material progress is manifest in the sky-scrapers, the modern factories, the network of new canals, and the grandiose hydro-electric installations which today bear witness to what may best be described as the Americanisation of Russia. But emancipation of the people has not accompanied these improvements. Liberty of the subject is more restricted than it was in the reign of Nicholas the Second and the price of it is severer silence. Indeed, in its ruthless disregard of human life and in its creation of a large privileged class, graded in rank and rich in titles, the Soviet Union has much in common with the Russia of Peter the Great. The loss of life among the slave workers who built the Soviet canals and who today mine the coal and gold in the Kolyma district of Siberia has its counterpart in the appalling death-rate among the workers who built St. Petersburg.

Certainly the contrast between the Soviet leaders of today and the men who made the October revolution is startling. Gone is the idealism, which in 1917 and 1918 inspired both leaders and rank and file and induced those foreigners who lived through the revolution to hope that from the turmoil a better Russia would emerge. Like many others I had been affected by the spirit of self-sacrifice and abnegation of personal ambition which animated the early revolutionaries. I find much to fear, but little to admire in the counter-revolution of Stalin.

Today I look back on the revolution with a profound consciousness of the power for good or evil which the strength of will of a handful of men can exercise on human destiny, with regret for my own sins of omission and commission, and with lasting gratitude to Fate which thrust me at a young and impressionable age into the centre of great events, put me in touch with men who were altering the history of the world, and, if it made me many enemies, gave me the best friends I have ever had. It is in adversity that one knows one's real friends, and mine stood by me.

Of these friends only Moura is alive today. She is now a naturalised British subject and has a wide circle of friends in this country. But there can be few who saw her in those stirring days in Russia when she was in the prime of her youth and good looks, tireless in her energy, magnificently indifferent to the loss of great possessions, highly intelligent and quick-witted, and with her dark, wavy hair and smiling, fearless eyes a *nonparella* of grace and beauty and indomitable courage.

I see her regularly and among the many Russians whom I know few have endured the long and difficult years of exile with such fortitude and selflessness as she has. Her interests are wide-spread, and because she thinks of others and never of herself she rises supreme over her own difficulties.

We talk rarely of the past, and our gypsy days are over. In life it is a good rule never to go back, but I broke it for the gypies on March 18, 1936. I had arrived in Paris from the Riviera at 10.45 p.m. and had just undressed when the telephone rang. It

E

was Moura. Would I come round to 72 Rue de la Fondarie at once? I went and found her in a Russian cabaret with her sister and brother-in-law Prince and Princess Kotchubey and M. Yazykov, a former Russian diplomat. The cabaret was tiny and rather dingy with lanterns casting crotchety shadows on the low ceiling.

As I came in, a young Russian with glassy, staring eyes swallowed a last vodka and staggered from the room. We now had the place to ourselves, and I sat down with some misgivings. I was tired after my journey and not in the mood to have my memories harrowed. Nor did the performers, only three in number, seem to promise much. I was mistaken. The tall pianist, an *emigré* aristocrat, drew wonders from his cottage piano. There was a competent Caucasian guitarist. The requisite gypsy element was represented by a dignified old lady in a plain black dress with a faded white lace collar and a long necklace of imitation pearls. The voice was genuine, as good as any that I have heard, and, as she sang all the old favourites in that deep quivering contralto which is the special gift of the real *tsiganka*, the mist between the present and the far-off yesterdays rolled away. As a finale to a long session she sang to an old tune the song of the exiles, *Molis Kunak*, "Pray, warrior, pray that God will give you strength to return to your own country."

The song, banned on the Paris radio in order to please the Soviet Government, was plaintive and in the dim light of the little cabaret very moving. I thought of Yesenin, the blond young peasant poet, whose brief flame of genius had flourished in Moscow during the early years of the revolution:

> "Bring the guitar that I have loved too well;
> Come, gypsy, play some song that will release
> And help me to forget these poisoned days
> Which brought no love, no happiness, no peace."

I looked at Moura. Her eyes were fixed on the ceiling, and there were tears in them. These gypsy songs did not help one to forget. They forced one to remember. And for Moura and for me there was no way back across the years.

Chapter V

MEMORIES AND PORTRAITS

"I've studied men from my topsy-turvy
Close, and, I reckon, rather true.
Some are fine fellows: some, right scurvy:
Most, a dash between the two."

IT has often been said with something more than a half-truth that the Russian is the pleasantest and most scintillating of casual companions, but hard to live with, and to do business with—impossible. Inevitably there are exceptions, for the Russian character is highly individual and combines frequently in one person extremes of expansiveness and reserve, frankness and suspicion, constancy and infidelity, and generous kindness and savage cruelty. Personally, I have always been fascinated by the variability of the Russian mood and, although since 1918 I have never been allowed to go back to Russia, I have followed with intense interest the subsequent careers of those Russians, politicians and poets, actors, artists and adventurers among whom my lot was once cast either by choice or by duty and who exercised a moulding influence on my character.

First must come Maxim Gorki whose works opened my eyes to the terrible contrast between wealth and poverty and prepared me for what was to come in Russia. I met him only once—in February 1915, in Moscow, when I was introduced to him and placed beside him at Baleiev's famous cabaret "The Bat". He was quite unlike the portrait drawn of him by Ivan Bunin, the Nobel prizeman, in his little book of memoirs which, was published in England in 1950. To me Gorki seemed the most modest and quietest of men. His face was full of feeling and sympathy; very rugged, too, except for the softness of the eyes. I saw none of the conceit and arrogance which Bunin ascribes to him. We sat at the back of the hall and between the various turns on the platform talked at random. Gorki spoke very quietly and avoided all mention of the War to which, as indeed to all wars, he was opposed. He smiled at the antics of Baleiev, the Armenian *compère* of the entertainment, but reserved his praise for the Russian performers and told me that all Russians were born with theatre in their blood. He seemed surprised that I could speak Russian and said that I therefore could read him easily in the original. I answered truthfully that I knew his play, *The Lower Depths*, almost by heart but that I found his novels difficult because he used so many peasant words. "Ah," he said, "if you want to understand Russia you must see something more of it than the cities."

In those days it was Baleiev's custom, when any distinguished person came to "The Bat", to make a short speech and call on the audience to drink the visitor's health with musical honours. He did this, of course, for Gorki, and I never saw anyone look more genuinely miserable.

I did not see Gorki in 1918 when for a time he criticised certain aspects of the Bolshevik *coup d'état*. In spite of his neutral attitude he did a noble job in persuading Lenin, with whom he had long been on terms of friendship, to spare and to release distinguished writers and scientists who were opposed to the régime. In 1921 a recurrence of the tuberculosis from which he had always suffered compelled him to leave Russia and return to Italy.

During his enforced exile he continued to remain in close touch with events in Russia and, though never abandoning his independent approach, became increasingly interested in the changes that were taking place in his country.

His absence, however, became the object of virulent attacks by the more rabid section of the Bolsheviks, and the Soviet critic Gorbachev characterised his attitude towards the revolution as one of "benevolent incomprehension". In reality it was an attitude of approval limited by the full right to criticise. He exercised this right on several occasions, although when he returned to Russia for good in 1928 his attitude hardened in favour of the régime and he attacked its enemies with almost vicious vigour.

When he died in June 1936, his passing was mourned by the

whole Soviet Union, and Stalin himself was a pall-bearer at the funeral. This proper and laudable commemoration of a great writer was marred by a subsequent and stupid attempt on the part of the régime to attribute his death to the machinations of the followers of Trotsky, who "instigated by their Fascist employers", allegedly either poisoned him or sabotaged the treatment which would have cured him.

Gorki's best work was written before the revolution, but today he is recognised throughout the Communist countries as "the creator of proletarian literature". By the end of 1951 59,155,000 copies of his works had been published in the Soviet Union alone, a total which puts him well ahead of Pushkin and Leo Tolstoy, his nearest rivals.

In spite of the violence of his later writing, I have always regarded Gorki as a most humane man who was incapable of hurting any living creature. In the last years of his life he was held in great honour by the Communists and was housed in splendour in the Moscow mansion of the late Michael Riabushinski, a member of the former well-known family of Russian millionaires and the father of Tatiana Riabushinska, the ballerina. Before the revolution forced Michael Riabushinski into exile, I knew the house well and dandled the future ballerina, then a baby, on my knee.

Gorki, I think, loses in stature for taking up his abode in a millionaire's house, although I do not suppose that he had much choice in the selection. His real name was Pieshkov, and during the last war many Whitehall officers and officials must have met Colonel (now General) Zinovy Pieshkov, a much decorated French officer and then an ardent supporter of General de Gaulle. Zinovy Pieshkov was the adopted son of Maxim Gorki. Here is the story.

At the time of the abortive revolution of 1905–6 Gorki was arrested during a manifestation of students in Nijni-Novgorod. Among those arrested was a street-urchin who had been caught distributing anti-Tsarist leaflets. When he was brought into the court to await the arrival of the examining magistrate, the boy saw lying on the desk a copy of the leaflet, the only incriminating piece of evidence against him. In the flash of a second he filched it

from the file and ate it.   The authorities had no other course but
to set him free.

When Gorki was released in his turn, he learnt of the boy's
remarkable presence of mind and was so delighted with it that he
adopted him as his son, and paid for his education.   In time the
young Pieshkov joined the French Foreign Legion, fought gallantly
in the First World War in which he lost an arm, became a French
subject, and transferred to the French army.

In politics Gorki and his adopted son were poles apart, but they
corresponded regularly until Gorki's death in 1936.

General Zinovy Pieshkov ended his career as head of the French
Diplomatic Mission to Japan and now lives in Paris.   His real name
is Sverdlov.   He is a younger brother of the late Jacob Sverdlov,
the first President of the Soviet Union and a fanatical Bolshevik
who in 1914 shared an exile's room with Stalin in the forsaken
Siberian settlement of Kureika.   His memory is perpetuated in the
city of Sverdlovsk, the new name for Ekaterinburg where the Tsar
and all his family were murdered in July 1918.

The last time I saw Jacob Sverdlov was in the Big Theatre in
Moscow when as Chairman of the Presidium he was vainly trying
to keep order in the rowdiest Congress of Soviets in the history of
the U.S.S.R.   The last time I met his French General brother was
over a cocktail in the St. James's Club in London during the Second
World War.

If I knew Gorki only from afar, I was on intimate terms with
Count Alexei Nikolaievitch Tolstoy who was by a long way the most
intriguing and amusing of my Bohemian acquaintances.   I met him
during the First World War when he was writing for the *Russkiya
Viedomosti*, a Moscow Liberal newspaper with a high standard of
literary excellence and erudition.   I got to know him really well
through a lucky chance.   Early in 1916 the war was going badly
for the Allies and especially for Russia, and both St. Petersburg and
Moscow were buzzing with the same malicious rumours that were
so widespread about the Second Front in 1942 and 1943.   The
English were not trying.   They were keeping their Navy in a glass
case.   England would fight until the last drop of Russian blood.

To check these lies the British Government decided to invite a party of distinguished Russian writers and journalists to visit the Western Front, see the factories of Britain, and, in general, write up the British war effort on their return. I was instructed by our ambassador to invite Alexei Tolstoy to be a member of the party. I got in touch with him at once and invited him to dine with me at the Hermitage, then a famous Moscow restaurant, and talk things over. Tolstoy, big, corpulent, and rather unhealthy-looking, with dark hair, clean-shaven, blue-jowled face, and an eccentric taste in dress, was a formidable trencherman even according to Russian standards, and, with admiration tempered by increasing anxiety over my ability to foot the bill, I wondered when his capacity for food and drink would be satisfied. It was an expensive evening, but long before it was over he had accepted the invitation to go to England. With each glass his enthusiasm expanded. England, he said, was the one country that he had always admired. These silly and disgusting stories against the English were invented by the pro-German swine in St. Petersburg. He was the one man who could expose their treachery and nothing would give him so much pleasure as doing it.

I see that I was not greatly impressed by his exuberance, for the entry in my diary for that night of February 12, 1916, is brief and uncomplimentary. "He seems a fat, sleek kind of a pig. I fear there will be trouble over his mission." I doubted if he would do a good job.

He came to see me before he left. He was dressed for his new part in a pair of sponge-bag trousers, a mongrel black coat that was a cross between a frock-coat and a short jacket, a stiff butterfly collar with the widest of wings, and a flowing bow-tie. He looked like a mid-Victorian dandy. When I saw him off, he was wearing a magnificent fur coat. On his head was a curiously shaped bowler which would have made Mr. Churchill envious. My doubts about his ability to succeed were not diminished by this flamboyance.

I was entirely wrong. He returned from England in high spirits. He had enjoyed himself and with every sign of genuine enthusiasm he wrote a series of articles on the English war effort, so vivid and so apparently sincere that all Moscow read them. From that moment he posed as the great Russian Anglophile, appeared at gatherings of the Society for Rapprochement with England, and interlarded his conversation with English expressions. I saw him fairly often. He called me by my Christian name and gave me his books.

To this extent we were friends. He possessed all the talents and could write novels, sketches and verse with the same facility. But he was completely un-moral, had no convictions and no loyalties, and was interested only in money, high living and his own success. He could therefore adapt himself to political changes with a speed and an ease which shocked his more conscientious compatriots. He was a distant relation of Leo Tolstoy, but his rivals always said that the legitimacy of his birth, and therefore of his title of Count, was doubtful. He was a man whom it was difficult to dislike and even more difficult to respect.

After the Bolshevik revolution he escaped, not to England which would have been too dull for him, but to Paris, and during this period no other Russian exile was more vehement in his denunciation of the Bolsheviks than Alexei Nikolaievitch. In Paris he led his usual extravagant life. Soon, however, his money ran out, and no money meant no gypsies and no vodka. I was therefore not surprised when, by writing a couple of plays against the Romanovs, he made his peace with the Bolsheviks and went back to Russia. He posed as the patriot who could not live away from his own country, and to do him justice it was perhaps not merely pose. He wanted literary fame as well as wine and song.

Certain it is that the return was highly successful. The Bolsheviks received him royally or at least as a Count, and soon he was back to his old life of wine, women, gypsy music—and work. For the man was always a worker, and a speedy and quick worker at that. His mode of living got him into trouble with the Bolshevik purists, and he was summoned before the Society of Authors to answer charges of leading a bourgeois life and of writing bourgeois books. Tolstoy, however, was no fool. He had taken pains to ingratiate himself into Stalin's favour and to obtain from the great man a flattering inscription to the first volume of his *Peter the Great*. Armed with this copy of his book, Tolstoy appeared before his inquisitors and said: "I never read reviews of my work, but here is one that may interest you." The charges of deviationism were dropped and never renewed.

At intervals I heard indirectly from Tolstoy, but I never expected to see him again. Then in the forenoon of July 10, 1935, I received a message. Alexei Nikolaievitch was in London and wanted to see me. We arranged to meet in the evening at Josef's, the little Serbian restaurant in Greek Street. It was one of those oppressive evenings of damp, thundery heat when London is more unbearable than Batavia, and I arrived sweating, dispirited—and late. I had no difficulty in recognising my old acquaintance. He looked older, of course. The smooth, flabby face was now lined, and the massive figure had shrunk a little. But the old vigour was still there, and, as he greeted me, his voice, rather like the sound of a train entering a tunnel, resounded through the almost empty room. He was already rather drunk, but in full possession of his senses, and his talk, which ranged over half the world and never flagged, was scintillating. He had made the journey to London by the Soviet steamer *Smolny* and had been ashore at Hamburg. On this scanty evidence he had formed the conclusion that not only Hamburg but all Europe were dead. But London was overwhelming by its beauty, its magnificence, and its charm. It had always been his favourite city, and now after years in the drabness of Soviet Russia how wonderful it was to see the pretty and well-dressed women, the shops full of marvellous goods, and the brilliantly lit streets thronged with happy, care-free people. But most wonderful of all for him personally was to sniff again the free air of a free city. He closed his eyes and breathed heavily as his hand reached towards the brandy bottle. Was he serious? I think that for the moment he meant what he said. He was in the mood when all the world was roses.

I tried to draw him out about the Soviet Union. For him silence was impossible, but he became more cautious. He had his work, and this was the great thing. Life was not gay. It was even difficult, but not intolerable. He reverted quickly to the safer theme of the glories of London.

At the end of the evening I drove him back to the Soviet Embassy where he was staying. In the taxi he became suddenly confidential. "I have a favour to ask you. There is a Communist girl in France, the daughter of a cardinal and a nun, whom I wish to take back to Russia. I have been refused a transit visa. Can you help me?"

He leant heavily against me, gave a great guffaw, and then lapsed into silence. I thought that his potations had overcome him. I had under-estimated his strength. When we entered Kensington Palace Gardens, he was wide-awake. "I think I'll get out here," he said. He embraced me warmly on both cheeks, staggered out and walked the remaining hundred yards or so to the Soviet Embassy.

After his return to Russia I studied the Soviet newspapers carefully to see what he would write about his English visit. In due course his articles appeared. The theme had changed. London had become a mean city in which the contrast between wealth and poverty was a disgrace to civilisation.

Alexei Tolstoy continued to pour out novels, plays and poems until he died. During the war he became one of the most powerful propagandists on the Allied side, attacking the Germans with bitter invective and again finding words of praise for the British war effort. His death in February 1945 came opportunely, both for his reputation and his personal safety, for had he lived a year or two longer, even his chameleon-like qualities might not have saved him from the literary purges which followed Zhdanov's denunciation of the "rootless cosmopolitans" and "deviationists" under the influence of the decadent West.

In this respect fate has dealt kindly with him, for today he ranks second only to Gorki as the greatest proletarian writer of the Soviet Union. His prodigious output is uneven in quality, but the best of it stands very high. Only thirty-four when the revolution started, he spent the greater part of his life as a writer in the new Russia. He never felt himself entirely free in it, and *The Childhood of Nikita*, the book by which he is best known in the Soviet Union and which will probably give him enduring fame, was written in exile. To us foreigners he is a better guide to the Russia of today than Dostoievsky.

One other fact remains to be chronicled. Alexei Tolstoy was a voluptuary who always needed money. In the Soviet Union he made it on the grand scale, for with the increase of literacy among the Russian people the sales and earnings of a successful Soviet writer far exceed those of even the most popular American or British author. The Soviet writer, too, is much less heavily taxed.

In 1917 and 1918 I was too preoccupied with other matters to make the acquaintance of the young poets of the revolution. On several occasions I met the exotic and flamboyant Mayakovsky, the founder of collective futurism and poet of the crowd. He forced himself on the attention of the Moscow public by his eccentric dress and wild escapades; but I cannot say that I really knew him. There was, however, one gifted young man whose poetry has influenced me deeply, and that was Sergey Alexandrovitch Yesenin. Although he began to write before the revolution, I never knew him and never even saw him. In 1918 he was just twenty-three, a flaxen-haired, blue-eyed son of the soil who had embraced the revolution with the fervour of a land-hungry peasant and who saw in Lenin the god who had created a new world. Unfortunately, he succumbed early to the temptations of the city, and even today he is best known to the Western world as the good-looking young man whom Isadora Duncan swept off his feet and married within three weeks of her forty-fourth birthday. The marriage, stormy from the first, lasted just over three and a half years and ended in the Hotel d'Angleterre in Leningrad in 1925 when, in the same room in which he had stayed with Isadora Duncan on their first visit, Yesenin cut a vein in his wrist, wrote a farewell poem to his wife, and then hanged himself.

The truth is that, while Yesenin could inspire others, he could not control himself. When drunk, he was a hooligan. When he was alone in the steppes which he loved and evoked so well, he was a child with a divine gift of song. His poems fall easily into three divisions: the early poems of the country-side, the revolutionary songs, sometimes graceful, sometimes turbulent, blasphemous and rebellious, and the final poems of disillusionment and despair.

Gratitude to Lenin is expressed in a poem of sincere admiration of which the following lines are a sample:

> "Not his the locks which win success
> With languorous women.
> Bald as a tray, most modest of the modest,
> Simple and kind and shy,
> He was for me a kind of sphinx.
> I never knew what force in him
> It was that shook the world,
> But shake the world he did."

The gratitude to the Bolsheviks did not last. After using the peasants to make the revolution, they had betrayed them, and Yesenin, an individualist who never was wholly able to cross the gulf between the old Russia and the new, became more and more restive and querulous. This new mood is expressed in his long poem, "The Russia That is Passing":

> "What have I seen?
> All I have seen is war.
> Instead of songs I heard the cannon's roar. . . ."

> "That I belong not to the 'new'
> Far be it from me to conceal.
> With one foot I remain within the past
> And, as I strive to join the ranks of steel,
> I slip and with the others fall behind. . . ."

> "I envy those whose life is spent in strife,
> Who steadfast stand for some inspiring cause,
> But I, my youth in ruins, grope and have
> Not even memories. . . ."

Just thirty when he ended his life, Yesenin, too, was perhaps fortunate in his death, for sooner or later he would almost certainly have run foul of the régime. Today some of his revolutionary poems are still included in Soviet anthologies, but danger stalks those who quote him indiscriminately. In his *Retouches à mon Retour de l'U.R.S.S.* André Gide mentions a Russian friend X.

who, in wine, recites Yesenin's poems with tears in his eyes. Gide's guide takes alarm and tells the emotional Russian to stop at once. Again, in *It Happens in Russia* Vladimir Petrov tells how he meets in prison seven Russian schoolboys of sixteen and seventeen who had been arrested for reading anti-Soviet literature. Included under the category of anti-Soviet were the poems of Yesenin.

Unlike his revolutionary contemporaries, Yesenin was a true lyric poet and, as such, will have a permanent place in Russian literature. During the last war I read him constantly, finding in the music of his verse a nostalgic echo of my own stormy youth.

Another poet who attracted me during the last war was Konstantin Simonov. Younger and less gifted than Yesenin, he wrote some moving war lyrics and, incidentally, sent the volume in which they appeared to an Englishman with the following dedication: "To Herbert Wells on whose books I was brought up from childhood, as a mark of my profound respect, K. Simonov, Moscow, 16th July, 1943." Today such a dedication would be dangerous to a Soviet writer, but Simonov has long ago sold himself body and soul to the Party line, is one of the spear-heads of the Communist attack on the West, and writes violent and rather stupid plays against the United States. As editor of the *Literaturnaia Gazeta*, he is in a position to conduct a witch-hunt not only of Soviet literary deviationists but also of foreign writers. He exercises his power to the full and on November 27, 1951, filled four long columns of his newspaper with a scarifying denunciation of Mr. J. B. Priestley whom previously he had obviously regarded almost as a fellow traveller.

Still on the right side of forty, Simonov has earned big money. He spends it lavishly at the expense of his literary reputation and, I imagine, of his own soul.

Denunciation of living Western writers as decadents does not mean that all Western literature is banned. Translations of Jack London sell in millions of copies and the works of Charles Dickens are a close second. Like the Germans, too, the Soviet Communists not only honour Shakespeare but claim him as their own, as the following quotation from Simonov's newspaper* shows:

* *Literaturnaia Gazeta*, 4th October, 1951.

"The great English poet, the proud Swan of Avon, has, as it were, crossed the sea. He feels himself more at home in the Soviet Union than he does in England where contemporary bourgeois society is retouching his sturdy features in the most scandalous manner. We know the real, unfalsified Shakespeare."

This boastful arrogance is part and parcel of the *Russland über Alles* theme of which Konstantin Simonov is the most perfervid exponent. To my mind it is a more sinister portent than the most violent political speech of M. Vyshinsky.

My next portrait is of a ghost that has come back to life. In *Memoirs of a British Agent*, I related how in the winter of 1918 I met in an underground cabaret in Moscow a young artist called Vertinsky, who enjoyed a brief popularity as the singer of defeatism. He had an almost feminine figure and, when he appeared on the stage with his face made up as white as his pierrot costume, he really looked like a ghost. He sang lugubriously of the uselessness of war, and the Moscow night-hawks, spending the last of their now useless money on champagne and melancholy, encored him again and again. He had talent. Indeed, of all the Russian entertainers he is the one whose performance, partly because of the circumstance and environment of time and place, I remember most vividly.

When Trotsky closed the cabarets in the spring of 1918, Vertinsky made his way to Paris. For a time I heard of him. He was faring badly, and I had long supposed that he was dead. Then in 1951 one of the members of our Moscow Embassy told me of the wonderful success of a Russian cabaret singer who had come back after over thirty years of exile. It was the same Vertinsky. His success was so great that the Soviet authorities became alarmed and stopped him singing. They permitted him, however, to play in films, and here, too, he has scored a big success. But it is his songs which make the irresistible appeal, and I am assured that on the black market of Moscow his gramophone records fetch a high price.

Today I have another living link with my Russian past in André Michelsen, the son of the rich Moscow industrialist in whose factory the fanatical young Jewess, Fanny Kaplan, fired two shots point-blank at Lenin. The attempt led to the arrest of all the French and British officials in Moscow and Petrograd, and while Lenin's life hung in the balance our own lives were in considerable danger.

The Michelsen father of course heard of the attempt as soon as it happened, left his house at once and after a series af adventures made his way abroad. The mother remained at home to look after André, then a boy of twelve, but she soon died from hardship. Some years later André, now a well-built and dangerously good-looking young man, was allowed to leave Russia. He inherited a fortune of £30,000 on his father's death and, as revolutions do not encourage thrift, spent it in three years. His experiences gave him the material for several successful books, of which *The Castle of Chillon* is the best.

I met André in London more than thirty years later. He is still an attractive and gifted man. Today he is a leading member of the B.B.C. team which broadcasts daily to the Soviet Union.

With Alexander Kerensky, whom I knew intimately in Russia in 1917, I have remained in friendly relations ever since, and have seen him frequently. Few men have risen to such heights and fallen so quickly. In 1917 not only many Russians but all the leaders of Britain, France and the United States expected from him a miracle which was beyond the power of any human being to perform. He did his best. He was then a sick man suffering from a diseased kidney, but he never spared himself. When he failed, as he was bound to fail unless he made a separate peace, his countrymen made him the scapegoat of their own mistakes. The world dismissed him with the same indifference with which it treats all fallen idols.

Kerensky has borne his eclipse and exile with dignity. He has recovered his health and does not look his seventy years. He bears no malice. Today he is interested in the million and a half Russians, mainly prisoners-of-war and deserters, who refused to go back to the Soviet Union after the last war. He is still an optimist. He gave to Russia six months of freedom—his critics would say six months of uncontrolled freedom—and he is confident that freedom once given is never forgotten. He believes that the end of Communism will come in Russia, but he has no illusions that it will come quickly.

Although he has long made his home in the United States, he has left a legacy to Britain in his two sons, both of whom are British subjects. Both have done well. Oleg, a brilliant engineer and a strong anti-Communist, built most of the bridges on the rail and road routes from Persia, which during the war carried Anglo-American aid to the hard-pressed armies of the Soviet Union. Oleg's son is at Oxford and, as a member of the Labour Party, was elected Secretary of the Union. Oleg's brother is with the British Thompson-Houston Company.

Alexander Kerensky has another tie with England. One of his best friends was a Russian political *emigré* who before the March revolution had spent many years of exile in our country and married an English lady. When Kerensky came into power, his old friend returned to Russia and became head of Kerensky's personal Secretariat. Six months later the Bolshevik revolution sent the friend back to England as an *emigré* for the second time. The friend's name was David Soskice. He was the father of Sir Frank Soskice, Solicitor-General and Attorney-General in the two Labour Governments of 1945–50 and 1950–51.

Chapter VI

THE RED TSAR

"One of the painful things about our times is that those who feel certainty are stupid, and those with any imagination and understanding are filled with doubt and indecision."

BERTRAND RUSSELL.

ON August 22, 1939, Hitler informed the German High Command: "I have decided to go in with Stalin, because there are only three great statesmen in the world; Stalin, myself and Mussolini. Mussolini is the weakest."

At that time Stalin was certainly a powerful figure. Lenin, who made the October revolution, died before he had completed it. Fourteen years after Lenin's death Stalin had carried out his counter-revolution and by a series of bloody purges had rid himself of the revolutionary intellectuals, most of whom had been the close associates of Lenin. He then proceeded to perform a miracle. Betrayed by his ally, Hitler, he was forced into a war which he had sought to avoid and, partly by good fortune, partly by the mistakes of his enemy and by the help of his new allies, but mainly by his own qualities of leadership, he enabled his country to win its first military victory for over a hundred years. Inevitably the man of the people became the people's idol.

Whatever one may think of his methods, Stalin's place in world history is secure. It is therefore an almost irresistible temptation to everyone who has been concerned with Slav affairs to try to analyse his character and to estimate the permanence or impermanence of his achievement. It is a difficult and, in many respects, an unprofitable task, for standards of comparison are lacking and no foreigners and few Russians have known him intimately. Foreigners who were well acquainted with Tsarist Russia are not welcome in the Soviet Union. Those, including the Western ambassadors, who are

F

tolerated there today, live in a kind of ghetto, are restricted in their movements, and seldom, if ever, see the Communist Tsar even at a distance.

Another obstacle which makes even an estimate of Stalin's popularity difficult is the systematic falsification of history which has taken place since Lenin's death. The history of the revolution has been re-written several times. Documents have been destroyed or altered. Names have been expunged or, like Trotsky's, retained only for execration and abuse. The figures of prominent revolutionaries have been removed from official photographs and even from films. Today Stalin is not only the victor of the last war but also the hero of the revolution, the favourite pupil and staunchest colleague of Lenin, and the creator of the Red Army.

His enemies deny him any part in the revolution or in the creation of the Red Army and point out with some justification that before his death Lenin was highly suspicious of the ambitions of his pupil. The truth, I think, lies somewhere between these two extremes.

When the March revolution of 1917 swept the Tsar from his throne, Stalin was in Siberia where he had been serving a sentence of exile since February 1913. Most of the revolutionary exiles, including Lenin and Trotsky, were abroad, and the only Bolshevik of subsequent prominence in St. Petersburg at that time was Molotov, who was editing *Pravda*, then as now the organ of the Bolshevik Party.

The Government which the March revolution ushered in was liberal and democratic. It believed in all the freedoms and it at once permitted the political *emigrés* and the Siberian exiles to return. One of the first to reach St. Petersburg was Stalin who at once took over the editorship of *Pravda* from Molotov.

The two men had much in common. Unlike the *emigrés* they had spent their lives in Russia. They were of the people and had worked with the people and from an early age had organised strikes and clandestine meetings. For the security of themselves and of their relatives they had long abandoned their real names. Molotov, which means "hammerer", was born Scriabin and is a distant relation of the famous Russian composer of the same name. The

Georgian, Djugashvilli, a mouthful even for gifted linguists, adopted finally from his numerous aliases the cognomen of Stalin, the man of steel.

Both men had never been on intimate terms with the intellectual *emigrés*, and Stalin himself was fully conscious of his own intellectual deficiencies at this time. This sense of inferiority explains his caution during the period from March 1917 until July 1918, when, during a critical moment of the civil war, he was sent by Lenin to Tsaritsyn (now Stalingrad) as political commissar. Till then his role was a secondary one and to the general public he remained unknown.

In John Reed's *Ten Days that Shook the World*, to which Lenin contributed a laudatory preface and which contains the most graphic account of an eye-witness of the October revolution, Stalin is mentioned only once—and then only in an appendix in which his name appears as Commissar of Nationalities.

Stalin was no coward, but he knew—and, indeed, has always known—how to wait. During the period between the March revolution and the November revolution he continued to write somewhat cautious articles for *Pradva*. He was the intermediary between the Central Committee and Lenin who, having been sent back to Russia in a sealed railway carriage by the Germans, was in a different category from the other returned exiles and was forced to go into hiding to avoid arrest.

Stalin was also a member of the Revolutionary Military Committee which, under Trotsky, organised the October revolution, but in the rising itself he took no active part, and the allegorical pictures which now figure in Soviet text-books and which portray him standing by the guns and directing the fire of the insurgents are inventions of his flatterers.

I have often been asked how it was that people like Robins, Sadoul and myself, who in 1918 had passes to Smolny and more or less free access to the leading Commissars, failed to appreciate the importance and, indeed, the greatness of Stalin. It is a question to which there is only one answer. If anyone had suggested at that time that Stalin would be the successor to Lenin as leader of the Party every responsible Communist in the country would have smiled contemptuously or given a hundred reasons why such a thing could never happen.

I met Stalin only once. The Central Executive Committee were holding a meeting in what was formerly and is, I think, once more the restaurant of the Metropole Hotel in Moscow. Trotsky was haranguing the delegates from the rostrum from which in Tsarist times Konchik, the Czech band-leader, used to play his violin, and ogle the pretty wives of the Moscow merchants. Raymond Robins and I were sitting as privileged spectators at a side table. Presently a short and stockily built man came walking along the narrow passage between the rows of chairs and the side tables. Alex Gumberg introduced him to us. It was Stalin. He was dressed in a high-necked Russian shirt with his trousers tucked into long Russian boots. He seemed to be taking no interest in the proceedings. We exchanged a few polite words. He asked us if we wanted some tea. Then he walked sedately out of the room. He looked like a man who was always master of his time. Our tea came quickly.

Doubtless, we could have seen more of him in those days, although I think that even then he had no relations with foreigners. It was a mistake on our part, but at the time there seemed to be so many more interesting and more important people to get to know. Compared with the brilliant and flamboyant Trotsky or even the cynical, caustic and unprincipled Karl Radek, Stalin seemed an unexciting figure.

As the civil war developed, Stalin became increasingly active on the military side and, backed by Voroshilov, began to criticise Trotsky. It was the first open sign of a personal antagonism that began on the day on which the two men first met, and, although the real test of strength was not to come until after Lenin's death, Stalin received sufficient backing from Lenin to enable him to maintain his position against his then far more powerful rival.

Stalin's great opportunity came when he was appointed the first General Secretary of the Central Committee in April 1922. In the days of the Byzantine Empire the Emperors in Constantinople were accustomed to appoint Georgians to high provincial posts because of their proven ability as administrators, and this ability

Stalin, the greatest of all Georgians, had inherited. Incidentally, he owed his own appointment largely to the efforts of Molotov who as one of the previous routine secretaries of the Committee had worked quietly but persistently for Stalin's nomination as General Secretary.

From the first day of his appointment, fortune played into Stalin's hands. Lenin's illness gave a new and quite unexpected importance to the functions of the General Secretary. When he was clearly giving too free a rein to his own ambitions and seemed to be building up a vast bureaucratic machine, Lenin, detesting bureaucracy and well aware of the dangers of the Stalin–Trotsky antagonism, rebuked Stalin but was too ill to exercise his former powers of control. When Lenin died on January 30, 1924, Trotsky was convalescing in the Caucasus. Stalin was not the man to neglect such remarkable opportunities. He used them to make himself master of the Party machine, and four years after Lenin's death the brilliant and gifted Trotsky had been ousted from the Party and sent into exile at Alma Ata.

The quarrel between Stalin and Trotsky was partly political and partly personal. During Lenin's lifetime Trotsky wanted to spread the social revolution to all countries in order to save the Russian revolution. Like Marx who had no faith in Slavs, Trotsky did not believe that the revolution could survive in one country only, least of all in Russia. Stalin took the opposite view. He wanted to create Communism in one country only, in order to ensure subsequent revolution in the rest of the world. Like all Communists, both men desired the universal triumph of Communism. Stalin's approach, however, was backed by Lenin, and no eye-witness of the events of 1917 and 1918 ever doubted that it was the correct one.

After Lenin's death the quarrel became a struggle for personal power, and Stalin won, mainly because Trotsky, in spite of his exceptional talents, was highly temperamental in character, had never been a good Party man, and lacked fixity of purpose.

I have dwelt on these early years of the revolution not only because they were the formative period of Stalin's qualities as a leader, but also because they reveal how important a part fate or chance plays in the rise of even the greatest men. Had Lenin been killed outright by the two shots which Fanny Kaplan fired at him on the evening of August 31, 1917, at Michelsen's factory in Moscow, Trotsky would have succeeded him immediately. Stalin was then eight hundred miles away at Tsaritsyn. Had Kaplan been arrested before she was able to use her pistol, Lenin would probably have lived several years longer, and it is a fair assumption that the extra span might have ruined Stalin's chances.

By the will of fate the course of events favoured Stalin. By 1938 he was the sole master of the Soviet Union. The victory of the Soviet arms in 1945 elevated him to the throne of a demi-god. He has been seen in the flesh by only a tiny fraction of his 200,000,000 subjects, but his portrait hangs in every school and every public building not only of the Soviet Union but also of all the satellite countries. Children are taught to praise and love his name. Poets write hymns to his glory. After his seventieth birthday the Moscow newspapers continued for nearly two years to print the millions of congratulatory messages sent to him from far and wide. The periodic reports which the *kolkhozniki* and industrial Committees send to him have now assumed the stereotyped form of an imperial petition. They are printed on the front page of *Pravda* and *Izvestia*. The great man's name appears in huge letters. The text of the report starts as follows: "With great joy we report to you, dear Iosif Vissarionovich that the *kolkhozniki* of the Kirov District, thanks to the immense help of the Party, of the Government, and of you personally, dear comrade Stalin, have achieved new successes in the development of our socialistic agriculture." Then, after a mass of detail, comes the ending:

"The workers of the Kirov District wish you, Iosif Vissarionovich, our dearly beloved friend and father, our leader and our teacher, good health and long, long years of life for the joy, happiness and welfare of the Soviet people and of all progressive humanity."

We have to go back to the days of the Roman Empire to find similar adulation and similar servility. Stalin is Augustus, the peacemaker of the world, the father of peoples and the guarantor of their safety. He is super-human, semi-divine. By any standard of comparison it is a remarkable position for a Georgian to have achieved; a Georgian, moreover, who still speaks Russian with a strong Georgian accent and who, like Hans Andersen, was born of a humble cobbler father and a washerwoman mother.

Admittedly, in Stalin's realm the privileges and class-barriers are in reverse to those of Tsarism. Under the Tsars the Jewry were kept within the Pale, and young Jewesses took the yellow passport of the prostitute in order to study at the University of Moscow. Today it is the daughter of a nobleman or an intellectual who has to plead for special privileges or resort to subterfuge to obtain them. In one respect Stalin is more Tsarist than the Tsars. The Tsarist censors told the writer what he must *not* do. Stalin's censors tell him what he must do: support the Communist dogma or stop writing.

In 1839 the Marquis de Custine wrote: "Two things and one person are worth seeing in Russia: the opera at St. Petersburg during the white nights, the Moscow Kremlin by moonlight, and the Emperor of all the Russias." Put Stalin in the place of the Emperor, and the statement is as true today as when it was written, for in the imagination of the Russian people, who never see their rulers in the flesh, Stalin is a more mystical and, above all, a more honoured figure than any Tsar. "Orthodoxy, Autocracy, Nationalism"— he represents all three in the eyes of the numerous races of his empire.

Nor are his praises sung only by cowed and servile subjects. Nearly all the high representatives of the Western Allies who met him during the war were impressed by his ability. In the fourth volume of his *War Memoirs*, Mr. Churchill refers to him as "the great Revolutionary Chief and profound Russian statesman and warrior". President Roosevelt was no less generous in his admiration.

How far has absolute power corrupted the purity of Stalin's Communism? There are many who say today that Soviet Communism and Soviet Imperialism are co-existent and indivisible. Outwardly at least, Stalin's power seems absolute. More than a hundred years ago a Russian nobleman described the Russian constitution to Count von Münster as "absolutism tempered by assassination". Stalin's régime is absolutism reinforced by periodic purges. At the same time he has created the very incubus which Lenin regarded as the greatest danger to the revolution: he has built up round him a large and privileged official and military caste which has a stake in the régime. In the early years of the revolution the military officers, shorn of their epaulettes and their medals, had over them a Soviet of soldier deputies to control their work; the factory managers were subordinate to a Soviet of worker deputies. In their short leather jerkins the clerks in the ministries looked more like thugs than officials. Today the generals wear medals as big as saucers and diplomats and officials as well as service officers sport the largest epaulettes in the world. The factory manager is now a boss with a high-powered car and a fat salary. The contrasts between wealth and poverty, between privileged caste and under-dog, which the Soviet propagandists never tire of emphasising as characteristic of Britain and all non-Communist countries, are now much sharper in Moscow than they are in London.

Powerful Tsars and famous generals, once condemned by the historians of Lenin's time, have been resurrected as national heroes and the works of the historians consigned to the bonfire. There is, too, a new type of Soviet man with bullet-shaped head, close-cropped hair and tooth-brush moustache who resembles in hardness of character, if not in facial appearance, the tough self-made man of Tsarist times like Lopakhin in *The Cherry Orchard*. Functionally at least, the Soviet scene bears an increasing resemblance to the Tsarist design, and the fact that the Soviet propagandists never tire of repeating that centuries now lie between the Russia of the Soviets and the Russia of the Tsars is in itself a proof that the Communists regard the resemblance as a weak link in their armour. True it is that at different periods of history, such as the November revolution, a year or a single day is equal to a century. Stalin's counter-revolution, however, has narrowed the gap and has introduced a strong element of nationalism into what has always been and still is an international movement.

Nevertheless, Stalin, in my opinion, remains a Communist. Moreover, he is in the remarkable position of being the one man in the world who decides who is a Communist and who is not.

The slightest deviation from Stalinist dogma or Stalinist opportunism involves the suspect in immediate denunciation as a traitor, a Fascist, and an agent of the West.

Quite apart from the problems of Hegelian and Marxist philosophy, there are, I think, certain simple beliefs which every orthodox Communist must hold. When I was on more or less intimate terms with Communists like Radek and Peters they invariably referred to the bourgeois of all countries as "the enemy". Today everyone who is not a Communist, and this includes the Left Wing Socialist, is "the enemy". As "the enemy" is an immoral enemy, any weapons, including the weapons of deception and lies, can be used against him. As long ago as 1920 Lenin, in his address to the third All-Russian Komsomol Congress, said: "We repudiate all morality derived from non-human and non-class concepts. We say that our morality is entirely subordinated to the interests of the class struggle of the proletariat." This principle governs the Soviet conduct of the cold war today.

The goal is the universal triumph of Communism, and for this end every Communist must train himself. The non-Communist countries must be expected to resist. A final clash is therefore inevitable. It is the task of the Communist to retain the initative of timing. The dogma therefore permits periods of opportunism during which a temporary co-existence with the non-Communist countries can be sought. Co-existence does not mean that the Communists will cease from encouraging nationalism in the Colonial dependencies of the so-called Western imperialists or from suppressing it in the satellite Communist countries. The tactics of opportunism are closely linked with the final strategy. The one constant is the policy laid down by Lenin and almost certainly still accepted by Stalin: to weaken the enemy by every means short of military war until the final blow can be delivered quickly and decisively.

These are the beliefs which, I think, are held by every Communist, and it would be foolish for any non-Communist to ignore them. They are inherent in every aspect of Soviet policy today, and they affect profoundly the issue of war or peace. They do not, and should not, rule out the possibility of negotiation and hard bargaining. They should, however, put a brake on wishful thinking in Western minds.

No one can say whether the Soviet Communists will start what they would call a preventive war and we an aggressive war. The clash may have begun before these lines are in print. But one thing is certain. Stalin expects an aggressive war against him before the final collapse of capitalism. The West lives in an age of anxiety and uncertainty. The East lives in an age of dogmatic certainty tempered by suspicion. Stalin is therefore prepared for this war and, indeed, has sacrificed the well-being of the Communist state to military requirements.

There is perhaps one consolation. Before the First World War the revolutionaries whom I knew had one fixed idea. In a country like Russia where distances between towns and villages are immense it is always easy for the central government to repress an incipient revolt. The only chance for a successful revolution is when the country is engaged in a foreign war, for war puts arms into the hands of the people. The principle was accepted by Lenin. I believe that in a reverse sense it influences old revolutionaries like Stalin who undoubtedly realises that the only possible danger to the Soviet state would be an unsuccessful war or, indeed, a war which did not start with a rapid victory.

Two questions are raised by these assumptions: are there weaknesses in the Soviet state and what will happen when Stalin, who has virtues of restraint, passes from the Soviet scene?

There are weaknesses in the Soviet state, but they should not be exaggerated. The standard of life is still very low. Moscow has the finest underground stations in the world, some vast new buildings, one or two luxury hotels and restaurants, and a few broad and impressive streets. But go into a house off a main street, enter a seven-roomed flat, and you will find three or four people living in each room and for all the household there is one small kitchen and one lavatory. The bugs and cockroaches of Tsarist times have not decreased. The people look drab. Nearly everything can be bought at a price, but it is too high for the masses. Shopping queues are as long as ever. When a foreign woman, the wife of a diplomat or an Embassy secretary, returns from leave, the one present which delights her Russian cook is a packet of needles and pins, a reel of cotton, and a piece of cloth.

In the provincial towns the contrasts between the privileged caste and the masses is even greater than in Moscow. Under capitalism the *Stakhanovite* system would be called sweated labour. In the Soviet Union it works only because the fixed wage or norm of the ordinary worker is kept at a bare subsistence level.

The maintenance of the vast organisation of secret police, the secrecy which surrounds Stalin's movements, and the curtained bullet-proof cars in which the leading Communists drive to their country houses are proofs that the régime still maintains itself by fear and force. There is no sign of the withering state predicted by Marx. On the contrary, it is further away than ever. And, hidden all over the remotest areas of the Soviet Empire are the forced labour camps. They are manned mainly by Socialists and Communist deviationists. No one knows their exact number, for not many return or escape. But there are few families in the Soviet Union who have not lost some relation or friend, and today there is a whole series of plaintive songs of exile which are gradually becoming widely known and are sung in secret even in Moscow itself. There is, too, the known fact that in 1941 the Ukrainians were prepared to welcome the Nazis as liberators and but for the folly of Hitler many more would have come over than the hundreds of thousands who enlisted in Vlassov's army.

On the other side, the régime is ruthless and all-powerful. Stalin may be genial in private life, but he has never been afraid to shed blood. In his *War Memoirs* Mr. Churchill describes how, when Stalin was telling him of the millions of Russian peasants who had been blotted out or displaced during the campaign for the mechanisation of agriculture, he had been minded to quote to his host Burke's dictum: "If I cannot have reform without injustice, I will not have reform." Had Mr. Churchill made the remark, I have no doubt that Stalin would have countered it with Richelieu's dictum: "I find it easier to tolerate injustice than disorder." It is the excuse of all dictators, and Stalin knows his Richelieu as the first man in history to enjoy the rank and title of Generalissimus. The fact remains that in the Soviet Union, there is no disorder, no sign and, in peace time, no possibility of active resistance. There is also no freedom, and in a country where the Government lies deliberately as a matter of policy the people are silent. This silence may indicate their disbelief in Soviet propaganda, but it is also a proof of their fear.

Fear, too, is behind the confessions which opponents or victims of the régime make at public trials whenever they are staged.

I am often asked if these confessions are obtained by so-called truth drugs, and in recent times great progress has been made in psychosomatic medecine. In the last war the Germans made wide use of a powerful amphetamine which enabled the troops to withstand fatigue beyond normal endurance.

It is known, too, that in certain conditions the injection of salts of barbituric acid can produce a twilight of the conscience which is favourable to confession. Pentathol is another drug which is supposed to act as a serum of truth. The whole subject, however, is in its infancy and still provokes polemics among doctors and scientists.

Personally I believe that the Soviet confessions are obtained by a process of attrition in which fear, exhaustion and finally indifference play their part. I am confident that constant interrogation, the repetition of the same questions by different inquisitors, a combination of brutality and cajolery, and, above all, the continuous interference with the hours of sleep will, in time, break the moral fibre of the strongest man and induce him to confess almost anything. The time varies with the man, but it is a fact that no victim is brought to trial without a long period of preparation. If the régime desires to get rid of someone quickly, it *liquidates* him quietly without trial and without trace.

I also accept the view that, at the trials of life-long Communists, confessions are sometimes inspired by a desire on the part of the victim to put himself right with history and to devote his last words to the cause to which he has sacrificed himself.

Nevertheless, I believe that many Russians resent being shut off from all contact with the outside world, do not swallow all the propaganda of their own Government, and, in particular, would like to know more about the Western way of life. I also believe that, like all other peoples, they have no wish for a third world war.

As for what will happen after Stalin's death, the prophets are likely to be wrong and those who expect immediate changes and blood to flow in the streets are almost certain to be disappointed. Nevertheless, I make bold to say that Stalin's disappearance from the scene will mark the end of an epoch in Russian and in Soviet history. Dictators rarely leave successors, and Stalin has been a dynamic dictator who has extended the Soviet Empire far beyond the limits of its natural frontiers. Such men are rare, and the mere fact of his personal ascendency has tended to submerge the individuality of his colleagues in the Politburo and to reduce them to the rôle of mere subordinates. Molotov, who on official occasions is generally ranked second to Stalin, has been little more than a loyal staff officer. Malenkov, a much younger man, has been trained in the same job which in very different circumstances brought Stalin to the front, and has experience of the Party machine. Then there is Beria with the whole vast organisation of the secret police under his control. Here are the three elements which will not mix easily or accept readily a single authority. None of these three is more than a tiny satellite in the constellation that is Stalin, nor is there any other personality in the whole Union who enjoys wide popularity among the masses. Given the man, others can elevate him to the pinnacle of a demi-god. They cannot put themselves in his place.

Moreover, the Soviet Union has not stood still since Lenin's death. Under Stalin it has seen more startling changes than any other country in the world. To take only one, an almost wholly illiterate people has become almost literate. It reads voraciously, and as it becomes more literate it will want wider mental horizons than it is allowed at present.

There is, too, a curious discontinuity in the rhythm of Russian history. It comes from the character of a people who, like their climate, tend to extremes and whose history has been marked by long periods of great passivity followed at intervals by short periods of violent convulsion.

With the disappearance of Stalin from the scene further changes must be expected, not only in the Soviet Union, but also in the satellite countries.   Under Stalin the whole energy of Communist policy has been directed from Moscow towards the extension of the rule of Communism.   Policy has been marked by the ruthless suppression of opposition at home and by the deliberate fomentation of disorder abroad.   In this sense it has been more imperial than domestic, and it is in the domestic field that the changes are likely to come.   The machine may continue to run for some time even when the master hand has been removed from the lever.   The changes themselves may be slow in coming, but, even if they are for the worse before they are for the better, they are inevitable.

BOOK II

RETREAT FROM PRAGUE

" There is no happiness without liberty, but no liberty without courage."

PERICLES.

Chapter I

THE RETURN OF THE EXILE

"I've wandered East, I've wandered West,
Through mony a weary way;
But never, never can forget
The love o' life's young day."
WILLIAM MOTHERWELL.

NOTHING in my life has affected me so deeply as the tragedy of the unfortunate Czechoslovaks. My connexion with them began in 1918 when I was instructed by the Foreign Office to negotiate with the Bolshevik Government the safe exit of the Czechoslovak army from Soviet Russia after the Brest-Litovsk peace. As a member of the British Legation in Prague, I witnessed the peaceful flowering of the first Republic under Thomas Masaryk. Twenty years later I was present when, after Munich, his son Jan, then Czechoslovak Minister in London, had to take down the portraits of his father and of Eduard Beneš from the walls of his Legation.

During the last war I was closely associated with the liberation movement started by Beneš at a time when most of the present rulers of Czechoslovakia were sitting safely in Moscow, denouncing the War as an imperialist conflict started by France and Britain. Long residence in the country and intimate acquaintance with the people have taught me to like both, and today, when the Republic once acclaimed by the West as a model democracy lies in the relentless grip of a Communist dictatorship, I share the sorrows both of the home Czechoslovaks and of those abroad, some of whom have suffered exile for the third time within the space of thirty-three years.

This Communist tragedy, I think, might have been averted. It began long before the end of the war and dates from December

G

1943, when Beneš made his first visit to Moscow and received from Stalin and Molotov the most implicit pledges of non-interference in the internal affairs of Czechoslovakia. Two hundred and fifty years before, Peter the Great, one of Stalin's heroes, had made a similar protestation of friendship to the Swedes at the very moment when he was preparing to attack them. Like Peter's, Stalin's pledges were of the thinnest pie-crust, but Eduard Beneš, eager to avoid the fate of the Polish Government in London, accepted them. Two years and two months later he was forced to pay a second visit to the Kremlin and to return to his country with a pro-Communist constitution foisted on him by Stalin.

Even then Czechoslovakia might have been saved. The war was won, but not over. As far as Prague was concerned, the Russian armies were still three or four days' march away. General Patton's army, fully equipped and eager to advance, was within easy striking distance at Pilsen and, expecting to be aided by the Americans, the Czechoslovaks in Prague rose on May 5, 1945, in open revolt against the Germans. Unfortunately, General Eisenhower had ordered General Patton to remain where he was.

At the time Mr. Churchill was Acting-Foreign Secretary in the absence of Mr. Eden in San Francisco and, quickly alive to the situation, he instructed General Ismay to get into touch with General Eisenhower and to urge him to order an immediate advance. General Eisenhower replied that he had made a military agreement with the Soviet General Staff not to proceed beyond his present line. Mr. Churchill sent a second message, and this time General Eisenhower ordered Major-General Deane, the head of the American Military Mission in Moscow, to take the matter up at once with the Soviet General Staff. In his book *The Strange Alliance*, General Deane describes his interview with General Antonov. It was stormy and ended with a blunt refusal, and, in the hope of placating the Soviet authorities and of facilitating an understanding between East and West, General Eisenhower took no action.

It was not the first attempt by the Anglo-Americans to woo Soviet favour by concessions, and like the previous efforts it failed. The Kremlin was not interested in saving Czechoslovak lives. It was determined to liberate Prague by its own forces and by so doing it not only increased its own prestige, but also gave enormous advantages to the Czechoslovak Communists. It was not the death of Jan Masaryk's "A free Czechoslovakia in a free Europe," but the obituary notice had been written.

After the war I had a standing invitation from Beneš and Jan Masaryk to re-visit Czechoslovakia and I was eager to accept it. To my distress I was too ill to travel and I missed several opportunities of flying back with Jan when he passed through London on his way home from the numerous international conferences. On these occasions he was reasonably cheerful, describing himself as a sober optimist and retailing with his customary frankness all his hopes and fears. When he went back to Prague after the war, there were no portraits, no busts, and no public mention of his father. On September 14, 1945, the anniversary of Thomas Masaryk's death and of Jan's birthday, the Communist ministers attended the commemoration service. Long notices were published in the newspapers. The portraits and the busts came back and remained in their place of honour. It was Jan's view that, if the situation was not so good as he would like it to be, it might be much worse. The democrats were regaining the lost ground, but the strain on Beneš's health had been severe. Closer acquaintanceship had bred in Jan the dangerous illusion that Czechoslovak Communists were not as other Communists.

In these days, as always, he was full of good stories, especially about the Soviet officials whom he saw frequently. They had, he told me, their own sense of humour. Their nickname for Molotov was Stone-bottom, because the harder you kicked him the more you hurt your foot.

My recurrent meetings with Jan stimulated my desire to re-visit Prague, but it was not until May 1947, that I was able to make the journey. It was an emotional return in more respects than one. It was my first sight of Europe since August 1939. Moreover, on the eve of my departure I received a message from the Czechoslovak ambassador in London informing me that Jan had been unexpectedly summoned to Geneva and that it was highly uncertain whether he would be back in Prague in time to meet me. Twice before I had made plans to go and had been forced to cancel them. This time I did not hesitate. Jan or no Jan, I would set out.

Fortune favoured me, for the weather was perfect and I travelled in great comfort with a compartment to myself all the way from Ostend to Prague. During the long journey through Germany I kept my eyes glued to the window and noted with increasing melancholy the contrast between the rich and smiling countryside and the desolation of the bombed cities and towns. In the almost tropical heat naked German boys and girls were bathing in the country streams, but every town I passed through marked the progress of destruction with scarcely an undamaged house and twisted and burnt-out trains blocking the railway sidings. At the stations old men in tattered clothes performed their duties with the listlessness of despair. I felt sad and ill at ease. After the war I had wanted eagerly to go to Germany which I had known intimately before the first war and between the two wars. I owed it a great debt, for it was there that I learnt how to work. Now suddenly all desire of return left me, and the disinclination has remained with me ever since.

From Nuremberg to the Czechoslovak frontier our train crawled with an irritating slowness that made me impatient. Moreover, I was by now a little anxious about my reception in Prague. Sir Philip Nichols, our ambassador to Czechoslovakia and an old friend, was away on leave. The Prague hotels, I knew, were over-crowded. If Jan were still in Geneva, where was I to stay?

As the sun was westering, we passed the frontier and I had my first glimpse of the Bohemian landscape with its undulating fields and plantations of birch and fir. In the little villages the gardens were a riot of apple blossom. At the top of a tall maypole the the Czech colours fluttered in the gentle breeze. Away to the north, forming a long background of mountain and forest was the wide vista of the Erzgebirge, almost blue, but softer and less majestic than the Cairngorms. It was in similar scenery that in 1916 Eduard Beneš, then a young man of thirty-three, made his way across the frontier under the nose of the Austrian police to start his first struggle for the liberation of his country.

When we reached Cheb, the frontier town in which Wallen-

stein was murdered and Henlein was born, the customs and passport officers were on a friendly alert and brought me *Horké parky*
(hot Frankfurter sausages) and a glass of beer. With more hope
than assurance I surmised that Jan was in Prague. In the dining-
car I sat opposite a Czech who told me that he had been born in
Russia. He was critical of the behaviour of the Red Army, but
he had plenty of blame for the British and the Americans. As we
passed Pilsen, he told me that the mayor of the town had been
very pro-American and had invited eight American officers to live
in his house. One night the officers went "on the batter" and,
returning home at 3 a.m., were unable to wake anyone. Not to be
done out of their comfortable beds, they found an axe and smashed
the front door in. The mayor lost his enthusiasm for Americans.

It was long after dark when I reached Prague, and there on the
platform was Jan to carry me off to the Czernin Palace which
dominates the Loretto Place in old Prague high above the New
Town and is assuredly the finest Foreign Office in the world.
Here, as Foreign Minister, Jan had his official residence on top of
the offices, and, although he himself lived, slept and worked in one
room, I was given a whole suite. We sat up till after one in the
morning talking of old friends and the youthful escapades in which
we had shared. Politics and a heavy programme, which included
a fishing-trip, were to come later.

Although I was dead-tired, I could not sleep. Indeed, I did
not close my eyes until the night was gone. It was one of Prague's
unforgettable dawns. With the first singing of the birds I was at
my window which took in the whole broad sweep of the city on
boths sides of the river Vltava. The sky was clear apart from a
small cloud in the north-east. The stars were still shining, and the
last quarter of the moon shed a ghostly light on the Petřin hill. I
waited and watched until the carillon on the old Loretto Church
just opposite had twice rung out its gentle hourly canticle.

While my vigil lasted, thoughts of the past raced through my
mind. In this old city I had nearly ruined myself by the extravagance of my follies after the First World War. Nostalgically I
wondered what had happened to the Russian gypsies and the little
Animier-Damen who a quarter of century ago had consumed my

substance. After all the tragedies since Munich did a new generation of Czechs still sit out the night in the *Nacht-lokals* round the Wencelaus Square? The Czechs, I knew, were not everybody's people. Without ever taking much trouble to study them, foreigners of the upper classes, not excluding the English, regarded them as *petit-bourgeois* and boorish. But I had always liked them and admired their qualities. They were a fine people, hard-working, highly-educated, rational, efficient and full of the virtues, and the faults, of the Lowland Scots whom they resemble. I felt not only a deep sympathy, but also a genuine affinity with them. The devil's dice had been too heavily loaded against them. It was far from being entirely their own fault that so much sorrow and disaster had overtaken them. Jan, whom I loved as a brother, was the symbol of all that was best and weakest in this unfortunate people, and now I was with him again in his own home.

These were my thoughts as I watched the small cloud change from black to grey, from grey to the palest of mauves, and from mauve to pink, until finally the rising sun chased all trace of cloud away and flushed the sky with red flame.

I felt happy and more at ease with myself. The memories of the past no longer haunted me with remorse. I was in love again with Prague. It was, I knew afresh, the most beautiful city after Edinburgh that I should ever see.

Chapter II

FLICKERING HOPE

*"Man has always been obliged to know not only that the
conditions of life are tragic, but also that he must fulfil them."*
ANDRÉ SUAREZ.

THE days that followed my arrival in Prague were a severe
strain on human endurance, and I marvelled how Beneš and
Jan survived it, for what was to me an exceptional effort
was to them their daily programme.

My very first day set a pace which never slackened. Dressed
in our summer best Jan and I set off to keep an appointment with
Beneš at the Prague Castle at nine in the morning. We were two
minutes late, and we found the President and Madame Beneš
already on the doorstep; Beneš a little older and greyer but looking
fit and very natty in a light summer suit and Madame Beneš as
gentle and as kind as ever. At once we jumped into the waiting
cars. Beneš had to pay an official visit to the Food Exhibition.

Throughout the longish drive to the Exhibition grounds the
streets were lined with cheering children and women. Customers
and shopmen left their counters and mechanics rushed out from
their garages to join the throng to give a wonderful welcome to
Beneš and to Paní Hana as every Czechoslovak used to call Madame
Beneš. There was also a lively greeting for Jan who, however
tired and melancholy he often was in private, was always at his
best on these occasions. Sitting in the second car with me, he
threw kisses to the girls, chaffed the men, and, in general, evoked
laughter and cheers. The welcome was clearly spontaneous.
We had with us no detectives and no police.

It took us two and a half hours to go round the numerous
exhibits. Never have I seen or consumed so much food. Beneš had
to taste everything. He submitted good-humouredly to the ordeal,

but refused all alcohol which ranged from various Czech beers to wine and plum-brandy. Jan at once intervened: "The President does not take alcohol," he exclaimed. "Here's our old friend Lockhart. He'll not refuse it." I, too, had to submit, although by then I had already consumed chocolate, ham, cheese, sausage, cakes, a bottle of beer, and a glass of milk, not to mention a sit-down luncheon at which I confined myself to a cup of soup.

Walking at the tail of Beneš's procession, I had as my guide and companion a Czechoslovak Under-Secretary of immense height and bulk. In the stifling heat he sweated profusely and looked, and, indeed, was miserable.

"I have not slept for three nights," he said to me pathetically, "and that is bad for the heart."

Expanding a little on the horror of insomnia, I expressed my profound sympathy. He drew nearer and whispered hoarsely:

"Pan Lockhart also used to like gypsy songs and wine. I have been listening for three nights to Russian gypsies."

Obviously the gypsies were still in vogue even if they were now of Soviet importation.

I was rescued by Madame Beneš who took me to see the exhibit showing what UNRRA had done for Czechoslovakia and what the Czechoslovaks had made out of the material supplied. Her gratitude was heart-felt. Without this aid, she told me, Czechoslovakia might easily have gone Communist at once and her husband would no longer have been President.

Meanwhile, Jan, who had touched neither food nor drink, was carrying the whole show on his own broad shoulders and keeping the onlookers in a high pitch of merriment. At the Slovak stand there was a huge pyramid of red sweet-pepper. Jan bought a packet and then raised his voice so that all could hear:

"Kopecky, Kopecky, come here, come here! I've a present that will please you. It's the colour you like—red paprika."

Kopecky was—and still is—the Communist Minister of Information and was therefore not popular with the crowd visiting the Exhibition. He shuffled up like a nervous schoolboy, and with mock gravity Jan presented the packet to him. Kopecky's face went deep red, but he took the packet with good enough grace. The crowd rocked with laughter, and I heard many comments such as, "Our Jan is in great form today."

He put on a second act at the model crêche where mothers who went to work could leave their children. It was equipped with every kind of contrivance and toy for the safety, amusement and comfort of the very young. We crowded into the spacious room, and Jan, taking a little girl into his arms, sat down on the extreme edge of a tiny baby's chair. The photographers flashed their bulbs. The children laughed and clapped their hands. Then Jan rose, kissed the little girl and handed her back to her mother.

If it was buffoonery, the Czechs liked it. Jan alone had turned the dullest of visits into an entertainment and had put everyone into the happiest mood. We drove away through lanes of cheering people, Jan and I racing back to his apartment where we had only a quarter of an hour in which to change our sopping shirts before going back to the Castle to a second and substantial lunch with the President and Madame Beneš.

Luncheon was an opportunity for Beneš to give me one of his famous *tours d'horizon*. It was like one of our weekly talks at Aston Abbots, his Buckinghamshire home during the war. I was a good listener, for after my enforced gluttony at the Exhibition I boggled at the mere sight of more food.

During the meal Beneš spoke more slowly than he used to do, and seemed tired, but, when it was over, he was his old self and for nearly two hours gave me a review of the whole situation. The burden of it was as follows:

Immediately after the liberation in May 1945, both the Russians and the Czechoslovak Communists were confident that they could establish Communism in Czechoslovakia without bloodshed and without protest. This was not only their conviction but also their intention. He, Beneš, was to be used for the time being. Then, if he did not toe the Moscow line, he was to be eliminated.

The Czechoslovak people, he said, were Westerners. They were not to be dragooned like Eastern peoples. There had been many anxious moments.   There were still difficulties, but the Communists were now losing ground, and today he could say that Czechoslovakia was out of the wood.

At this point Jan and I instinctively crossed fingers, and Beneš made some reservations.   The Communists, he admitted, were the best organised Party.   He had to reckon seriously with them, but today they realised that they could not achieve their aims without violence, and he was confident that the Soviet Government would not attempt violence.   He praised the realism of some of the Czech Communists, notably of Gottwald, then Prime Minister, Nosek and Dolansky, who, he said, had their share of Czech rationalism and of Czech commonsense.

Turning to the international situation, he emphasised the harsh difficulties under which small nations must continue to labour as long as there was no understanding between the Soviet Union and the United States.   In his view Stalin was convinced that within a year or, at most, eighteen months, the United States would be in the throes of a disastrous slump which would paralyse her activities abroad.   On the other hand, the Americans believed that the Soviet Union had been so weakened by the War that it was now negligible as a military power.   Both sides were, therefore, aggressive.   Because of her geographical position Czechoslovakia was the chief sufferer from this tension.

I asked Beneš what he would do to promote a Soviet–American understanding if he were in Mr. Ernest Bevin's place.   This time the logically-minded Beneš astonished me, for he began what seemed to be a *non sequitur,* and a moment or two passed before I realised that he was being ironical.

"There is," he said, "a vast difference between the situation after the First World War and the situation today.   We have achieved a far greater progress in democracy."

Then came the sting.

"We have made such an advance in democratic government that today two Powers, the United States and the Soviet Union, decide everything.   The small nations do not count.   They are never consulted.   Yesterday we signed a Treaty with Poland.   It was not our Treaty.   I did not want it in that form.   It was a

Soviet Treaty, and because it was a Soviet Treaty we were forced to sign it."

Then came the turn of the Americans. They were, he said, full of good intentions, but they did not understand Europe. Their policy was to offer money to enable countries threatened with Communism to oppose it. The conditions of their loan were that the country which was to receive it must expel all Communist ministers from its government. This was not possible in a delicately balanced country like Czechoslovakia. If the Americans were wise, they would realise that the best way of defeating Communism was to give a loan to Governments like the Czechoslovak Government in which the Communists, though strong, had not an absolute majority. With such a loan Czechoslovakia would go ahead so rapidly that within a year or two the Communists would be reduced to impotence.* The Russians had made many blunders in Czechoslovakia. The barbarous behaviour of the Soviet troops had cured the people of their enthusiasm for their liberators. This did not mean that the American policy was intelligent.

Beneš never answered my original query as to how he would further the cause of Soviet-American understanding, for I interrupted his train of thought by asking another question: would the situation be different today if General Patton had been allowed to liberate Prague?

Never in the course of our long acquaintance have I seen Beneš agitated, but this time his face flushed, and he brought all his arms into play as the words flowed from his mouth in short staccato sentences. He was nonplussed. The decision not to advance was a major disaster, perhaps a decisive one. He had been assured that the liberation movement was to be co-ordinated with the advance of the Anglo-American armies. He had been dumbfounded when he learnt at the crucial moment that nothing could be done. He had never understood and could not now understand the reason for the decision.

The President would have gone on talking for another hour, but

* Five days later Mr. Laurence Steinhardt, the American ambassador in Prague, told me that he agreed with Beneš's view on the loan and had tried to convince his own government of its wisdom.

Jan cut him short by saying that he and I had another engagement. In point of fact, he wanted Beneš to rest before his audiences which were due to start in less than an hour's time. Beneš surrendered, but accompanied us along the corridor still talking and still enumerating all his arguments on the tips of his fingers.

Back in the Czernin Palace, Jan himself retired to rest, but I went off into the city to buy some books and to see the damage to the old Town Hall near which many Czechs had been killed in the last days of the rising when the eager Patton had not been allowed to come to their relief. The damage was considerable and the famous Apostles' clock was ruined beyond repair. This apart, Prague had changed less than I expected since my last visit in 1936. In 1945, my driver told me, the hammer and the sickle had been everywhere. Now the Czechoslovak flag had replaced it.

Then I drove to our Embassy in the former Thun Palace. Nothing had altered, and as I passed through the great arched gateway my thoughts went back to Plachy, the aged white-haired porter, whom after a late night I used to wake at some unholy hour. He never complained. Out he would come from his little door, wipe the sleep from his eyes, and say gently: "Late home again, Pan Lockhart. Late home again."

Plachy died many years ago, and I expected to find no other friends, for Sir Philip Nichols, our ambassador, whom I had known for many years, was still absent on leave. When he was appointed Minister to the Czechoslovak Government in London in October 1941, he had not wanted the post. Closer acquaintance with the Czechoslovaks brought mutual liking and respect, and both Phil and his wife had learnt Czech before they came to Prague. They were as popular with the Czechoslovaks as Sir George Clerk had been in my time.

Feeling rather like a shy schoolboy, I asked the new unknown porter if I could see the Chargé d'Affaires and found him to be Bill Barker, the son of Sir Ernest Barker and a brilliant linguist who had studied at Prague University and whose knowledge of Czech and Russian is unequalled by any British subject. I had met him in the war when he was attached to the Czechoslovak Army in Britain.

He had a surprise for me. "There are some old friends here who want to see you," he said, as he pushed the bell. In came Rosenberg, Sir George Clerk's butler, looking little changed after all the years that had passed. He rocked my self-confidence not only by recalling episodes of my past but also by engaging me in a Czech conversation in front of such an expert as Barker. Next came Olmer, the old Chancery servant of my time, who had served in the British Army during the First World War. Fortunately he spoke English, and I recovered my nerve. I should like to have stayed longer and gone all over the house by myself, but I had to hurry back to the Czernin Palace to dress. My impressions had been good. Much as I respect the modern American diplomatic service, I felt that with Sir Philip Nichols and William Barker we had the best-informed Embassy in Prague. And this indeed was the verdict of Jan Masaryk and many other leading Czechoslovaks.

At seven o'clock I was in the National Theatre with Jan to attend the first performance of Janacek's opera *Kat' a Kabanvoa*. We had a box to ourselves, and I saw that both Madame Beneš and Beneš himself were in the President's box.

The house was packed, and in the stifling heat I found the opera long and dreary. When the curtain fell on the last act, I turned mechanically to the door, but Jan called me back in a fierce whisper. He was standing up in full view of the audience, and clapping his hands and calling "Talich, Talich" with frenetic energy. In a second the whole audience, including the President, was standing and following Jan's example.

Jan was, in fact, leading a demonstration. Talich was the great Czech conductor. He had been under fire from the Communists for having conducted for the Germans during the occupation. Largely through Jan's efforts and much to the satisfaction of the anti-Communists, he had been reinstated, and tonight was his first appearance in his old place. The demonstration was long, fervent and, of course, political. If there were any Communists in the audience, they made no counter-demonstration.

When we returned to Jan's quarters, he was well-pleased with himself, and I took the opportunity of questioning him closely about Beneš's health which was causing some anxiety to the British Foreign

Office. There were disturbing rumours that he was a sick and rapidly ageing man suffering from diabetes. I also knew that Sir Philip Nichols, our ambassador in Prague, who was thoroughly acquainted with the situation, had always held the view that the fate and future shape of Czechoslovakia depended on the physical fitness of Beneš.

Jan told me that the diabetes story was complete nonsense. As a boy Beneš had slight ear trouble which had the effect of upsetting his balance. During the years 1945–6, when he had to work night and day, there had been a recurrence, and he had one black-out in public when he had to leave the platform without finishing his speech. He had lived a wonderfully abstemious and regular life and, provided he could be stopped from over-working, he was good for another decade.

I was only partially reassured. It had been a long day for Jan, but a far longer and more strenuous day for Beneš who had started it with an hour's riding before we were up. I was sure, too, that before the ride he had read *all* the morning newspapers. He was the world's greatest and most methodical worker, and, apart from the twelve months after Munich, he had been in office in one capacity or another for nearly thirty years. Not even method and abstinence could maintain this pace for ever.

Chapter III

THE CZECHOSLOVAK STALIN

"It is the wisdom of crocodiles that shed tears when they would devour."

FRANCIS BACON.

M Y programme in Prague was too heavy to permit me to indulge freely in my favourite occupation of retracing lost footsteps and seeking the ghosts of the past. Nevertheless, I found time to go about on my own, to see old friends, to meet the new generation, to gossip with the shopkeepers, and to listen to the views of that most knowledgeable and sceptical of men, the Prague taxi-driver. In all foreign countries and especially in revolutionary times, the atmosphere of the streets is more instructive than theories derived from books or an intimate knowledge of official policy.

One of my first visits was to Julius Firt, my Czech publisher, who had now become an important political figure and a member of Parliament. He was not so optimistic about the future as were Beneš and Jan Masaryk and still feared much trouble from the Communists. He was, however, proud of his country and of the progress that had been made since the liberation. On the subject of Beneš and Jan he was enthusiastic. He told me that up to the time of Munich there had been a goodly number of Czechoslovaks who said of Beneš that he was the protégé and nominee of Thomas Masaryk, and of Jan that he was the son of his father and the "Playboy of the Western World". Now that since and during the war they had proved their own worth they were immensely popular. He saw no signs of new leaders arising from the present Parliament or from the youth of today. This was no more than the truth. As a small nation Czechoslovakia had been fortunate to produce in two generation two pairs of great men: Thomas Masaryk and the young Beneš and now the elderly Beneš and Jan Masaryk.

Firt took me to the Vyšehrad cemetery, where all the famous Czech writers, painters and composers are buried, to see the grave of Karel Čapek, a faithful disciple of Thomas Masaryk and the most gifted writer of Central Europe between the two wars. The last time I ever saw him alive was in March 1938, when I came to Prague hot-foot from Vienna where I had been an eye-witness of Hitler's entry into the Austrian capital. Karel Čapek was plunged in gloom, for he knew instinctively that Czechoslovakia's turn would come next. Some of his friends were present, and in front of them he asked me whether I thought Britain would fight if Czechoslovakia were attacked. He begged for a candid answer. I told him that he could not count on it. Three months after Munich he died at the early age of forty-eight.

The grave, designed by his brother Josef who died in a German concentration camp, was simple: a granite block at the foot of which rests a stone book with the dates of Karel's birth and death on the open pages. As I stood before it I remembered Karel's sparkling wit and his belief in small nations, and his passionate hatred of all cruelty. He had foreseen so much that had unfortunately come true. I recalled how, ten years before, in 1937 I had seen Hugo Haas and Olga Scheinpflugova in his play, *The White Sickness,* which portrayed the vileness and evil intentions of a dictator. I thought of Karel's strange romance with Olga, who was not only an actress but also a poet and writer of distinction. He had discovered her, had helped her in her stage career and had fallen in love with her. At the time he was suffering from serious spinal trouble, and his doctors told him that marriage meant certain and early death. Several years later he found a Swiss doctor who cured him. He then married Olga, and they lived very happily together until Munich and the Nazi whirlwind destroyed his spirit.

Firt, who was his publisher, told me that Čapek's works, which of course had been banned by the Germans during the occupation, were now in great demand. Today his books are banned again, this time by the Communist Government of his own country.

I also had a long talk with Hubert Ripka, who was a member of the Czechoslovak Government in London during the war and was now Minister of Foreign Trade. He was considerably less optimistic than Firt, let alone Beneš and Jan Masaryk. He had travelled widely in Europe in the course of his duties and spoke with horror of the régime in Yugoslavia. (At that moment Tito was the hero not only of Moscow but of all the Czechoslovak Communists!) Foreign trade, he told me, was becoming increasingly difficult and was likely to be much worse before it could improve. He was also perturbed by the inefficiency of the politicians who had been put in charge of the nationalised industries. They were quite inexperienced, and the Socialists, he said, were even more inefficient than the Communists. Much to my surprise, for he was a violent anti-Nazi, he admitted frankly that in certain industries the former German managers and technicians were sorely missed and could not be adequately replaced for many years. He also emphasised the loss to trade through the Nazi slaughter of the Jews.

Ripka agreed with the view that the Communists had lost ground since the liberation, but he qualified his optimism with the comment that the danger was not past, that recovery was too slow, and that the Communist decline would be very gradual. He looked tired and was obviously over-worked.

In one respect the highlight of my visit was my interview with Klement Gottwald, then Prime Minister and today President and the real dictator of the country. The meeting was arranged by Jan and took place in the Cabinet offices. I was shown up to his ante-room where I found two attractive lady secretaries, both of whom spoke fluent Russian. I was received by M. Gottwald almost immediately and saw before me a short, stocky clean-shaven man of fifty with a typical Czech face, black close-cropped hair and dark glasses. He was dapperly dressed in a well-cut lounge suit. It was my first view of the creator of the Czech Communist Party.

His greeting was quite cordial, and when we sat down round a table he offered me cigars and cigarettes. He himself filled a pipe. I later found that nearly all the Czech Communist ministers

H

smoked pipes in imitation of their "great leader and wise teacher, Josef Stalin."

Before we began our talk, he asked me if I objected to his bringing in his Press Secretary in order to have a record of the conversation. It was, he said, his usual method. It was also, I knew, a check on me.

In 1918 I had always felt quite at ease with the Bolshevik leaders in Moscow. With Gottwald it was more difficult. I had to ask questions in order to get him to talk. I opened with a query about Czechoslovakia's recovery. He replied frankly enough that after seven years of occupation by the Germans things could not be put right in a year or two. Recovery might take many years. Czechoslovakia had now no capital reserves. She could import only what she could pay for by exports. She had to buy her raw materials with dollars and to pay dollars for the transport of goods through the American zone of Germany. This was a sore point with all Czechoslovaks, for formerly the transport of such goods had been paid in Reichsmarks.

I asked him if an American loan would help. He said yes. A loan of $250,000,000 would lighten the economic burden very considerably. He would welcome the loan if there were no political conditions attached to it. He was not to be drawn into any criticism of the Americans.

I then asked him how far he thought the uncertainties of the international situation retarded recovery. He began by reminding me that from 1919 to 1920 the Western Allies had tried to intervene in Russia and had failed. The Russians had never forgotten this, and we should do well to remember it. They were infinitely stronger today. He then expressed his confidence that after two or three more conferences an understanding would be reached. After the First World War there had been a quick peace, and all the troubles had come after it. Now we were having the troubles before the peace. Perhaps it was better so. The Soviet Union and the United States had come out of the war far stronger than any other Powers. Now they were engaged in a diplomatic struggle for the major spoils of victory. The future of Germany, he said, was the real crux of the international problem.

I asked him how he saw the future of Czechoslovakia as a small nation half-way between East and West. He said at once: "We are making our revolution in our own way and all we request is no interference from outside."

"From both sides?" I asked.

He replied very mildly: "The Russians do not interfere."

I then told him that we in Britain were interested in the Czechoslovak experiment which seemed to me to be an attempt to find a synthesis between political liberty and economic democracy. I added that I disliked the manner in which the word democracy was abused today.

He shrugged his shoulders. "You have been here," he said. "You have seen for yourself."

I then asked him how his programme of nationalisation was progressing. Was it true that the programme was now completed? He confirmed that it was finished and added proudly that the Government had carried out its reforms at once.

It was now his turn to interrogate me about Britain which he had never visited. To my astonishment his first question was: "How is Mr. Churchill?" I replied that, although he was now in his seventy-third year, his energy and his remarkable health were the admiration and the envy of all his contemporaries. Gottwald, who had spent the war in Moscow, was reputed to like vodka, and was not too fit physically; he seemed to share the envy and was certainly interested. I therefore gave him an account of a typical Churchill day. For the first time he permitted himself a wan smile, which seemed to indicate both admiration and incredulity, and turned at once to the sufferings of the Czechoslovaks during the occupation. Two hundred and fifty thousand Czechoslovaks, he told me, had perished under the Nazi persecution. To this figure had to be added the losses by death, imprisonment and expulsion, of the Jews, of whom there had been 180,000 in Czechoslovakia. Not much over 20,000 now remained.

He then stood up to indicate that the interview was over. He repeated to me his assertion that Czechoslovakia would go her own way. Of course there was the military alliance with the Soviet Union. This was essential to Czechoslovakia's security. The

Czechoslovaks had not forgotten Munich. I might have retorted that the Communists took immense pains to ensure that the people should not forget, but said nothing. Although Gottwald had lived up to his reputation, as given to me by Beneš and Jan, of being a cautious and correct realist, I found him tough, sure of himself, and deeply grained with suspicion, only partly acquired during his long residence in Soviet Russia. Three hundred years of domination by a foreign Power had taught all Czechs born under the the Austrian ægis to dissemble their real feelings, to smile with their lips when they were crying in their hearts and to feign sorrow when laughter tickled their stomachs. Gottwald was born in 1897 and had served his apprenticeship as a carpenter in Vienna.

The unfortunate Dr. Vado Clementis, whom I met after an official dinner at the Czechoslovak Foreign Office, was much more expansive and affable. He was dressed in a dinner-jacket that fitted his plump, well-fed figure excellently, sported a carnation in his button-hole, and had a glass of brandy in his hand. Like Gottwald he had a large pipe in his mouth from which he puffed great clouds of smoke. He looked sleek and cheerful. He was then Assistant Foreign Minister. He had spent the war years in England and had worked for the Czechoslovak Government in London—today a serious crime in Moscow's eyes. Although I had never met him, he greeted me almost as an old friend.

"Well, what do you think of our revolution? What differences do you see here since your last visit?"

I replied that I saw very few, that here was the same law and order, the same equitable distribution of wealth, and the same hard-working, cheerful people that I had always found.

His face fell. "But what about our social changes?" "Yes," I said, "of course there have been changes. We are making changes ourselves, and they are more noticeable than the changes here." Then to please him I added quite truthfully that I had seen no signs of an iron curtain in Czechoslovakia.

He was at once happier and repeated to me what Gottwald had said. Czechoslovakia was making her revolution in her own way. He talked at some length on the necessity for Czechoslovakia of a balanced economy between East and West. As he himself was a Slovak, I turned the talk to Slovakia. He admitted that there were some matters to be adjusted and some grumbling, but asserted that Czech and Slovak relations were now much better than after the First World War. Slovaks would not be Slovaks if they did not grumble occasionally.

I again expressed my satisfaction with what I had seen during my visit. He was pleased and much to my surprise said the good order which existed was the result of careful planning during the war both in Moscow and London. All the changes had been agreed beforehand by all the political parties.

When the guests had left, I asked Jan about him. Clementis, he said, was easy to manage. He was a Slovak first, a Czechoslovak second, and a Communist third! This was a euphemism of Jan's subsequent remark to my American friend, Hamilton Fish Armstrong: "I almost like the little bastard. He lies to me only when he has to."

Poor Clementis. Although he was a great friend of Gottwald, he was arrested early in 1951 on a charge of counter-revolution. I would swear on oath that he was physically and mentally incapable of engaging in any subversive action. His real offence was committed before the Soviet Union was forced into the war. In 1939 he criticised the Ribbentrop–Molotov Pact and in 1940 he denounced the Soviet Union's attack on Finland.

At the time of writing (June 1952) he is presumably languishing in some Czechoslovak Communist prison. In their more violent speeches his former colleagues denounce him as a traitor and an agent of the West. Sometimes they hint at a trial, but it has not yet taken place.

Vado Clementis is not the only Czechoslovak Communist who has suffered or who will suffer from the long memory of Moscow.

Chapter IV

HIGH NOON AT MNICH

"Do not consent that Anthony speak in his funeral;
Know you how much the people may be mov'd
By that which he will utter?"

As everyone in Prague from Beneš to the youngest boot-
black talked politics and each had his own particular view,
I determined resolutely to defer judgment until my visit
was over. I also did my best to tap as many unofficial sources as I
could. My pleasantest and, in some respects, my most fruitful
experience was my reunion with the Bubela family

Borek Bubela had been the first Czech secretary of our Legation in 1919. Lila, his wife, had been my personal secretary and
had taught me Czech. Their marriage was the stepping-stone to
a successful career, for Borek Bubela left the Legation to join the
Anglo-Czechoslovakian Bank, and later his good work earned
him a senior post in the largest coal firm in Czechoslovakia. At the
time of my arrival in 1947 he was Coal Controller of his country
and was away from Prague on business. Both he and his wife
were very pro-British, Lila, indeed, passionately so, and their three
fine boys had been brought up almost as Englishmen.

Of all the Czechs whom I met Lila was the most pessimistic.
She warned me earnestly against official optimism. The Communists, she said, held all the internal key-posts in the Government
and controlled the secret police. If it were true that they had lost
favour with the electorate, they nevertheless were highly organised
and had hidden stores of arms. The other Parties were not organised in the same way and were in no position to counter a Communist coup if and when it came. The physical power, she insisted,
was already in the hands of the Communists. She was afraid for
her sons. Her husband's job, she told me, hung by a thread.

She took me to the Stavovské Theatre to see *The Cloud and the Waltz*, a war-play by Ferdinand Peroutka, a brilliant journalist, who had spent four years in a German concentration camp, and a fierce opponent of Communism. After the Communist *coup d'état* of February 1948, he made a daring escape to London, and is now in the United States.

The play itself is grim, has apparently no moral, and consists of a series of harrowing war pictures. One depicts a scene outside the Prague prison with two Czech wives waiting drearily in the hope of seeing their husbands' faces at the window. There are also several scenes of life in the cells of the concentration camps, one showing a Czech receiving the priest before execution and another portraying a Gestapo brute terrorising a Jew and making him sing an anti-Semitic song. The most gripping and the most horrible scene is in the study of a Czech intellectual who, knowing that the Nazis have discovered his connexion with the underground, sends for his doctor, begs him to give him poison, and, finally, being afraid of last-minute cowardice, insists that the doctor inject the poison into his veins.

The final scene is in a Gestapo room in North Germany. Two Nazi officers have just heard on the radio that the British troops have taken Hamburg and Bremen and are close at hand. The two officers take off their jack-boots in the hope of disguising themselves. Then the younger goes into another room and shoots himself. The elder officer remains. There is a noise outside, and in burst two English officers followed by a girl of the A.T.S. They put a record of the Blue Danube on the gramophone and dance. The German officer grins.

In each scene there is either a cloud or a strain of the "Blue Danube". Although the play would bore a London audience, it gripped me. It certainly fascinated the Czech audience which remained silent throughout, but cheered when the English officers made their entry.

On my last night in Prague I had a severely practical experience of Britain's decline as a financial power. I took Madame Bubela to dine at Barandov's, a luxurious restaurant built with terraces on the high rocks overlooking the river Vltava. I had no Czech money with me and, when the bill came I produced three English pound notes. The waiter hesitated. Then with many apologies he said that he could not accept them. Sadly I remembered my life in Prague after the First World War. The English pound was then coveted by all and was changed readily at higher rates than the official quotation. Now nobody wanted it.

Incidentally, Barandov's was full of English and Americans, nearly all of whom were members of the Diplomatic Corps. Their presence provoked Madame Bubela to strong comment:

"What do they all do?" she asked. "My husband went to the British Embassy recently and when he came back he said to me: 'In Sir George Clerk's time we were only seven and we were a respected and representative Legation. Now the place is like Selfridge's!'"

In point of fact, the British Embassy was highly popular with the Czechoslovaks because its staff was small in comparison with the swollen staffs of the Soviet and American Embassies. Jan Masaryk told me that we would be even more popular if our staff were still smaller. Nevertheless, there was some justification for Madame Bubela's comment, for the law of diminishing returns applies to the size of diplomatic staffs perhaps even more forcibly than to economic matters.

After the Communist *coup d'état* of February 1948, the Bubelas escaped quickly, and I was glad to be able to expedite their journey to Britain. They are now in Peru where they have made a brave and successful effort to start a new life. Of course I could not have mentioned them if they were still in Czechoslovakia.

Naturally, it was with Jan Masaryk that I spent most of my time. He put himself out to make my visit a success. Perhaps he realised that it would be my last. Certainly I felt closer to him during this short stay than in all the years that I had known him.

We had one week-end that I specially remember. It began on the Saturday of May 17. We had only one official engagement: tea with President and Madame Beneš at Lany, their official country residence twenty-five miles West of Prague. Immediately after luncheon Jan and I set off alone by car on a long excursion. First we went to Lidice or rather to where Lidice was, for of the village itself not a vestige remains. In their rage over the assassination of Heydrich, the brutal Nazi Protector of Czechoslovakia, the Germans not only shot all the men of the village, but also destroyed all standing stone including the old village cemetery. As we stood in the barren undulating field we saw relations of the dead searching for graves and putting up little wooden crosses and decorating them with flowers. At the bottom of a sloping hill is the communal grave of the victims of the Nazi savagery and a notice in three languages, Russian, Czech and English, marks the spot. The grass plot was like a flower-bed. At the head of it stood a tall wooden mast which Czech workmen were then removing in order to make room for the permanent stone tablet. The memorial was erected by the Soviet military authorities who, as soon as they entered Prague, sent a unit under a colonel to perform this task. Here again was a Soviet success made possible by the failure of the Americans to liberate Prague.

At the time of our visit there was an eyesore behind the memorial, an ugly wooden tribune for Communist orators. Jan said to me very firmly: "I shall have that removed if I lose my job for it."

My own reactions to Lidice, which even before its destruction was never beautiful, were depressing. Jan, however, was very moved and said not a word until I muttered what savages and what fools the Nazis were.

"I should say they were," said Jan quietly. "I was in the United States at the time and was making no progress. No one seemed interested in Czechoslovakia. Then came Lidice, and Czechoslovakia was on the map again."

From Lidice we drove to the village of Lany, all gay with lilac, and stopped at the village cemetery where Thomas Masaryk is buried. The atmosphere is peaceful, and rustic. Masaryk's grave is a little rectangular plot jutting out from a leafy wall. There is no stone, no cross, no plaque; nothing, in fact, to show that it is the grave of Masaryk except the wreaths, some faded, some with elaborate ribbons bearing the names of the donors, and the little posies of country flowers which Masaryk lovers used to bring every day.

There was no one else in the cemetery that afternoon except the guardian. Jan took him aside and, putting his arm on his shoulder, asked him quietly to remove the faded wreaths as quickly and as decently as possible. "My father," he said, "hated everything elaborate, especially flags and ribbons. He liked simple things." The guardian, a simple peasant, was in full sympathy with the request. I could see that he worshipped Jan, who was himself at heart a peasant, always at his best, not with the Czech bourgeoisie, but with the people of the villages.

We went on to Lany Castle which I had not visited for fifteen years. We were already late for Beneš, but Jan was not to be hurried and, before taking me to see the President, he led me upstairs to the room in which his father died. It was large with windows on two sides and an enchanting view over the park and forest. On a table opposite the bed was a cast of Masaryk's head and another of his hand. Otherwise, everything was severely simple. I remembered only the book-cases. They were plain, rather ugly and more suitable to an undergraduate's rooms than to a President's suite. But Thomas Masaryk was simple, and being President never changed him. He liked working and living in one room and in this respect Jan, who loved him and revered his memory, imitated him.

He told me that during the occupation the Germans never touched his father's bedroom and never pulled down his portrait anywhere. Nor did Hitler ever curse him or mention him in any speech.

Today Klement Gottwald, who now reigns in Lany, has dismantled the Masaryk room. The Masaryks were decent folk, but, as A. J. P. Taylor aptly wrote, decency against Communism is not enough.

We went downstairs to find the seemingly tireless Beneš full of politics and full of plans.

"I had horses all ready for you to ride in the park," he said at once. I explained hurriedly that we had experienced tyre trouble. I knew now why Jan had dawdled by the way and was grateful to him. His riding days were past, and so were mine.

Beneš questioned me about my interview with Gottwald and,

when I gave him a brief account of it, rubbed his hands. "Just as I expected," he said. "Gottwald is not bad. He is correct, reasonable and infinitely preferable to Fierlinger."

Here Jan broke in and told Beneš with great glee that Fierlinger had incurred the wrath of the Communists by his speeches in favour of the West during a recent visit to England.

Fierlinger, the only man whom I think Jan really hated, owed his whole career to Beneš. As ambassador in Moscow he had betrayed his benefactor during the war by intriguing with Gottwald against him. As Prime Minister after the liberation he had again worked against Beneš. He was to betray him a third time when the Communists made their *coup d'état* in February, 1948. A Social-Democrat, he succeeded in splitting his Party and, by lending the support of his section to the Communists, gave to the putsch a semblance of legality.

Once again I listened while Beneš gave us another run over the political course. He covered much the same ground as before. He expressed the same confidence in the future. When he had finished, he said to me earnestly:

"Give us a fair chance in the international field, and we'll pull through. But tell Mr. Eden, tell Sir Orme Sargent, that every minute has been hard work—the hardest work that I have ever done."

He seemed to thrive on it. Obviously it was still hard work, for the next morning he was setting out on a four-days' tour of Western Bohemia. It was to include his first visit since 1938 to Kozlany, his birthplace. I knew that it would be a triumph. I also knew that he never spared himself. I wondered how long he could stand the strain.

He came out to the door to see us off, and the sun lit up his grey hair and the quizzical sad smile on his lips. I felt instinctively that I had seen him for the last time.

On our way back to Prague we passed a village, and I noticed the words "Our Saviours" splashed in huge letters on the wall of a house. The rest of the sentence had been obliterated. I said to Jan: "What on earth is that? Do you have the Salvation Army here?"

"That," said Jan bitterly, "is one of the messages scrawled on the walls by the villagers to welcome the soldiers of Patton's army on their way to Prague. When they did not come, the villagers blotted them out. You will see lots more."

That same night Jan gave a party for me and opened his reception rooms. We were sixteen all told, and the guests included the Hurbans, Ferdinand Peroutka and his wife, Kopta, another well-known Czech writer, Sir Philip Nichols, our ambassador who had returned that evening from his leave, Olga Scheinpflugova, Karel Čapek's widow, and Marcia Davenport, the famous American novelist, who was an ardent Czechophile and devoted to Jan.

There was a superb buffet and vodka galore with every other kind of alcohol. The party was slow to begin, but a conspiracy among the guests finally set it going. They insisted that I must get Jan to the piano. His old gaiety, they said, was gone and he never played now. My visit to Prague was the big chance. It took me some time and a fair amount of vodka to bring him to the keyboard, but when he began he played for over an hour.

The spell of his father's memory was still on him, and he started with the minor Slovak melodies which corresponded so well with his mood. Then Madame Hurban and he sang numerous Czech and Slovak folk-songs, plaintive and nostalgic in their appeal, and as they sang the tears welled in Jan's eyes.

I had always been fascinated by Jan's sudden and endearing changes of mood. At almost all times he could switch from tears to ribald laughter and back again in a few seconds. And so it was that night. As though ashamed of himself, he broke into the wildest Russian drinking-songs, and we all joined lustily in the singing. With the dramatic instinct of the born actor he reserved his best effort to the end. Prokoviev had been in Prague a few days before, and Jan, who played and improvised well enough to take off any composer, gave a superb imitation. He began with a magnificent series of discordant thunder-claps on the bass with a twittering of birds in the treble. Suddenly he smiled. "Now a little melody," he said and played a few bars. Then, pretending to be very frightened, he raised his left hand, bit his little finger, looked round anxiously and whispered: "No, no, Stalin doesn't allow it." Up went his arms into the air and with both hands working like sledge-hammers he crashed into a finale of cacophonous discords. It was a brilliant parody thoroughly in keeping with the political views of his friends.

At one in the morning the guests wanted to go, but Jan made them wait. He had a surprise: hot sausages with horse-radish and French mustard. The sausages arrived in two huge silver tureens of boiling water. We seized our forks, picked out the sausages in pairs and ate them with relish. Not for years had I seen Jan so gay and so genuinely light-hearted.

When all the guests had gone, Jan and I sat up till nearly three and talked about almost everything except politics. It had been a wonderful party, but not perhaps the best preparation for the strenuous day that lay before us. The week-end was not over. On the Sunday that was already with us Jan had to speak at a vast open-air Slav meeting in commemoration of the partisans of South Bohemia who fell in the struggle against the Nazis. It was to be, Jan told me, almost entirely a Communist manifestation, and Mnich, where it was to be held, was eighty miles or more from Prague.

On the Sunday morning Jan and I left the Czernin Palace soon after nine, picked up Marcia Davenport at her hotel, and set out on our long journey. There was a heavy pall of cloud over Prague, and rain was falling in a dismal drizzle. Even Slavs have hangovers, and Jan was tired, depressed, and silent.

He had, I knew, made no special preparations for his speech, but on our return from Lany just before the party he had found a parcel on his table. It contained a Bible annotated by his father. Thomas Masaryk had given it to M. Šamal, his Chancellor and the leader of the Czech underground movement in the First World War. In the Second War the Nazis had arrested Šamal and had tortured him to death in Berlin. Mainly through Jan's efforts, his ashes had been found and had been brought to Prague a few days before my arrival. In gratitude Madame Šamal had sent the Bible to Jan. He had opened it at hazard, read for a moment, and then jumped up. "I've got a text for my speech tomorrow", he said to me.

As soon as we were clear of Prague, the scenery became more and more beautiful, and by the time we reached Tabor the rain had stopped. In this old Hussite town we were given a heavy luncheon by the Committee of Partisans. Our host was a big and rather flabby man with beautifully kept hands. His dark suit looked as if it had come from Savile Row. He was most affable. To my surprise Jan whispered to me that he was a Communist and a typical sleek bourgeois who had joined the party for personal security and advancement.

During luncheon I had some talk with a genuine Communist, a youngish man who had spent three years in a Nazi concentration camp. I asked him how he had been treated. He showed me his teeth. They were false and nearly all gold. The gentlemen of the Gestapo had knocked his real teeth out.

After luncheon we set out in a procession of cars for the meeting. The sun was now shining, and when we reached the little village of Mnich we saw in the distance the site of the manifestation. The setting was imposing. The monument which was to be unveiled was draped in black and stood on a small plateau half-way up an undulating hill. Here in a large grassy rectangle were assembled over 20,000 people: peasants in their national costume, legionaries of the First World War, troops and officers and military bands, and the diplomatic representatives of the Soviet Union, Poland, Yugoslavia, and Bulgaria. The Communist element was strong. Marcia Davenport and I were the only non-Slavs in the large gathering.

To the right of the monument was a long seat for the widows and mothers of the fallen. On the left was a small stand with a wooden tribune for the speakers. From the stand itself there was an enchanting view across a wide stretch of country composed of meadows and corn-fields and undulating hills topped with woods. Far away in the distance was the blue line of the Ratibor mountains.

We took our seats in the second row of the stand directly behind the Slav ambassadors. Jan was as nervous as a frightened puppy, fidgeted incessantly, and kept asking me for cigarettes. His turn to speak came rather late, and I had ample time to observe and listen to the various Communist orators.

The big gun was Rudolf Slansky, then the General Secretary of the Czechoslovak Communist Party, but now, like Clementis, purged, dismissed from his high post, denounced as a traitor and, of course, as an agent of the West, imprisoned or dead. I was introduced to him on the tribune before his speech. Erect, sandy-haired, with the burning eyes and lean, ascetic look of a fanatic, he struck me as a man whose integrity and faith were unassailable. Nor do I believe that he was in any respect a traitor to his cause. He was, however, the chief rival to Gottwald, and in a Communist dictatorship there is no place for two "bosses".

When he rose to speak, he stood as stiff as a ramrod and harangued the vast audience in a harsh staccato voice. At his first mention of Yugoslavia there was a roar of applause, and a section of the crowd began to chant: "Ti-to, Ti-to, Ti-to" with the same mechanical rhythm with which the Fascists, when marching, kept time with an incessant Du-ce, Du-ce. The whirligig of Communist favour moves with incredibly rapidity. Yugoslavia was then a Communist state and Tito himself the darling of the Communist gods! To outward appearance at least Czechoslovakia was still a free democracy.

For the most part, however, Slansky was heard in silence, and the greatest applause that he received came when he ended his speech with the customary slogan: "Long Live President Beneš." Like all the other Communist speakers, Slansky made the serious error of delivering a fierce political speech at a meeting which the sober crowd regarded as a commemoration of the dead.

This gave an advantage to Jan who, when he mounted the tribune, lost all trace of his previous nervousness. He began slowly. He was, he said, a minister without a Party. Some might say that he was above Party. He could assure them that he was very much under the Parties. There was laughter and loud applause. Then after the laughter came tears as he spoke of the two thousand patriots of South Bohemia who had died for their country. His language was simple and came from the heart.

On the widows' and mothers' benches two old women wept quietly and continuously. Below the tribune was a group of young peasant girls whose bright national costumes made a colourful ring round Jan. In the bright sunlight I watched one pretty girl whose eyes were fixed on him in adoration. Her face was trans-figured with the faith that one sees in pilgrims at Lourdes.

Then he spoke of the Pan-Slav manifestation. He paid his tribute to it. Every time there was a war, it was the Slavs who had to pay. This should and must not happen again. He went on to say what the Slav brotherhood must be. It must work for good and not for evil. Its corner-stone must be love. There must be no militancy, no hate. Then he quoted the verse from Šamal's Bible about mercy and humility. He spoke of the brotherhood of man and the United Nations. There was one more reference to the men who had died that others might live. With a final exhortation to *makat*—a Czech slang word meaning "to work" which he illustrated vigorously with his whole body—he sat down.

When the end came with the singing of the solemn Hussite hymn "All Who Are God's Warriors", the crowd surged round him, and Marcia Davenport and I had the greatest difficulty in following him to his car. His triumph had been complete. No one else counted, and at every village on the way back from Mnich to Tabor the peasants came out to cheer him. He had a smile and a joke for all.

On the long drive from Tabor to Prague he changed completely. In his elation he seemed to have lost his previous tiredness, and all the way home he regaled us with a stream of anecdotes, personal reminiscences and rather bawdy stories. If I had not known him so well, I could not have believed that it was the same man that I had been plying with cigarettes before his speech. When we reached the Czernin Palace Jan was again dead-beat. To round off one of the most strenuous week-ends of my life I went to the theatre.

Chapter V

THE LONG HAND OF MOSCOW

"Nobody who reflects on the conditions under which a Russian universal monarchy would be established will be astonished at me for looking upon it as an unspeakable evil, an endless immeasurable misfortune. . . . . It would mean nothing less than the violent overthrow, the total subjugation and enslavement of all educated Europe, the suppression and suffocation of all free-minded and noble thoughts and endeavours in the human race."

F. PALACKY.

I LEFT Prague with the melancholic reflection that I should never see it again. The feeling was instinctive. I had little apprehension of the disasters that were to come so soon. Indeed, my impressions, which I put down on paper on the slow journey home, were not wholly pessimistic. I had seen a large number of people of every shade of sentiment and, if hopes and fears of the future were equally divided, there was general agreement among the non-Communists that the situation was much better than it had been immediately after the liberation.

The bourgeois elements were far from cowed. Their newspapers were free and attacked the Communists vigorously. Anti-Communist jokes had a wide circulation, and there were many stories about Madame Gottwald, who, as the wife of the Communist Prime Minister, had acquired a bourgeois taste for fine clothes, rich food and good wine. Two of her alleged "gaffes" were current during my visit. On one occasion she visited the Art gallery and, having muddled the painters of the pictures with the young Czech artist who was showing her round, returned home and told her friends: "I met a delightful young painter today called Rembrandt."

Her dinner parties, at which cognac was served in immense

I

bell-shaped glasses, supplied the material for the second story. At a party at which important guests were present, she was alleged to have whispered to the butler, as he was about to pour cognac into her glass: "Don't fill it up to the top today, Jiří. We've got foreign diplomats."

Jan Masaryk told me that the stories were almost certainly invented, but illustrated her character.

Gottwald himself, however, was respected and regarded as reliable, and what perturbed me most was the conviction of both Beneš and Jan Masaryk, and doubtless many others, that of all peoples the Czechs were the least likely to accept Communism and that Czech Communists were not as other Communists.

In general, the situation was aptly described by Father Riquet, the famous French preacher of Notre Dame, who visited Czechoslovakia about this time.

After his return to Paris he was interrogated by the journalists: "How do the Czech people react to the régime?"

"As people usually do when things are going badly. There are pessimists and there are optimists."

"Can you distinguish them without difficulty?"

"Yes, it is very simple. The pessimists are learning Russian and the optimists are learning English."

As for myself, I accepted the views of the British and American ambassadors that, while the present was a marked improvement on the past, the future depended to a large extent on the state of President Beneš's health. In their opinion he was the only person who could steer Czechoslovakia through her troubles. I had seen Beneš for myself. As always, he was doing too much. He was, however, in good heart, and his energy seemed in no way diminished. I was not unduly alarmed.

Indeed, I was more concerned about the health and state of mind of Jan Masaryk. Politically he was not then unhopeful. He was afraid of the Russians and did not trust them. The attitude of the Americans irritated him, although he was half-American himself and understood them well. They tried so hard to help, but did it so often in the wrong way. He was, however, more or less confident that Czechoslovakia was safe and quite certain that the Communists were on the down grade and would lose many seats at the next election. He told me that he could handle them easily, and more than once I saw him do it.

His popularity with his own people was immense. In my presence he said to Beneš: "You are the most popular man in the country; I come second, and David (then the Speaker), and not Gottwald, is third." In his heart, however, he knew, and he told me privately without a trace of arrogance, that he came first in the hearts of the people. I am convinced that he spoke no more than the truth.

Apart from the fact that he belonged to no political Party, his chief weakness as a politician was his inability to say no. He made more promises than any man could fulfil. He did his best to keep them, and the simple people who came to him with their troubles never went away empty-handed. His day, however, was not long enough for all to benefit. It began early in the morning in his bedroom where from eight o'clock onwards the telephone rang incessantly. Sometimes he was kept so busy that he could not get dressed before noon. Then began the long round of visits and conferences which lasted all day and half the night.

While I was staying with him, his doctor gave him a thorough overhaul, and the result, Jan told me, was satisfactory. Whatever the doctor may have said, I knew not only that Jan was tired but also that in the mornings he had a racking catarrhal cough. He had great reserves of physical and nervous energy and drew freely on them. In public he never showed irritation and, however weary he might be, his natural charm, which few could resist, could always assert itself. He could dictate a speech—I heard him do it for a Czech delegate who was leaving at once for an international Rotary conference in Chicago—in five minutes. It was brilliantly done, for he could always find something original to say or give an original twist to a commonplace. But if ever a man was suffering from physical and nervous exhaustion, it was Jan in that summer of 1947. I had seen him with the mask off, when the melancholy which afflicted nearly all the Masaryks lay heavy on him and he said to me in all sincerity: "I wish to God I was rid of it all."

I knew that, although he meant what he said, it was only a half-truth. He carried on because he felt it was his duty to his country and to his father. I was also sure that since he had become a great public figure on the international scene he would have found it hard to leave it and would have been unhappy if he did. He belonged to the public, and whoever belongs to it rarely leaves it without regret.

Yet almost the last words that he said to me in Prague were about Winston Churchill whom Jan admired greatly, although his political sympathies were with Labour.

"Curious, isn't it," he said to me, "how politicians never know when to quit. First, there was Lloyd George and now there's Winston."

"During the war," he went on, "Winston invited me to Chequers and in the course of conversation he said to me suddenly: 'What do you think, Masaryk, that I ought to do after the war?'

"I replied: 'I hope, sir, that you will write your memoirs of it.'

"Like a flash Winston came back at me: 'Is that all you suggest that I should do?'

"I explained at once that this was only one suggestion."

Resignation and escape were never wholly absent from Jan's mind. On my last evening in Prague Marcia Davenport and I had cocktails alone with him in his room before an official dinner. He looked ill and depressed. *Apropos* of nothing he said suddenly and quietly:

"I can't go on much longer; I can't stand people. I like you and you," he went on, pointing to us in turn, "but there are very few others that I care for."

At the subsequent dinner no one could have imagined that he had a care in the world.

We British, I found, were not unpopular in Prague. The harsh memory of Munich remained, but it had been softened by the support which we had given to the Czechoslovak Government in London and to the thousands of Czechoslovak exiles who had found a welcome and a homely refuge in Britain. The liberation movement had begun in London at a time when the Czech Communist leaders were sitting in Moscow, supporting the Ribbentrop–Molotov Pact, and denouncing the war as an imperialist venture started by Britain and France.   The non-Communists were proud of the Czechoslovak airmen who had fought with the Royal Air Force throughout the war.   Above all, they wanted us to be strong.   They had seen how unprepared we were in 1939.   They feared the Russians.   They hoped that, if the occasion ever arose, we should be firm enough to prevent another Munich, this time with Stalin to dictate it.

Even before the war Czechoslovakia had been the European democracy with the least contrast between wealth and poverty. Most Czechoslovaks sympathised with the policy of the British Labour Party and mistrusted certain Conservatives who, they felt, disliked them and whom they regarded as largely responsible for Munich.   In 1947 these sympathies were even stronger now that the country had become almost equalitarian.   Nevertheless, at this time Winston Churchill was by far the most popular foreigner; and not only with the non-Communists who then represented about seventy per cent of the people.   Jan Masaryk told me that, not long before my arrival, he had addressed a large meeting of Communists in Prague.   He had said to them: "I may not always agree with the policy of Winston Churchill today, but I say here and now that for the winning of the war and for our own liberation we owe more to Winston Churchill than to any other man."

The Communists, Jan told me, had cheered his words with fervent enthusiasm.

I myself had an ocular proof of Mr. Churchill's popularity. On my last day in Prague I went to Topič's bookshop to send back by post the numerous books which I had bought.   As I entered, one whole window of the wide shop-front was being prepared for dressing.   Across the back ran a huge ribbon with the words "Churchill's Speeches Second Volume".   The window space was being filled exclusively with Churchill in Czech.   Astonished by the number of copies, I asked the manager:

"How long will you take to sell these volumes?"

"They will be gone in three days."

Throughout my visit I had a constant stream of visitors.   Most of them were young people whom I had never known. Nearly all were profuse in their gratitude to Britain. One clever journalist, Miss Bernaškova, who wrote for Karel Čapek's old newspaper, talked to me for an hour in the most glowing terms of Czechoslovakia's recovery and of the heroic work done by Beneš and Jan Masaryk. She spoke with admiration and apparent sincerity. Today she writes the most violent Communist propaganda against the West, but whether from conviction or for her daily bread I cannot say. There were others who have remained more resolute and whose names I dare not mention for their own security.

Much as I had longed to see Prague again, my visit gave me more regrets than happiness. I had acceded to an ardent nostalgia, but the flame had flickered feebly. Prague looked much the same, but it was not my Prague. The houses in which I had lived were now inhabited by strangers. Above all, the friends of my younger days were gone. Many of them were among the 250,000 Czechoslovaks who perished under the Nazi persecution and who comprised the cream of the Czechoslovak intelligentsia. Prague was full of ghosts.

I came home apprehensive of Jan's strength, uncertain of Beneš's endurance, but quite sure that the future shape of Czechoslovakia depended on the maintenance of the fragile understanding between East and West.

After my return to Britain events in Czechoslovakia moved swiftly. General Marshall had already outlined his proposal of American aid, and in order to give practical effect to it the states of Europe were invited to a conference in Paris. On July 4th, 1947, the Czechoslovak Council of Ministers met under the chairmanship of Klement Gottwald, then Prime Minister, and, on Jan Masaryk's proposal, accepted the invitation. The decision was unanimous, and little time was wasted on discussion.

Five days later a Czechoslovak political delegation composed of M. Gottwald, Dr. Drtina and Jan himself left for Moscow, nominally to consult the Soviet Government on the proposed Franco-Czechoslovak Treaty. The next morning brought a thunderbolt from Moscow. Stalin had forbidden the Czecho-

slovak Government to take part in the Paris conference. Acceptance of the invitation, he told Gottwald, was a hostile act against
the Soviet Union.

Jan came back shattered. Later he told me: "I went to Moscow
as the Foreign Minister of an independent sovereign state; I returned
as a lackey of the Soviet Government."

In that same month of July Beneš had his first stroke. Although
it was concealed from the public, the Czech Communist Ministers
were well-informed and, fearful of losing the general election
which was to be held in the spring of 1948, began to prepare their
plans for retaining power at all costs. The first inkling of what
was to come was the affair of the "surprise packets". On September 11th, 1947, the three leading non-Communist Ministers, Dr.
Zenkl, Dr. Drtina and Jan Masaryk, received through the post
secret boxes which contained bombs. Fortunately one box was
opened by an official expert. No damage was done, and the three
Ministers were warned. The guilt was fixed firmly on the Communists who, however, were able to obstruct and delay the official
inquiry.

Meanwhile, the Communist leaders, who controlled the secret
police, "discovered" a plot in Slovakia where the Communist
strength was weakest. On the flimsiest of evidence they were able
to reduce the representation of the Slovak Democrats, the largest
Party in Slovakia, and to reorganise the Slovak Board of Com-
missioners to their own satisfaction. This little putsch was the
rehearsal for the *coup d'état* of February 1948.

During this summer I heard a good deal about Jan Masaryk, but
little from him. Indeed, since my visit I had received only one
hastily scrawled note to thank me for my broadcasts, for on my
return to England I had accepted an invitation from the B.B.C. to
deliver a weekly talk to the Czechoslovaks, a task which I have
performed ever since without missing a single week no matter
where I have been. Towards the end of September Jan went to
New York to represent his country at the meeting of the United
Nations at Lake Success. I had always regretted his frequent
absences abroad at international conferences. His presence at these
meetings was equivocal, for his delegation voted almost automatic-

126

RETREAT FROM PRAGUE

ally with the Soviet delegation, and, much as he was liked by the
Anglo-Americans, I knew that there were some who did not
understand the difficulties of his position. His absence from home
enabled the Communists to plant their own henchmen in the
Czechoslovak Foreign Office. The Uno autumn session of 1947
dragged on almost interminably, and I wondered when Jan would
return. I guessed that he must be unhappy. Then on December 3
my telephone rang. It was Jan. He was at his flat in Westminster Gardens. Could I come to see him?

It was a dull and gloomy afternoon, and I found Jan terribly
tired. He was in a dressing-gown with his left arm in a sling
underneath the sleeve. Shortly before leaving for Lake Success
he had torn a muscle in his left shoulder. It still gave him pain.
His American friends, he told me, said jokingly that he had hurt his
shoulder leaning too hard against the Iron Curtain.

He had been tortured by doubts in the United States. There
had been published rumours that he had made a fortune on the black
market and was not going back to Czechoslovakia. The truth
was, he said, that some American friends had urged him to give up
his political career and become an American citizen. He had been
tempted and had refused. "You can leave your country twice,"
he said to me, "or as many times as you have strength, to fight a
foreign enemy. You can't do it, to fight your own countrymen."

He had one thought: to go back to Czechoslovakia as quickly
as possible. But for the fog which had delayed the aeroplane
coming from Prague to fetch him he would have been there already.

He talked wearily of the Uno meeting. He gave high praise
and credit to General Marshall. Hector McNeill had done well.
The Soviet delegation had behaved badly, and Vyshinsky had been
the most abusive, partly because he had been a Menshevik, and
partly because abuse was in his blood.

Did I know Dann, the former Menshevik and Marxist scholar
who had died that year in the United States?

I said I did.

"Well," replied Jan, "I had a Czech friend, a Menshevik, who
went to see Dann not long before his death. My friend asked Dann
why Vyshinsky was always so violent.

"'Violent,' said Dann. 'He was always violent. When he was a Menshevik, we had to pull him up continuously for abusing his opponents. His reply was always the same: 'What's wrong? They're only Bolsheviks.'"

In spite of his depression Jan was quite optimistic about the coming Czechoslovak elections in the spring. The Communists were not nearly as strong as people thought. Although a non-Party man he himself was going to enter the contest and was going to attack as soon as he returned to Prague. To me this was cheerful news, but he spoilt the effect by adding gloomily: "Of course, if the Russians interfere, we are finished."

He was quite frank about Beneš's health which was, he said, much worse than the official statements implied, but possibly rather better than rumours whispered. There had been something in the nature of a real stroke, only slight perhaps, but dangerous to a man who worked as hard as Beneš did. He, Jan, was going back to take some of the load off Beneš's shoulders.

I looked at him with fear in my heart. He was in no physical state to carry his own burdens, let alone somebody else's.

The next day I took him to meet Bob Dixon, who was to replace Phil Nichols in January as our ambassador to Czechoslovakia. Jan was more cheerful and made a good impression. He drove me back to his flat and I went upstairs with him. He had brought back from America little Christmas presents for his friends, and there was soap and a carton of Chesterfield cigarettes for me. As we said good-bye, he made a great effort to be cheerful, clapped his hand on my shoulder, and smiled: "Never mind, old boy, we'll beat the bastards yet."

They were the last words I ever heard from his lips.

Chapter VI

THE MASARYK TRAGEDY

"For we fight neither for glory nor for wealth nor honours, but only and alone for freedom which no good man surrenders but with his life."

THE New Year of 1948 dawned damp and muggy. I spent the day in London by myself and wrote strenuously. My usual broadcast to the Czechs was going out a day earlier, and the European Service of the B.B.C. had sent me a mass of information including a copy of Beneš's New Year's message to the Czechoslovak people. It contained the statement, more courageous than encouraging, that the greatest achievement of the Czechoslovaks in 1947 had been the maintenance of parliamentary government. In the evening I went to the Beefsteak Club. The place was deserted, and I dined alone and read my mail. There were numerous letters from known and unknown friends in Czechoslovakia. Among them was an attractive card from a Czechoslovak painter with an original drawing and a little note saying: "Your book was on many Czech Christmas trees this year and it was on ours."

There was also a letter from Lev Braun, my former Czech teacher and an attractive young man of erudition backed by natural intelligence. He wrote sadly. He had given up all hope of returning to Czechoslovakia, was taking out his naturalisation papers for British citizenship, and wanted me to sign them. His private news from home was of increasing Communist violence. The secret police, he said, was full of a new type of thug who were more akin to the brutes of the Gestapo than to any Czechs that I had ever known. The world which began with the Pax Britannica and the First Republic was ended. The age of the Barbarian was beginning. If I wanted to see Czechoslovakia again I must go at all costs before the elections. It would be my last visit.

Although I did not believe all this, my confidence, already shaken, was shattered. Throughout the autumn of 1947 the inside news from Czechoslovakia had been distressing. Sir Orme Sargent, then the permanent head of the Foreign Office, took an increasingly pessimistic view of the future, and the American newspapers, with more money than our own to spend on foreign news, openly predicted disaster. On November 10 Joseph Alsop, writing in the Paris edition of the *New York Herald Tribune*, of "the creeping terror" in Czechoslovakia, had declared: "Beneš is aged and ailing and Jan Masaryk is a paunchy man who makes jokes." At the end of the year, however, the British Government were too preoccupied with troubles in Palestine, civil war in Greece, and increasing Soviet pressure on Germany and Rumania to add to their burdens, and on December 31 the B.B.C. review of 1947 was overcharged with optimism. At that time there were few people in Britain who realised that the next European convulsion would take place in Prague or that it would come so quickly.

On February 14 I received from President Beneš a bound copy of his new volume of memoirs. On the title page there was a generous inscription, but the writing was shaky and irregular and sadly different from the bold hand of three or even two years ago.

On February 20 I was present at a luncheon given by Major-General Ian Jacob to Sir Philip Nichols, who was in London on leave after Prague, before taking up his new appointment at The Hague. There was much conversation about Czechoslovakia and about Jan Masaryk. I told those present of my last conversation with him and of my fears lest he should be unable to bear the strain.

After luncheon I went home to my rooms in Hove. The town was deep in snow. That evening I turned on my radio. The big news came from Prague. The National Front had collapsed. The non-Communist ministers, with the exception of the Social-Democrats, had resigned. Gottwald was demanding the formation of a Communist Government. Beneš was said to be resisting the request. It was the end.

The Czechoslovak Communist *coup d'état* of February 1948 was a revealing example of the ease with which a minority party, prepared to use violence, can triumph over majority parties which rely solely on parliamentary procedure. The crisis began when Prime Minister Gottwald refused to act on a majority Cabinet decision demanding the removal of recently appointed senior Communist police officers. Believing that on this issue President Beneš would dissolve Parliament and proclaim a general election, the twelve ministers of the bourgeois parties resigned. Their action was ill-prepared and perhaps over-hastily taken. But they were in a serious dilemma. In preparation for the spring elections the Communist Minister of the Interior had been packing the Police Department with Communist supporters. If the bourgeois ministers had tolerated this irregularity without protest, the elections would have been faked and Gottwald would have obtained the fifty-one per cent majority which, he had boasted publicly, was all that he required for the complete Communisation of Czechoslovakia.

The Communists were well-prepared. Denouncing the resignations as a prelude to a bourgeois putsch, Gottwald sounded the Communist tocsin. Armed workers appeared as if by magic in the streets. Action Committees took control of the factories and the radio. To give a Moscow blessing to the coup and to ensure its success, Zorin, the former Soviet ambassador to Czechoslovakia and then Deputy Foreign Minister of the Soviet Government, had arrived in Prague on the eve of the crisis with the alleged mission of *supervising the arrival of grain deliveries to Czechoslovakia from the Soviet Union.*

Bullied incessantly by Gottwald, Beneš hesitated. There was, however, no substance in delay. The situation had been irretrievably lost in the first twenty-four hours, and, in order to prevent a disastrous bloodshed, the ailing President approved the new Communist Government on February 25. By obtaining the adherence of the Fierlinger wing of the Social-Democrats, Gottwald was able to give a mask of legality to Communist violence. Almost overnight the free democracy of Czechoslovakia was transformed into a totalitarian State of the recognised Soviet pattern. Demoral-

THE MASARYK TRAGEDY 131

ised by Munich and by seven years of Nazi occupation, bereft of decisive leadership, and with no hope of help from the West, the Czechoslovak people succumbed almost without resistance. Only the students manifested their loyalty to the ideals of Thomas Masaryk.

Out of loyalty to Beneš, Jan Masaryk, who had been ill during the crisis, remained in the new Government for fourteen days. His action was criticised both by his Czechoslovak admirers and by some of his Western friends.

I did not expect him to stay long at his post. At the end of February I received a message from him through a safe hand. He begged me to do my best to keep his name out of all broadcasts and newspapers. He knew, the message said, what he was doing. Sunday, March 7, was the anniversary of his father's birth, and I was shocked by the manner in which the Communists celebrated the commemoration. Full honours were paid to Thomas Masaryk, the man who, above all others, detested violence, but the theme of the official speeches was that, if he were alive, he would have approved the Communist coup.

On the Monday morning I was called to the telephone in my Hove apartment. It was Marcia Davenport. She had come straight from Prague with messages for Sir Orme Sargent and me. She had instructions, she said, to see me first.

I told her that I would be in London on Wednesday morning, but offered to come at once if the matter were urgent. She hesitated for a moment, then said quietly: "Wednesday will do." She told me that the situation in Czechoslovakia was far worse than the outside public realised and that the plight of Beneš and Jan was terrible.

On the Wednesday morning I was in my club in London before half past ten. I was called to the telephone at once. A voice from the *Evening Standard* said: "Can you tell us something about Jan Masaryk?" "Why?" I asked tremulously, "what has happened?" Back came the answer. "He has committed suicide. He was found dead outside the Czernin Palace at 6.30 this morning."

With a heavy heart I went to Claridge's to see Marcia Davenport. Her distress was agonising, and at first she was incoherent.

Jan, she said, had sent her to England with instructions to see me first and to ask me to help her to see Sir Orme Sargent. Jan was going to escape. He wanted us to think well of him.

She broke down. "What are the use of messages now!" she sobbed, and tears filled my own eyes.

I stayed with her for two hours, and she told me all she knew. Jan had sent her to England on Sunday, March 7. The message to Sargent and me was that he would escape later at some international conference. The resignations of the twelve ministers had been a mistake and had made his position much more difficult. He was now being spied on by his own people, and that he could not stand. On no account was I to come to Prague. My life would be in danger.

On the Saturday he had been to Sesimovo Usti to see Beneš, and Beneš had said to him: "I had to bear the brunt of Munich when you were abroad. Now that I am old and ill you must stay and help me and the country." Jan had come back from the meeting in deep depression and had told Marcia that Beneš would never see the Hradčany (the Prague castle) again. When the crisis came, Jan had stayed at his post, partly to support Beneš and partly to help and save others who were in danger. He had failed.

It is unlikely that the mystery of Jan's death will be solved in the near future. Most of his compatriots believe that he was murdered, and a considerable volume of circumstantial evidence points to this end. As soon as the body was discovered, M. Nosek, the Minister of the Interior, who was then in control of the Security Police, and Dr. Clementis, Jan's successor as Foreign Minister, arrived on the scene, and these two Communists took complete charge. All approaches to the Czernin Palace were barred, but the police doctor, who was called at once, was said to have given a verdict of suicide. A few weeks later he was found dead in his office in the Police Department, and the Communists announced that he, too, had committed suicide.

No public inquiry into the cause of Jan's death was ever held. Moreover, the bathroom window beneath which his body was found was awkwardly placed for a man of Jan's physique. He had in his possession easier ways of taking his life; sleeping tablets and a revolver. Those who knew him best maintain that jumping from a window was the last means which Jan would have attempted unless, of course, he had been suddenly surprised by the secret police.

If the Communists had discovered Jan's alleged intention of leaving the country, they had every motive for silencing him for ever. Known to the whole populaton by his pet name of Honza, a Czech diminutive of Johan or Jan, he was the one person whose arrest might have provoked civil war. Once abroad and free, he would have been a formidable opponent, for, as one of the best broadcasters in the world, he might have made an irresistible appeal.

On the other hand, the tragedy seemed to have taken the Communists by surprise, and there was some delay before they were able to elaborate their official explanation. Obviously they could not admit murder or even attempted escape. They therefore announced Jan's death as suicide and at the same time released a spate of propaganda which fixed the blame on the West. At the funeral during which hundreds of thousands lined the streets in silence, M. Gottwald declared that Jan had been driven to his death by the alleged abuse which his Western friends had showered on him for remaining in the new Communist Government. This view had already been expressed by Nosek in his statement to the Czechoslovak Parliament and was promptly taken up by the Communist Press and radio and broadcast to the world. The Communists went even so far as to produce at great speed a new version of *The Story of the Happy Honza*, a popular Czech fairy-tale, in which Jan, having realised the perfidy of his Western friends, finds the true light and "in this happy time of his people departs neither to the West nor to the East, but to the land from which there is no return."

These hypocritical attempts to fool the people met with no success and were soon abandoned. In point of fact, there was no hostile or abusive criticism from Britain and very little from the United States where Jan's friends were well aware that he was trying to save something from the wreck of Masaryk democracy. Moreover, the instinct of the Czechoslovak people was sound. They knew very well that he was no Communist. "No man shall dictate to me what books I shall read, what music I shall hear, or what friends I shall choose." This and similar phrases they had heard too often to be deceived, and to every Czechoslovak his death, following hard on the commemoration of his father's birthday, told its own story. There was no place for the son of Thomas Masaryk in a Government which had used violence to seize power and was already terrorising its opponents.

During the celebrations of his father's anniversary Jan did not go with the other ministers to the grave at Lany. Later, he went alone and stood there for an hour. What he thought or felt no one will know, but of one thing I am sure. The knowledge that his father's birthday was being celebrated hypocritically for purely opportunistic reasons by the men who were undoing his work must have been agony to Jan, and I think it probable that during that lonely vigil he made his final resolution. I do not doubt that he had made his plans to escape. I also do not doubt that he had come to the end of his physical and mental strength, and, although I have no proof, my knowledge of him and my instinct tell me that, having lent his name to the new Government in the hope of restraining it, he found collaboration impossible and gave his own life in protestation against the outrage done to his country. Like Prince Charles Edward after the failure of the Forty-Five, he had found that "to live and yet not to live is far worse than to die".

Eduard Beneš, now suffering from arterio-sclerosis in an advanced form, lingered on for six months. He had burnt himself out with incessant work and the strain of the post-war years. Today many of his anti-Communist compatriots blame him for his hesitancy and weakness at the time of the coup, but there was little that he could have done. The Communists were prepared and armed; the non-Communists were disorganised and had no weapons. A mere spectre of his former self, he was present at Jan Masaryk's funeral. On April 8 he made his last public appearance at the six hundredth anniversary of the Caroline University of Prague and spoke for freedom. His voice was so feeble that he was heard with difficulty, but the matter was good and will be remembered. Refusing to sign Gottwald's new Communist constitution on the ground of its undemocratic nature, he resigned as President and left Prague never to return.

His whole policy had been based on an understanding between East and West. It was the only possible policy for a democratic country situated in the perilous geographical position of Czechoslovakia. Through Western weakness, as much as through his own, the policy had failed.

He retired to his country home at Sesimovo Usti, and from now until the end his life was a living death. His mind was occasionally fogged, but at most times was as clear as ever. At intervals I received oral messages from him through faithful friends. They were uniform in their content: that he stood by the principles which had always guided him and by his speech at the Caroline University; that he was a prisoner in his country and not allowed to leave it.

Shortly before his end he had a long talk with an old friend to whom he gave his last message. It contained a bitter denunciation of Stalin and Gottwald who had betrayed him by breaking all their solemn pledges. The message is not positive evidence, but I do not doubt that it represents his final views.

Today Eduard Beneš is buried in the peace and solitude of Sesimovo Usti and Jan Masaryk rests beside his father in the grass grave at Lany. Eduard Beneš had no children; with Jan's death the male line of the Masaryks is extinct. The Communists have long abandoned their attempts to claim them as supporters of the February *coup d'état* and they now denounce both men as bourgeois reactionaries and traitors who betrayed their country at the time of Munich. Every conceivable lie or half-truth is used to blacken their memory. All books which praise their work have been removed from circulation, and in the schools young children are taught to revile their names. In Communist eyes their sin was that they were not Communists; their chief fault that they placed too much reliance on the West.

Of the two men Beneš had the stronger character and by far the finer intellect. The son of a small farmer, he owed his success to great natural ability and to an immense capacity for work. He

K

lived for politics, made few friends, and to the end retained the reserve and shyness of a man who has no aptitude for social graces. In this respect he was a lonely and at times pathetic figure, craving sympathy, yet not knowing how to evoke it, but finding it always in his gentle and courageous wife who, during the First War, suffered imprisonment and gave the whole of her little fortune to the cause of liberation. In spite of his unrivalled knowledge of European politics, Beneš never really understood the English upper classes who, with some notable exceptions, he felt mistrusted him, but to England and to the English people whom he had learnt to know during his six years of exile after Munich his gratitude was sincere.

His chief weakness as a statesman was perhaps his conviction that all difficulties could be solved by negotiation, in the arts of which he had few equals. In some quarters his skill was regarded as akin to guile, but once his word was given I never knew an instance of his going back on it. Nor is it fair to blame him because, through the weakness and unpreparedness of others, negotiation ended in disaster.

Two qualities he possessed in abundance: natural kindness and real courage. When after Munich the blows fell thick upon him he bore them with exemplary fortitude. In the end tragedy overwhelmed him, for, more than any other man, he had helped to liberate his country twice only to see it betrayed again by his own compatriots into the domination of a foreign power.

I knew both Beneš and Jan Masaryk intimately for nearly thirty years. For Eduard Beneš I shall always retain respect, affection and gratitude for many kindnesses, but Jan I loved as a brother. He had several weaknesses: a volatile temperament, a lazy disposition, an ultra-sensitive nature which inclined him to melancholy, and a certain instability of purpose which forced him in times of crisis to lean on others rather than on himself. His gifts came from the good fairy. His charm was irresistible. He could be eloquent in half a dozen languages and evoke tears and laughter when he liked from any audience. He had a deep-rooted sympathy with all who were in sorrow or trouble, to whom his kindness was equalled only by his generosity. A naturally good "mixer", he could suit his stories and his conversation to the lowest company, but fundamentally he was both in his heart and by his actions a Christian.

By temperament and by his natural gifts he should have been a musician. The needs of his country and the wish of his father made him into a politician. When Thomas Masaryk was approaching death, he sent for Jan and said to him: "You know Beneš understands me and understands us; work with him", and this precept Jan carried out faithfully to the end. The two men formed an admirable combination. Beneš made the policy and Jan, with his gift of words and of psychological insight, popularised it all the world over. Although he had the artist's dislike of politics, he was, in fact, Beneš's ambassador-at-large, and in this capacity he served his country as no other Czechoslovak could have done. He sleeps, but his voice, which Trygve Lie said aptly was the voice of the United Nations, still sounds in the secret hearts of his countrymen. To millions he is today a symbol of what a decent world might have been and, pray God, will be again.

He was, indeed, the most lovable of men with a deep and generous affection for Britain and the British people. It was not merely a legacy from his Anglophil father. It grew with years of long residence and tested experience when he was the Czechoslovak Minister in London. Although Americans will dispute my judgment, I have never doubted that in his heart England came next to Czechoslovakia, and many of those Czechoslovaks who knew him best share my opinion. To give only one example, Klima, who served him for twenty-four years, told me that on Jan's last visit to London in December 1947, his parting words were: "I'll be back here in the flat in February. It's the only place where I can get a real rest, and I need a long one." Although destiny had claimed him for his own country, he kept his Westminster flat to the end.

Since his death countless tributes have been paid to his memory by men and women of all races, for he was in the finest sense a world citizen. But his best epitaph was never meant as one and came to my notice by chance. One of his London servants, a Czech who had been with him for many years, sought a post with a friend of mine. She asked him about Jan as an employer. "I don't know," replied the Czech simply. "He was never my employer; he was my friend."

The Communist coup of February 1948, rendered one valuable service to the free world. It roused the democracies of Western Europe to a livelier sense of their own peril. Unfortunately the awakening came too late to help the Czechoslovaks whose tragedy is the most poignant of our times. Here was a sturdy people, decent and democratic by existing standards, hard-working and highly educated, Western-minded and progressive by tradition, and deeply imbued with the love of liberty. To regain that liberty they struggled for three hundred years. When it was won they made the best use of it only to lose it twice within ten years to the two worst tyrants that Europe has produced since the Dark Ages. For these two losses the Powers of Western Europe bear a heavy responsibility.

Today the Czechoslovaks, of all people perhaps the least likely to accept Communism willingly, are again in the grip of a foreign power, with some of their noblest patriots in exile for the third time, and the home Czechs crushed under the heel of a ruthless minority. They are restive and miserable under their new tyrants, and the European Services of the B.B.C. estimate that from seventy to seventy-five per cent of the people are opposed to the régime.

The resistance is passive. The Czechs are a rational people and not given to romantic self-sacrifice. But, if they do not fight uselessly in the streets, they know better than most peoples how to put water in the petrol of the Communist machine, and during the past year there have been more savage sentences for sabotage and more purges in the Communist Party in Czechoslovakia than in any other satellite country.

The people, too, have their anti-Communist jokes which pass by word of mouth from one end of the country to the other:

"What nation has the largest cow in the world?"

"Czechoslovakia, of course."

"Why?"

"Because its head is in Prague and it's milked in Moscow."

"Jesus, and not Caesar," said Thomas Masaryk and the words, repeated often by his son Jan, are known to every Czech. In Central Europe the Czechs and Slovaks have suffered from various Kaisers and Tsars, words which are of course derived from Caesar, but none has been so hated as the Red Tsar under whose tyranny they now groan and whose viceroy, the Gottwald whom Beneš and many other Czechs and foreign ambassadors found reasonable, now reigns in Prague.

The Communists are not a Party, but a conspiracy. Communism is not a policy but a creed which is more dangerous than Nazi-ism because, although the god-head is in Moscow, its appeal is international.

BOOK III

HOPES AND FEARS IN THE WEST

Chapter I

NOT SO NEUTRAL SWEDEN

"One enemy is too many, and a hundred friends too few."

GERMAN PROVERB.

I HAVE a warm place in my heart for the Scandinavian countries which I have often visited, though I have never stayed longer than a few weeks. I like the people. I like their food and I like their akvavit which, after whisky, is the best of all spirituous liquors. I like the sea journey, and especially the evening departure from Tilbury with the Turneresque sunset over the Thames. Above all, I like the northern landscape and the northern light, some aspects of which awake in every Scot memories of his homeland.

Indeed, there is a natural affinity between the Scandinavian and the Scot and their history has been closely intertwined. In the days when the Norsemen were the boldest and fiercest of searovers they ravaged our mainland and our islands. For over four hundred years they occupied part of Scotland and they have left to this day the imprint of their language in the place-names of our rivers, mountains, and townships of the North and West. Later, when Scotland was torn by civil and religious wars, Norway and Sweden offered asylum and an honourable career, generally in the army, to both Scottish Catholics and Scottish Covenanters. Today in both countries there are men of Scottish origin whose families have been Swedish or Norwegian subjects for generations but who celebrate St. Andrew's Day and who, when they die, remember their link with the old country by leaving money to Scottish institutions and charities. To give only one example, Harald Grieg, director of the Norwegian National Theatre and a descendant of the great composer, was imprisoned by the Germans during the last war. He spent his time in writing, on tiny scraps of paper which he managed to smuggle out, the Scottish origins of his family from a proscribed Macgregor who changed his name to Greig and fled to Norway. Harald's brother, Nordahl Grieg, is Norway's great war-poet and, indeed, war-hero, for he was shot down over Berlin when flying for us.

Today the Norsemen, the Danes and the Swedes, once the curse of Europe, have long abandoned their warlike pursuits and, although they still cherish the memory of great warrior kings like Gustavus Adolphus and Charles XII, they have developed a peaceful and humane civilisation which other nations must envy and admire. Indeed, Sweden, which escaped the horror and devastation of two world wars, has some claim to be regarded as socially and economically the most advanced country in the world. When I first went there thirty-five years ago, Swedish electrical engineers used to go to the United States to learn their job. Now it is the American electrical engineers who come to Sweden.

There are some British people who find this Scandinavian civilisation dull and unexciting. In point of fact, Scandinavian civilisation resembles what most of us would like our own civilisation to be, for it maintains successfully that delicate balance between the desire for change and the need of tranquillity which is or used to be the prerogative of British political genius. In almost every respect except that of language the Scandinavians are more akin to us than any other race. Their way of life is like ours. Their Socialists are like our Socialists, their Conservatives like our Conservatives. I have no patience with those of my countrymen who are never happy unless they can put a stick into the smoothest-running wheel and who pretend to believe that civilisation is the exclusive privilege of the Great Powers. In this connexion I prefer the verdict of Karel Čapek, that keen observer of the foreign scene, who in his *Journey to the North* wrote:

"I don't know what those nations (the Great Powers) are up to all the time with that power and greatness of theirs. Well, well, don't you burst with all that pride. Here I have been to look at three nations. They are called small, and you see that their system is good; and if one were to count perfect things one would find them there in greater number than among the larger terrestrial kingdoms.

"And here also history has produced any amount of hostilities, conquests and wars, and nothing of them remains; they were all to no good. Some day people may come to realise that no victory is worth while, and, if really they are in need of heroes, they might take one like the small doctor from round about Hammerfest who in the Polar darkness runs his boat around the islands where a woman is in child-birth and an infant cries. All the time there is scope for brave and complete men, even when one day the war drums cease to roll."

I share these views of my old friend, and in 1947 I went back to the three small Scandinavian countries to see how they were faring. The first that I re-visited was Sweden. It was autumn, the driest and sunniest that the country had experienced for many years, and the tints of the maples and birches shed an iridescent radiance over land and water. This strange beauty appealed more to me than to the Swedes. The long drought had caused an economic crisis. The rivers were almost dry, and for lack of water power and British coal, many factories had been forced to close or to work on short hours. Cattle—again for lack of water— were being slaughtered in such numbers that the cold storage depots could not take the carcases.

My first port of call was Göteborg, which, known as "Little London", is the most pro-British city in Sweden. Here the drought had not affected industry, and the shipbuilding was in full swing, the only limits to expansion being the shortage of man-power. Several of the big shipyards, I found, were employing Italian labour and were well satisfied with the experiment. Indeed, nearly all the nations of Western Europe, with the exception of Britain, seem to have made excellent use of Italian workmen.

In Göteborg I received a warm welcome from several old friends. The one I wished most to meet again was missing. This was Segersted, the famous editor of the *Göteborgs Handelstidning*. Erudite literary critic, fearless political commentator, he was a man whom to meet once was to respect for all time. Some years before the war he had taken me under his wing, and there are few men whom I have admired so much. Always valiant for truth, he became during the war a sore thorn in the flesh of the Swedish Government, for he took the view that in the struggle against Nazi Germany his country's place was beside the Western Allies and not on the side-lines of a neutrality which, if Germany were victorious, would not save Sweden. What Segersted believed, he wrote, and in a series of brilliant articles he attacked both the Germans and his own Government. He was subjected to considerable persecution. Everyone whom he saw or who entered his office was watched by the police. His military expert, a former Swedish naval attaché in London, was reduced in rank. The Swedish Government tried every means of persuading Segersted to moderate his attacks. Finally King Gustav sent for him and begged him not to compromise Sweden's policy of neutrality. Segersted paid little or no attention to these requests and continued daily to denounce the Germans. In Mr. Churchill he saw the one man who could save Europe and, *ipso facto*, Sweden, and, as he strode, a lonely and fearless figure, through the streets of Göteborg, he was accompanied by a powerful British bull-dog which he called Win-stone.

He died early in 1945, and I like to think that he died happily, for he knew then that victory was assured and had, I hope, no knowledge of the bitter fruits that it was to bear afterwards. Later, many Norwegians told me that Segersted's stand for the Allies just prevented them from utterly despising Sweden's record during the war. He was a great man who will have his place in the history of his country.

In Göteborg nearly all the Swedes whom I met were pro-British and, whether or not they approved the Swedish policy of neutrality, had been pro-British throughout the war. The atmosphere of Stockholm was different. I stayed at our Embassy. The weather remained superlatively fine, and the view from my bedroom window was enchanting. I lived in two worlds. At the Embassy I met members of the nobility, leading politicians, and high officials. In its courteous formality it was like a return to the England of Edwardian days. My private friends in Stockholm were my Swedish publishers, a Socialist firm presided over by Gustav Moeller, then Minister of Social Welfare and for many years a leading figure in the Swedish Social-Democratic Party. And in this informal world I was among friends and admirers of the British Labour Party.

Sir Bertrand Jerram, our ambassador, had only recently presented his credentials, and I was amused to learn from him that the ceremony is still based on the procedure laid down by Whitelocke, the first British ambassador to Sweden. Whitelocke was appointed by Cromwell and, on arriving at the Palace to present his credentials to Queen Christina, was received by the Grand Master of Ceremonies to whom he handed a beaver hat and a new pair of gloves. The Grand Master was displeased and said bluntly that on these occasions he was accustomed to receive better presents. Whitelocke pointed to the gloves. The Grand Master was mollified when he discovered that they contained forty golden sovereigns. New British ambassadors still present the pair of gloves, but the golden sovereigns are no longer included, and the ambassadors themselves lack the power of Whitelocke who, free from the thraldom of Foreign Office telegrams and telephone calls, was never afraid to make his own decisions. He had no hesitation in admonishing Queen Christina when she wished to claim precedence for the Danish ambassador because he was the representative of a closely related monarch whereas Whitelocke was merely the representative of a Protector. Whitelocke had his way, and I make bold to say that there is not one Swede in a thousand today who would not like to see England as strong and as vigorous as she was in Cromwell's time.

Stockholm is misnamed the Venice of the North, for its beauty, cold and ascetic, lacks the warmth of the South, but it looked good to me and, indeed, was very attractive. The contents of the men's shops made my mouth water. There were stacks of fine English poplin shirts, silk ties, and bundles of the best English cloth including one roll labelled "Harris tweed woven in Tarbert." The tailors had English cutters, and today the Swedes boast, not without just cause, that they have supplanted the English as the best-dressed men in the world. By contrast with post-war London Stockholm was like those model cities which we plan but cannot see for many years. Indeed, for the cleanliness of its streets, its plumbing and housing, its excellent traffic bridges, and the smokeless purity of its air, which brings a tingle to the cheeks and puts fresh energy into old veins, Stockholm has no rival, and presents a vivid contrast with post-war London.

Most of these benefits are the fruits of neutrality, and I found that, like the Irish, many of the Swedes had a neutrality conscience. I noticed it in their apologies for the hospitality which they lavished on me. They were careful to explain that this was something special and that, if I went to an ordinary eating-house on my own, I should find the food neither so plentiful nor so good. According to Swedish standards, but not to ours, this was true. I was told later by an old Swedish friend that after the war the Swedes had lived very well until they gave their best to a group of American editors who were "doing" Europe. The American editors rewarded them by writing in their papers that the Swedes were rolling in fat while the rest of Europe was starving. The Swedes then introduced a mild form of austerity.

Their neutrality conscience was also visible in their generosity to the refugees from Eastern Europe and, in particular, to the unfortunate Esthonians. The contrast between the prosperity of the Swedes and the plight of the refugees was brought home to me forcibly in our own Embassy. Bertrand Jerram, who had spent several years in the Soviet Union, had some remarkable pictures painted by a Russian *emigré* of the 1920 period. One picture portrays an aristocratic family in one room of their country mansion. The old countess is cooking potatoes over an improvised stove. The light of the fire shines on the red lapels of her husband's tattered uniform. The room is filled with ramshackle odds and ends including one sign of former wealth in a grand piano. The village bagman who has brought the potatoes illicitly is standing by waiting for payment. The old countess has no money. She offers the grand piano in exchange for the potatoes. The bagman hesitates. Then a happy thought comes to him. The piano may amuse his children. The second picture shows the children hammering discordant noises on the piano in the bagman's barn.

I think it true to say that Sweden has shown a more generous and friendly attitude to the refugees than any other European nation. It is also true that she can best afford it.

In domestic politics I found that the Conservatives and Liberals complained mildly of high taxation and of Socialist measures which they feared would lead to Communism. The Socialist Ministers whom I met seemed to me to be moderate and cautious men. The Swedish business men looked and undoubtedly were rich. Because of her wealth I concluded that Sweden had carried out her social revolution more gradually and less painfully than we had. I think that few Swedes will disagree with this verdict.

Between the Sweden of 1917 and 1947, the dates of my first and last visits to the country, there is one great difference. In the 1914–18 War, the Swedish upper classes were predominantly pro-German and only the Socialists under Branting were pro-Ally. In the Second World War the vast majority of the country was anti-Nazi. There were, however, certain Army officers who in their deep-rooted suspicion of Russia and in their traditional admiration of the German Army were far from being pro-Ally. There were also business men who as neutralists did big business with Nazi Germany, though, when the war was ended, they were the first to slobber over the British and Americans and to give exaggerated expression to pro-Western sentiments. But, by and large, few Swedes wished to see the triumph of Nazi Germany.

Sweden's passion for neutrality is dictated by her geographical position. For a Western European this is difficult to understand. For a Swede it seems natural. Stockholm is the best window in Europe for a view of both Germany and the Soviet Union, and the Swedes are quick to note the first signs of danger. In 1914 they refused to accept the fatality of a war for which Western Europe, and Britain in particular, refused obstinately to prepare in spite of numerous warnings. They saw the same lack of preparation in 1939, and if today they have not joined the North Atlantic Treaty Organisation and, indeed, did their best to prevent Denmark from adhering to it, the reason remains the same.

It would be easy to say that the Swedes take the selfish view and argue that, if war comes and Sweden is attacked, the West will come to her aid and eventually liberate her. But the argument is unfair.

It is true that Sweden does not wish to provoke the Soviet Union, but she has always realised the danger not only to herself but also to Finland in whose independence she has a vital interest. In this respect she is perhaps in the most delicate position of any European nation. But she is spending large sums on rearmament and has, in relation to the size of her population, the largest and best-trained army in Europe, a small but efficient navy, and a modern air force. If she holds back today from committing herself to the West, it is again because she sees strength on her doorstep and weakness in the West.

In this connexion I had a long talk with General Douglas who in 1947 was Commander-in-Chief of the Swedish Army. Justly proud of his Scottish descent which he can trace back in a straight line for several centuries, he could not have been more friendly. There were, however, two things which he could not understand: (1) why, when the Anglo-American forces were at their greatest strength, they allowed the Russians to occupy Berlin, Prague and Vienna and (2) why, when it was clear that the Soviet Government would not disarm after the war, the British and American Governments demobolised their forces with such reckless rapidity.

His views, I found, were shared not only by most Swedes, but also by many people in all the small nations of Western Europe.

One of my pleasantest experiences in Sweden was my visit to Uppsala, the Swedish Oxford and one of the oldest universities in the world. I dined in the local hotel with Professor Liljegren, the President of the Swedish-British Society, a sturdy old man of over seventy although slightly deaf and blind in one eye. He held strong views and expressed them with voluble vigour. He was a good talker, but my ears were elsewhere. On a platform on the other side of the room a little orchestra was playing Viennese music with a soft and languorous melancholy which filled me with nostalgia. My wildest and happiest years had been spent in Central Europe, and the haunting melodies brought back memories which I thought I had put away with other childish things. I was fascinated by the leading violinist, an elderly Apollo whose dress clothes fitted him perfectly and who played divinely. With his fine features and his iron-grey hair, he looked more like a stage diplomat than an artist.

When our dinner was finished, I went up to the platform to thank him for his performance. He told me that he had been a prosperous Esthonian banker. As an amateur he had played the violin since his boyhood. Now, after the misfortunes that the Soviet Union had inflicted on his country, what had been a hobby had become a profession. He had no complaints. His violin had stood him in good stead. He was more fortunate than many of his compatriots.

After my lecture to the students, several of them came back with me to my hotel, and we sat up until long after midnight discussing many subjects, but mostly Britain and the world of today. They were not so fluent in English as the Danish and Norwegian students, but they struck me as keen, healthy young men with few inhibitions and no complexes and with little or no abandonment of their spiritual inheritance in favour of the ruthless materialism of today. They were, too, well-informed and much more tolerant in their views than the students of many other countries. Their conversation can be summarised in one sentence: fear of Russia, the European instinct that the Americans did not understand Europe, the desire to see Britain strong, and an uncomfortable feeling that she had been wounded beyond recovery. I did my best to reassure them.

I was up early the next morning and to my astonishment found not only that my breakfast, which I had ordered for 8 a.m., was not ready, but also that there was no one about to prepare it. I assumed that the Swedes rose late. I discovered later that conditions in the post-war Swedish welfare state are similar to those in Australia. Hours of work for domestic service are strictly regulated, and except in the big towns one must dine at tea-time or eat cold. Snaps or akvavit is rationed. In restaurants one glass is permitted for luncheon and two for dinner. Those who buy their snaps in a liquor shop have a ration book which entitles them to two bottles a month. Anyone who falls by the way of drunkenness can have his ration book taken away for whatever period the magistrate may decide. These regulations have made for greater sobriety, but would not seem to have eradicated entirely the innate desire of the Swede and incidentally all Northerners, including my own countrymen, for strong drink. On Saturday nights Stockholm, at other times a quiet city, is raucous with songs and revelry, and in private houses I found that on other nights—and days—of the week snaps, if not served in a Viking's wassail-horn, was never in short supply.

My happiest day in Sweden was spent with my Swedish publishers, who gave me a luncheon at the Golden Fleece in Stockholm. This restaurant, once frequented by Bellmann, the father of Swedish poetry, is world-famous. It is situated in the old town and is now owned by the Swedish Academy. The building in which it is housed has vast wine-cellars and dates from the thirteenth century.

We sat down sixteen to food and wines such as no Parisian restaurant could surpass. I was placed between Minister Moeller, the President of the publishing firm, and Gustav Hellstrom, the well-known Swedish novelist and critic. But the host was Carl Ollsen, the managing director, and his presence moved me deeply, for he was a doomed man, mortally ill with angina pectoris, and had come that day from his sanatorium to give the luncheon. He had been for many years a very good friend to me and a wonderful salesman.

Both Gustav Moeller and he paid the warmest tributes to England for saving the world for freedom and expressed the usual pious wishes for her recovery and her strength. I replied as best I could and expressed my conviction that all would be well with us, assuring my hosts that a nation which had shown such courage, defiance, inventive power and genius for improvisation during the war could not have become decadent within the few years of so-called peace.

I was glad when the speeches were over, and I could talk to Gustav Hellstrom whom I have always admired and liked. He was then sixty-five, and like Ollsen had a bad heart. He had therefore to live carefully, but loved his snaps. "Wherever I go," he said, "I hope there will be snaps. I hate and despise cocktails." He was then the Christopher Morley of Sweden, vastly erudite, a brilliant talker with half a dozen languages at the tip of his tongue, including Latin, and a most resolute champion of England. He told me that he had cancelled his subscription to *Time* because it was always denigrating the British effort.

He also informed me that Burns was admirably translated into Swedish by Fröding, Sweden's greatest poet, and was read with delight because Burns was the poet of everything that Swedes liked best in life: wine, women, and song.

Talking of the folly of man whose character had not changed one whit in thousands of years, Gustav Hellstrom told me a consoling story of a Swedish friend of his who at the age of sixty-four was going to marry a young woman of twenty-four. Gustav said to him gently: "Is it wise?"

"Wise!" replied his friend. "Of course not. Who on earth would expect wisdom from man? But I'm old and it may last two years. What greater happiness can a man expect at my age?"

Apart from the professional politicians and a few outstanding exceptions, people conform to much the same pattern in most European countries, but two Swedes made their own individual impression on me. They were Dr. Hallgren, the famous amateur yachtsman, and Esbjornson, then the nineteen-year-old chauffeur of the British Council.

Dr. Hallgren reminded me of the doctor hero of Čapek's *Travels in the North* and I imagine that he was the very man. He had spent some time in the north of Sweden and in the lonely islands and had sailed his boat single-handed round the long, heavily dented Scandinavian coast. He was proud of Sweden's health services, but sarcastic about international medical conferences at which for scientific terms Latin is the official language. Written, he said, it was all right, but, when spoken, it was gibberish because every nation had a different pronunciation. I assumed that he was having a dig at England and said at once that for a long time we had adopted the "new" pronunciation and that the younger generation of doctors could be easily understood.

"It isn't only the English," he said. "We Swedes and, indeed, the other nations are just as bad. What do you think our philologists would do if they could not tinker with pronunciation and produce a new one every few years."

In the course of his travels Dr. Hallgren had eaten almost every known and unknown dish. One, however, had always defeated him. In the far north of Sweden the inhabitants have a delicacy called syrstroming. Stroming is the Swedish for the little baby herring which, when cooked fresh, is delicious. Up north, however, the locals let this herringlet go absolutely rotten before they eat it. Like the Malay durian which trained gourmets regard as the finest of all fruits, the syrstroming has a terrible stench, and the difficulty is to get it into one's mouth. Hallgren, who is rarely defeated, never overcame this obstacle.

Esbjorn Esbjornson, who was my interpreter and driver during my stay in Stockholm, was a remarkable young man, with blue eyes, fair hair, and the tall muscular frame of a typical Swede. He had good manners and a quiet self-confidence. He was a stickler for punctuality and methodical organisation, and, although he had never been abroad, spoke excellent English. I talked to him freely and derived more information from him than from all the politicians. What amazed me most was his initiative. At nineteen he had already planned his life with the same precision with which a German staff officer plans a strategic operation.

He worked very long hours by day for the British Council; for five evenings in the week he went to night school. I asked him if he was taking some technical examination. "No," he said, "I am finishing the ordinary state school. My father, a small farmer, died when I was sixteen and I had to go home to keep my mother and my brothers and to work the farm."

Now that he was free again, I asked him if he intended to remain a chauffeur. "No," he said quietly, "I am going to be an officer in the Swedish army."

Brigadier Stronge, then head of the British Council in Sweden and a former military attaché, thought very highly of him and was confident that Esbjorn would achieve his ambition. I hope he has won through. He was certainly a fine product of Swedish education and the Swedish welfare state.

.   .   .   .   .

I parted sadly from my Swedish friends, for I knew that with some of them it was a last farewell. By and large, the Swedes are a virile and healthy people who have great virtues and great potential assets for the free world, and we should be wise to understand patiently the peculiar difficulties of their geographical and exposed strategic situation. It is this which actuates their neutrality policy, their fear of Russia and their constant anxiety about Finland. Admittedly, they seem to many Western Europeans, especially to those in whom a desire for feverish excitement has become almost a mental disease, to lack glamour and, except at football matches, to be over-solemn, but they have a keen sense of humour of their own.

When Sir Edward Appleton, the great physicist and now Principal of Edinburgh University, went to Stockholm to receive the Nobel Prize, a dinner, at which the Crown Prince (now King Gustav Adolf) was present, was given for the prizewinners. Sir Edward was placed next to Princess Margaret, wife of Prince Axel of Denmark, on the opposite side of the table to Lady Appleton. The dinner was a solemn and ceremonious affair, and the speeches were long and heavy. Just before Sir Edward's turn came, the Princess said to him: "Your wife is trying to tell you something. I think that she is saying 'humour'. Does that mean anything to you?"

It did, and in the course of his speech Sir Edward warned his audience how unwise it was for amateurs to dabble in science. To illustrate his point, he quoted the instance of the man who resolved to discover by scientific experiment the causes of drunkenness. He therefore took four glasses, one containing brandy and soda, one rum and soda, one gin and soda and the fourth whisky and soda. Finding out by prolonged experiment that all four made people drunk in approximately the same time and proportion, he applied his dangerous little learning to the finding of the common denominator which, of course, was soda.

Sir Edward's audience rocked with delighted merriment and continued rocking for several minutes. Gratified, but a little surprised, he waited until the laughter ceased and then went on with his speech.

When he sat down, the Princess whispered to him delightedly:
"Do you know why the audience laughed so much at your
story?"

"No," said Sir Edward modestly.

"It was because the Crown Prince is a keen amateur scientist
and never drinks anything but soda."

Chapter II

NORWAY STANDS FIRM

"I believe in the value of small nations; I believe in the value of the minority. The world will be saved by the few."

From the last testament of ANDRÉ GIDE.

I SPENT my boyhood in Broughty Ferry, now virtually a suburb of Dundee, and our house had a wide view over the Firth of Tay. Three-masted whalers still sailed under canvas to far northern waters. Norwegian ships put in at Dundee, and several of my father's friends had business interests in Norway. My parents never went to England, and inevitably as small boys my second brother and I heard more about Christiania and Bergen than London. Our interest was roused to enthusiasm when my father, more adventurous than my mother who was happy only in the Highlands of Scotland, left us one summer to visit Norway on his own.

He brought us back Norwegian knives and a book with fascinating pictures of fjords and mountains, lakes and swirling rivers wilder and more majestic than those of Scotland, although I was then far too patriotic to admit it. My favourite author of those days was R. M. Ballantyne, and from his *Erling the Bold* and another book whose title I forget I learnt more about the land of the midnight sun.

Norway was therefore the first foreign country to make any concrete impression on my youthful mind and Norwegians were the first foreign sailors and probably the first foreigners that I ever saw. Since then I have visited the country several times, and I still think that of all European capitals Oslo has the most beautiful surroundings. Today the city has suffered from too rapid expansion and lacks harmonious symmetry. Indeed, one of our ambassadors described it to me as "Six Suburbs in Search of a Centre".

Nevertheless, it has easy access to superb country, and on a keen winter's Sunday it is a stirring sight to watch the sturdy rosy-cheeked young men and women of Oslo tramping through the snow to the mountain railway which takes them in their tens of thousands to the magnificent ski-ing grounds at Holmenkollen.

During my first visit in 1917, Norway was neutral. Ship-owners were making vast fortunes almost overnight, and in the Grand Hotel in Oslo, where Ibsen once held solemn discourse with his friends, champagne flowed like water at eleven o'clock in the morning. When I went back in the autumn of 1947 to stay with Sir Laurence and Lady Collier at our Embassy, the atmosphere was wholly different. After a German occupation which had inflicted great hardships on the whole population, a Norwegian Labour Government was striving with commendable energy and success to create order out of chaos. Very like us both in char-acter and in physiognomy, the Norwegians never accept defeat, and, although Norway bred the original Quisling, Norwegian resistance during the last war was dour and determined. Through-out the war many Norwegians undertook the hazardous journey across the sea in order to fight for us, and their little army, quar-tered in Scotland, made many friends. Indeed, there is a close affinity between the Scots and the Norwegians, and Scottish nationalists are fond of quoting the many advantages which Norway has gained from her separation from Sweden as a strong argument in favour of Home Rule for Scotland.

My first day in Oslo was a Sunday. I woke early and pulled up the blinds. It was a glorious morning, and from my Embassy window I had a superb view of the fjord with the sun turning the sea to silver, and shedding a rich glow on the autumn colouring of the trees. With the possible exception of Rio no other British Embassy has so enchanting a setting. The house, too, is impressive and has a history. It was built by a rich Norwegian banker who entertained King Edward VII in it when he was Prince of Wales. King Edward liked the house and in 1905, when Norway became independent, he persuaded the British Government to buy it. By then the banker was dead; the next owner was in financial diffi-culties, and the Government obtained the house very cheaply.

On the afternoon of my first day Sir Laurence and Lady Collier took me for a drive to Sunoya on the Tyrifjord, a large fresh-water lake studded with islands and lying between wooded hills. The drive is a noble one, for most of the way the road skirts the precipitous bank of the fjord. At one particularly steep place where the high slope down to the lake was almost sheer, the Norwegians were erecting a monument. I asked what it was for. Here is the story. In the early days of the German occupation three Norwegian drivers were ordered to take three bus-loads of German soldiers to Sunoya. When they reached the precipice, the first driver hurled himself and his bus-load over the cliff. The second driver did the same. All the occupants of the two buses were killed. The third Norwegian driver was about to follow the example of his compatriots, but the Germans behind him, now alive to what was happening, shot him dead and saved themselves.

The history of Norwegian resistance is replete with similar grimly heroic stories. The Norwegians are tough fighters, good men to have beside you in a tight corner and stern enemies. Quisling and his friends had split the country, and, although most of them had received their deserts before my visit, collaboration was a dangerous subject to discuss. Hate of Germany was still strong, and most Norwegians were openly critical of Sweden's neutrality during the war, although, to be fair, the Swedes did much to help the Norwegians, especially towards the last stages of the struggle.

I met one Norwegian who was grateful—Mr. Ditlar-Simonsen, a magnificent specimen of manhood with a head like a Viking. He was imprisoned by the Germans and then exiled to a small seaside town called Frederichstat. One winter's night he seized a small boat, put his wife and children into it, and rowed over to Sweden. They arrived nearly frozen with no possessions and no money. The Swedes were good to them and looked after them until the end of the war.

In Norway I gave several lectures and, as in Sweden, enjoyed most my talk to the university students. I had addressed them in Oslo two years before the last war and had found the going hard because their knowledge of English was inadequate. Now I was amazed by the progress they had made. English had become the popular foreign language, and the young student who introduced me made a brilliant and witty speech without a single note. After the lecture I went down into the bowels of the University to the British Council Club where the students met every Thursday, had tea and cakes, spoke English with one another and sang English songs. I stayed two hours, talked to many of the students, and would have been glad if at their age I could have spoken any foreign language as well as most of them, without ever having been abroad, spoke English.

This remarkable progress is a tribute not only to the initiative of the British Council and to the success of the B.B.C. lessons in English, which have a vast audience, but also to the good work of the English Department of Oslo University. The Department has doubled since the war, but the supporters of English had a hard struggle, for, although politically and economically Norway has always been Western-minded, academically it had been accustomed to follow the line of Ibsen and Björnson and to look south towards Germany. I was told by a high authority that at Oslo University there were still several professors who spoke no English and maintained that no original thought had ever come out of England!

This was certainly not true of Dr. Keilan, Norway's most remarkable professor, whom I met both at our Embassy and at the dinner which the Norwegian Pen Club gave to me. Small in stature with bent shoulders and a harsh voice, he is a lyric poet and a doctor of economics, civil law, international law, and history. He has an encyclopædic mind and a marvellous memory. His Norwegian colleagues say of him that he is prepared to admit that there are more erudite men in the world than he is but that he cannot account for the fact. He talks like a Norwegian mountain torrent, but the flow is brilliant and sparkling.

His speech at the Pen dinner was a fine tribute to England and to the English genius for compromise which he described as prompt for compromise when compromise was feasible but firm for rejection when no compromise was possible. In spite of Dr. Keilan's erudition I hope rather than believe that his judgment on this matter is infallible.

Having been head of our propaganda to enemy-occupied countries during the war, when my main task was to obtain as free a hand as possible for the regional experts, I enjoy in the now liberated capitals the reflected credit of the work of others. As I gave to the Norwegians the freest hand of all the Allied Governments who broadcast from London during the war, it was perhaps inevitable that I should be invited to broadcast from Oslo. When I had recorded my talk, I was taken round the Oslo broadcasting station by Major Littler who during the war had been with the Norwegian Government in London. The building, started before the war and finished at great expense by the Germans in 1942, is or was then the most modern in Europe and in the latest devices for sound reproduction and for controls was far ahead of Broadcasting House in London.

Afterwards, Major Littler took me for a drive all round Oslo including the saw-mill district where over a thousand years ago Norwegian lumber-jacks established the first settlement. We finished up at Eckeberg on a high hill with a superb view over the harbour. Here over a sumptuous luncheon we had a good talk about Norway's progress since the war. Although not a Socialist Major Littler gave generous praise to the Norwegian Labour Government which, he said, was doing a good job and was on what he called "the swing forward". It had, he said, no fear of the Communists who since 1945 were on the down grade. He told me that on King Haakon's seventy-fifth birthday *Frijheid*, the Communist newspaper, had published on its front page three columns of eulogy of the King. This, he assured me, was the measure of the King's popularity and of Communist weakness. By his conduct in the war King Haakon had become the best-loved man in the country, and the Communists were far too feeble to attack him. Although I have learnt by sad experience to suspect such wishful remarks as "our Communists are not as other Communists", everyone whom I met in Oslo, including our own ambassador, endorsed Major Littler's opinion. Incidentally, Sir Laurence Collier, much beloved by the Norwegians, came a good second to the King in popularity.

I should perhaps point out that, although the Norwegians have now mastered their Communist problem, they had considerable trouble and anxiety immediately after the war. In particular, fear of the Soviet Union, whose extended frontier in the far north now borders on Norway, was widespread and gave rise to an unfortunate incident. In the first flush of liberation the Norwegians invited Mr. Churchill to visit their country. Mr. Churchill accepted the invitation. Before the visit could take place, Soviet pressure was so strong that, in order to prevent possible unpleasantness, the Norwegian Government felt itself forced to beg King Haakon to write to Mr. Churchill and to suggest a postponement of his visit. Much against his will the King acceded to the request.

Fortunately, as they gained renewed strength, the Norwegians sent a second invitation. With his customary magnanimity Mr. Churchill accepted, came to Oslo, and received a welcome which neither he nor the usually unemotional Norwegians will ever forget. In his long political career he has had to wait many years for popularity, but when it came it was in fuller measure than any Englishman has ever received, and in Western Europe it is perhaps even greater than in his own country. Wherever he goes, General Eisenhower is a deservedly popular figure. In the Communist world adulation of Stalin is obligatory. But in Western Europe the name of Winston Churchill is enshrined in the grateful hearts of all people.

In Norway I heard what was to me a new Churchill story and, as my informant was in a position to know the facts, I assume that the incident has a solid substance of truth.

When the first oranges were being brought to England during the war and were being distributed by regional areas, a large consignment was on its way to Liverpool for delivery at Bristol. Owing to lack of dock facilities and transport at bomb-harassed Liverpool it was impossible to land the oranges without considerable delay, and Lord Woolton, then Minister of Food, fearing lest they should go bad and receiving a good offer from Eire, was alleged by the Press to have closed the deal. Inevitably the Press made the most of the outrage of sending oranges destined for the sorely-tried people of Britain to neutral Eire. A cutting was shown to Mr. Churchill who promptly minuted it: "Minister of Food. A report pray. W.S.C."

According to my informant the Ministry of Food then switched the ship back from its course to Eire and ordered the oranges to be landed in England even if they were rotten. Lord Woolton then reported that the Press story was inaccurate and that the oranges were being distributed according to plan.

Back came another Churchillian minute: "I am glad that you are not sending oranges to Mr. de Valera. He does not deserve them. You may send him some raspberries."

One thing I was determined to do before I left Oslo: to visit Gimle, the monstrous and gigantic house begun after the First World War by a Norwegian shipping millionaire who went smash before he could complete the building, and finished by Quisling at a cost of 4,000,000 crowns to the Norwegian tax-payers and inhabited by him during the German occupation.

The house was then tenanted by Baron Koenigswaerter, the Counsellor of the French Embassy, and his English wife, who is a sister of Lord Rothschild. Thanks to our ambassador, I was able not only to visit the house but also to be shown over it by the Baron and Baroness.

Gimle means the Vikings' heaven, but there was nothing celestial about its appearance. The approaches were riddled with machine-gun posts and dug-outs hidden cunningly among the bushes. The entrance was a vaulted hall which led immediately into a much larger Gothic hall with two long dining-tables. In this Vikings' dining-room Quisling's guardsmen ate their meals and awaited his orders.

The house itself was a maze of vast reception-rooms and, by contrast, rather small and poky bedrooms. There was an immense bathroom for Madame Quisling, who is a White Russian, and a somewhat smaller bathroom for Quisling himself with the bath in the centre of an otherwise bare room to leave proper space for the physical jerks which he practised daily. A curious collection of weighing-machines bore witness to the attention which he paid to his figure. There were no corridors in the house, and one passed from room to room as in a picture gallery. The Koenigswaerters had brought no furniture, but had rented the house as it stood. It was therefore almost exactly as it had been in Quisling's lifetime. Most of the furniture, china and pictures were junk—expensive junk and mainly German.

For his work Quisling had his own special apartments: a study, a library, and a tiny dining-room with a table for two where he could talk in privacy with a would-be convert or an intended victim. The library was the most interesting room, and the books revealed the tastes and megalomania of the man. Nearly all had to do with military campaigns and the lives of great commanders. In one corner stood a huge globe of the world with Germany's conquests marked in blood-red. There used to be another present from Hitler, an unwieldy copy of *Mein Kampf* printed on the heaviest parchment, but this has been removed by the Norwegian Government. The whole house and its contents were a sorrowful illustration of the folly to which ambition can drive a man. The only things which I should have cared to take away were two attractive Russian landscapes which presumably belonged to Madame Quisling. The Norwegian Government and the Koenigswaerters were kind to her, and from time to time she used to come to the house and claim some small personal belonging.

At the end of a long inspection I went down to the cellars to see Quisling's bomb-proof air-shelter equipped with air-conditioning and a telephone exchange. Off the main room was a sinister cell in which there was barely room to stand, and I wondered how many recalcitrant followers or victims had spent their last hours in it.

In his life Quisling had been almost everything from a Communist to a Nazi and at each time had believed sincerely in every creed that he adopted. It was his visit to Soviet Russia as a member of the Nansen Relief Committee which turned him into a follower of Hitler. The Norwegians put him to death quietly and decently. I do not know what they will do with the house, for it is too large for anyone or anything except a museum or a government department.

Today there is no trace of Quislingism in Norway, but during my visit I came across a crusty old shipping magnate who had a low opinion of England. I met him casually at a party, and he mistook me for a Canadian and therefore spoke freely. "England is finished," he said. "I do not see how she can recover." To reassure him I gave him a long list of our war inventions. He grunted.

"You do not believe me?" I said.

"I believe you, but I do not believe that you know."

It was not very polite, but worse was to follow.

"You have lost the art of building ships," he said. "You lost it after the First World War. Now you have bad construction, bad workmanship, and bad materials. Norway has to go elsewhere for her ships: to Göteborg and Genoa. Today the Italians are better shipbuilders than the British."

He was very old, and I let him talk because, as Scott said, the old have not much longer to talk.

Moreover, he was a single exception among Norwegians who are not only pro-British but also stout friends who are able to strike a firm blow for freedom. At the end of the war they had one valuable asset in the mercantile marine which suffered heavy casualties both in ships and men. For the use of it we owed them £70,000,000, and this debt has been met by the building of Norwegian ships in England. Otherwise, with fewer resources than the Swedes and a big mess to clear up after the German occupation, they have made steady progress towards recovery.

Nor is their steadfastness their only virtue. They have the courage to face the sternness of realities, and today if Denmark and Norway are both members of the North Atlantic Organisation the credit and the courage are Norway's. During the preliminary negotiations the Swedes wanted a Scandinavian Pact outside of NATO. The Danes hesitated. The Norwegians said bluntly: whatever you do we are going in. The Danes came too, and that was that.

This Norwegian people, numbering just over three millions, is a great little nation, and no other small country has influenced so profoundly the cultural and sociological conditions of European life during the last hundred years. It has produced Ibsen, Björnson,

Johan Boyer, Jonas Lie, Knut Hamsun, and Sigrid Undset, and of these, Björnson, Hamsun and Sigrid Undset won the Nobel Prize for Literature. In music, too, Norway has given us Grieg and Sinding, and in painting Munch, the one original European painter of modern times who owed nothing to Paris. Hitherto numbers have had little or nothing to do with intellect. Indeed, if mere numbers meant a greater proportion of intellect, how much better the world would be. Unfortunately, they tend merely to provide more men to man machine-guns, to fly aeroplanes, to drop bombs, and to serve the ambitions of dictators. That is why the small civilised nations love peace. That is why the Great Powers slip so easily into the temptations of vainglory and war.

Chapter III

THE PLEASANT LAND OF HAMLET

"And let thine eye look like a friend on Denmark."

IN my younger days I liked Sweden best of the Scandinavian countries, admired Norway most, and relegated Denmark to third place in my affections. Today I have reversed the order. Denmark, often described as "a jig-saw puzzle of islands", grows on one with the ripeness of acquaintance, and of all the Western European countries it is the one in which I find myself most at home. I have re-visited it several times since the war and I hope to return as long as the travel bug remains in my blood. What an enchanting capital is Copenhagen with its richer and warmer beauty than the colder charms of Oslo and Stockholm!

On all my post-war visits I have been the guest of my good friend, Sir Alec Randall, the British ambassador. The Embassy, an old house where Nelson stayed after the Battle of Copenhagen, has a fascinating site. It is in a fashionable street not far from the Amelienborg Palace, the residence of the King. Almost within a stone's throw is the landing stage at which the steamers dock, and only a few hundred yards away is Nyhavn, the sailors' quarter and the most colourful street in Copenhagen. Just round the corner opposite the Embassy is the editorial office of *Land og Volk*, the daily newspaper of the Danish Communist Party. Within a few minutes one can be in three different worlds.

Today most of our Western European Embassies have a Churchill room and a Montgomery room in commemoration of their post-war visits. Field-Marshal Montgomery is a frequent visitor and the most popular of guests, for he gives no trouble, is punctuality itself, up early and early to bed, and does his own

M

washing. The Copenhagen Embassy has a Nelson room as well as a Churchill room and, as the house is small, even the humblest guest is certain to sleep in one of them. It is a noisy Embassy, for, true to its reputation as the Paris of the North, Copenhagen lives by night and day. Every morning I was wakened at 6 a.m. by the clang of trams carrying workers to their factories and by the raucous shouts of revellers staggering home to their rest.

Danish hospitality is unstinted and gargantuan. Almost every Copenhagen Dane speaks some English; the university students excel; and virtually all Danes are pro-British. As they need our coal and cannot obtain it and as we force them to sell us their agricultural produce at an unproductive price, the pro-British sentiment must be sincere. It has been put to a severe test. Like nearly all Western Europeans the Danes regard Mr. Churchill as the greatest man of our time and cannot understand why the British electors rejected him in 1945. Of all the receptions that he has ever received few can have equalled the ovation given to him when from a balcony of the Town Square of Copenhagen he addressed a hundred thousand Danes.

I was not lucky enough to witness it, but I saw something of Danish fervour and British energy when I accompanied Mr. Eden on his visit to Copenhagen in September, 1948. I am a keen sight-seer and have an exaggerated reputation for being an early riser and a late sitter, but I could not keep pace with Mr. Eden.

We took off by air in the afternoon of September 1st and, arriving late at Copenhagen, were rushed to the Embassy where the Ambassador had organised a large party. It lasted late. The next day was my birthday, and we set out early. Mr. Eden was determined to see as much as he could, and we went first to Fred-eriksborg, once the palace of the Danish Kings and now, thanks to the munificence of M. Jacobsen, the founder of the Carlsberg brewery, the national and historical museum of Denmark. Mr. Eden was interested in the modern murals portraying King Knud's (Canute) conquest of England, and in the chapel which houses the shields and banners of the Knights of the Elephant. In a panel by a window hung a shining new shield with a coat-of-arms showing on one side a mailed crusader and on the other a soldier in British battle-dress. It was the shield and banner of the latest Knight, Field-Marshal Montgomery.

With my taste for the exotic and grotesque I found a special pleasure in a picture of a Danish royal shoot. In the foreground of a country road stood the royal guns: King Christian IX of Denmark, known as the father-in-law of Europe, his two sons-in-law King Edward VII, then Prince of Wales, and the powerfully built Alexander III of Russia. Beside them stood the youthful and frail figure of the Duke of York, afterwards King George V, smoking a cigarette. The day's bag was laid out on the grass at the side of the road. It included several deer, numerous hares and partridges, and on the right in the place of honour half a dozen foxes!

From Frederiksborg we went on to Fredensborg where at the famous Store Kro we had a sumptuous birthday luncheon with the greatest display of Smoerrebroed as hors-d'œuvres that I have ever seen. Many writers have extolled the wonders of the Russian "zakuski", and I agree with their verdict, but like many other good things in Russia "zakuski" were introduced by the foreigner; in this instance the Scandinavians. Danish hors-d'œuvres are more than a feast in themselves, and the post-war British stomach rebels against the main meal of three or four courses which follows. We did a good best, but I could read in the eyes of the Danish *maître d'hôtel* that we had disappointed him. We were no longer he-men.

The ambassador's son and his wife were our cicerones and had obviously received instructions from Sir Alec Randall to show Mr. Eden everything. So on we drove to Hornebeck and the coast without a minute's rest, and here, while the sun beat down on the blue waters of the strait, Mr. Eden and the two Randalls bathed. Two of our party were already dead-beat; young Nicholas Eden and myself. While the others swam, we lay down on the warm sand and slept soundly. Helsingör or Elsinore came next with Kronberg Castle and Hamlet's battlements but, to Mr. Eden's disappointment, no "beetling cliffs". Today Elsinore is the great centre for tunny fishing, and that keen and proficient angler, Prince Axel, has landed some fine specimens.

After a long day we returned to the Embassy just in time to

dress for a large dinner-party given by M. Rasmussen, then the Danish Foreign Minister. Most of the Danish Ministers were present, and it was late before we got to bed.

The next day was even more strenuous, and the sun shone as fiercely as ever from the cloudless sky. Mr. Eden was up early, and faint yet pursuing, off I went with him—this time on foot— to show him the Fish Market which is, I think, the most attractive in the world. It is a Danish Venice. On one side of the sea canal is the Thorwaldsen Museum; on the other the market itself with a background of charming eighteenth-century houses with attractive gables, fascinating long latticed windows and walls of the brightest colours. The canal is packed with small boats, each with a large tank in which the fish are kept alive. When the market opens, the fish are passed from the tanks to the fish-wives, very attractive in their white caps, on the pavement. The fish are still alive, and not only lobsters, eels, crabs, and other shell-fish, but also cod, flounders and whiting. I do not think there is any Society for the Prevention of Cruelty to Fish, but, although I am not squeamish, it was a shock for me to see a huge cod gasping and throwing himself out of his box on the pavement in a last paroxysm many hours, if not some days, after he had been caught. The Danes, however, would not buy them dead. They are proud of their sea-fish, and maintain that in London we don't know what fresh fish is. If the Scandinavians do not know the sea and what lives in it, who does?

Mr. Eden was not so interested in fish as I was. He had another objective: the superb Gauguin collection, another gift of the great Carlsberg brewer, in the Danish Glyptothek. When Gauguin went off to the South Sea Islands, he left his wife, a Dane, to fend for herself. Gauguin's two sons are still alive. Both are artists: one a painter and the other a sculptor. One lives in Copenhagen and one in Oslo.

From the Glyptothek we raced—this time, fortunately for me, by car—to the Tuborg brewery whose managing director, M. Jerichow, is president of the Anglo-Danish Society. Having seen the brewery before, I remained discreetly in the background while Mr. Eden climbed steep ladders to inspect the top of the gigantic vats and clambered up countless narrow stairs. At the luncheon which followed Danish hospitality excelled itself, and even Mr. Eden was pleased by the prospect of a rest in the afternoon. The prospect soon vanished. Dinner at the Embassy was to be early because the same evening Mr. Eden was to make his big speech to the Anglo-Danish Society. No sooner had I lain down than Alec Randall came in to tell me that Beneš had died.

For a moment I was numbed with grief and wanted to be alone. The final tragedy had wiped out, momentarily at least, the long years of his success. The Communist *coup d'état* had hastened his end, but had he lived he would have been paralysed and helpless, and my head told me I ought to be glad that he had been spared this humiliation.

I had little time for reflection. I dressed quickly and told Mr. Eden. During dinner the telephone began to ring incessantly. The correspondents of the London newspapers desired a message from Mr. Eden. The *Sunday Times* wanted him to write an article. I had to deal with them. I prepared a message. Mr. Eden altered it and approved it. An article was impossible. There was no time.

The fine Oddfellows' Hall was crowded to hear Mr. Eden. In the middle of his speech he referred with some emotion to Beneš's death and to their long friendship. Hardly were the words out of his mouth when, to my surprise, the whole vast audience stood up as one man and observed two minutes' silence. The triple tragedy of Czechoslovakia had been not only a lesson to the Western Great Powers but also a warning full of foreboding to the small nations. The Danes took it to heart, and from that moment Communism in Denmark received a formidable set-back.

Mr. Eden's speech, a judicious mixture of exhortation and encouragement which included a warm tribute to Ernest Bevin, made a deep impression on his Danish audience, and he received an ovation which I thought would never stop. His task, however, was not yet over. After the speech there was a long and tiring reception. Moreover, Mr. White, the able correspondent of the *Sunday Times*, had not abandoned all hope of extracting an article on Beneš and, late at night, he suggested that Mr. Eden might write his appreciation in the aeroplane. The *Sunday Times* would pick it up at Northolt on his arrival on Saturday morning. I expressed my doubts, but promised to do my best.

I was up early the next morning and at 8.30 a.m. went to Mr. Eden's room. He had already written more than half of his article. At nine he took a Press Conference in the Embassy. Then we raced to the aerodrome to catch the 10 a.m. plane. As Mr. Eden's Viking rose off the ground, a voice from the loudspeaker resounded: "All passengers for South America please take their places." M. Rasmussen, slim and dapper but looking pale and tired, turned to me and said quietly: "I do not think I feel strong enough to go to South America this morning, so, if you will excuse me, I shall go back to my Foreign Office."

I wished that I could have gone with him. Instead, I went off to lunch with the leaders of the Danish resistance movement, whose presiding genius, M. Federspiel, is an old Harrovian. A former Danish Minister, he speaks perfect English and would pass for an Englishman anywhere.

I come of a games-playing family. I have lived a hard and tough life. But how modern Foreign Secretaries in general and Mr. Eden in particular survive the whirlwind of flying, feasting, and speaking which are now an essential part of their daily life is to me a constant source of wonder.

The Danish attitude towards politics is similar to our own. There are a few rich Danes and some Left-Wingers who like to believe that the Soviet Government has no aggressive intentions and that Denmark would be prosperous if it had remained outside the North Atlantic Treaty Organisation. But the bulk of the country is sound. The Socialists and Trade Unionists think more like Mr. Attlee and the late Ernest Bevin than like Mr. Aneurin Bevan. The other Parties are pro-Churchill and pro-British. Some of the farmers are naturally sore about the low prices which we pay for their agricultural produce. With the exception of the Communist *Land og Volk* the Press is patriotic and, in particular, M. Terkel Terkelsen, the editor of the *Berlingske Tidende*, which has by far the largest circulation in Denmark, is a firm supporter of the North Atlantic Treaty. During the war he was a leading member of the Danish section of our Political Warfare Executive and today frequently broadcasts in English for the B.B.C. on Danish affairs.

Strategically Denmark lies in a very exposed position, and inevitably many Danes feel anxious about the possibility of war. Would they be over-run at once and left to their fate until the Western Great Powers were in a position to liberate them or would the West at once come to their help? It is a comprehensible question. On his first visit to Denmark General Eisenhower did not answer it very well, but since then Field-Marshal Montgomery, almost as popular a figure in Denmark as Mr. Churchill, has done much to reassure the Danes.

Like all the small European nations the Danes want to see a strong Britain, and most of them believe in our powers of recovery. As for their own troubles they bear them bravely and even gaily, for they are essentially a gay nation. Nor has any Danish Government since the war indulged in truckling to the Soviet Union. When M. Rasmussen was Foreign Minister, the Soviet ambassador came to see him to protest against an anti-Soviet article in a Danish newspaper. As usual, the Soviet complaint was delivered in violent terms. M. Rasmussen turned to his visitor and said quietly: "The last person who used such language to me was the Nazi Governor of Denmark during the occupation." And this was all that the Soviet ambassador got out of him.

As in all the countries which were occupied by the Nazis during the war, the bitterness between collaborationists and resisters dies hard in Denmark, harder, in fact, than elsewhere, mainly because the original conditions were different. Early in the morning the Danes in Copenhagen awoke to find the Germans already there. The surprise was complete, and at first the Nazis tried to make the occupation as light as possible and, contenting themselves with rounding up and imprisoning some Jews, left most things undisturbed. Had the occupiers been any other nationals but Germans, the policy might have succeeded. But Danish memories are long. Schleswig-Holstein and the war of 1866 were not forgotten, and, gradually as Danish obstinacy re-

asserted itself, the Nazis realised that their policy of partial con-
ciliation had failed and resorted to their customary methods of
violence. It was, in fact, the Danish resistance groups who provoked an increasingly tense situation. Danes made their way to
England and Danish sailors gave their services and their lives to
the Allied cause. Danish ships were also an asset of great value.
Fighting as volunteers in the British Army several Danes won high
distinction. For the small but bloody Commachio operation in
Italy two Victoria Crosses were awarded. One was given posthu-
mously to the Danish hero, Major Anders Lassen who, after silencing
single-handed four German pill-boxes, was shot as he advanced
to take the surrender of the fifth which had hoisted the white flag.
I myself witnessed a moving scene when, during Mr. Eden's visit,
he met Madame Christmas Moeller, the widow of the former
Danish Prime Minister who came to England during the war to
lead the anti-German movement. She had lost everything. Her
son, who joined the Grenadier Guards, was killed.

In Denmark itself the resistance grew in strength and boldness
until long before the end of the war it not only supplied us with
valuable intelligence but became a very sharp and deadly thorn in
the flesh of the Nazi occupiers. Admittedly, the resistance left a
bitter taste after the war, and many bogus elements indulged in
witch-hunting. In particular, the Communists, who up to the
Soviet Union's enforced entry into the war had collaborated most
heartily with the Nazis, tried to make political capital out of their
own subsequent persecution against the Socialists, some of whose
leaders had remained in the Danish Government during the occupation. The Danish resistance movement, however, was composed
almost entirely of non-Communist elements. Nor did they lack
"guts". I give only one example which I know to be true. The
Danish translator of several of my books was Peter Gudme. He
was deeply engaged in the resistance movement and knew many
of its secrets. He was captured by the Gestapo and taken to its headquarters. He was subjected to the usual Nazi torture and, fearing
lest under more pain he might betray a secret, he burst free from his
persecutors as he was being led from the torture chamber and dived
over the stair banisters from the fifth floor and was killed instantly.

Today, as the last war recedes into the deeper recesses of memory, the differences between Dane and Dane have lost much of their bitterness. In countries where Governments lie deliberately, the people do not speak. Their silence is a proof not only of their fear but also of their disbelief in what is forced on them. The Danes are a voluble people, and nearly always there is laughter in their voices. They have some reason for their genial attitude towards life, for not only are they a free and progressive people, but they have also performed something of a miracle which must often puzzle the professional historian. Once a powerful and conquering race, they have survived numerous perils as a small nation during the centuries since their greatness. Although the future events of history are as unforeseeable as those of the theory of probability, they believe that they will continue to survive. It is an attitude against which I have no grudge. Denmark always strikes me as a singularly pleasant country and the Danes as a people who, given even the smallest opportunity of tranquillity, will continue to make a valuable contribution to European civilisation. There is nothing of Hamlet in their character. They are conscious of their European obligations and will fulfil them.

One difficulty they have. Their popular and democratic King, a sailor with a sailor's breezy way with all his subjects, has no son. Prince Knud, the Heir Apparent, is unlikely to make a successful monarch, and almost all Danes would like to ensure the succession of the King's eldest daughter. As Denmark has the Salic law, the constitution would have to be altered. For several years the matter has been discussed officially and unofficially, and a new constitution is being slowly prepared. Delay has obvious dangers, for only too often time forestalls dilatory action.

On all my visits to Denmark I have been favoured with exceptionally fine weather and in this respect must count myself fortunate, for the climate is inclement although the winter is mild in comparison with that of Norway or Sweden. Denmark, too, differs greatly in aspect from its northern neighbours. Sweden is a country of lakes, forests and mountains inhabited in fancy by trolls with hair as gnarled as the oldest trees. Norway is a land of deep fjords and high peaks, of sturdy women and strong men. Denmark is the country of big eaters and doll's houses, doll's farms and doll-like horses. It is also the land of Hans Andersen and should therefore be seen through rose-coloured spectacles. This involves no effort or difficulty, for his home town of Odense radiates hospitality and friendliness.

Odense is the chief town of Fyn, an island which has the shape and flatness of a pancake and is known as the garden of Denmark. The town itself is most attractive with a sleepy atmosphere of timelessness and a lovely square in which stand the fine Town Hall and the Cathedral of St. Knud. A little beyond is the delicately-spired Catholic church and sloping down to the right is the charming Hans Andersen garden with a stream running through it. I find this square, which is not square, and this garden quite enchanting, and to me they seem haunted by Andersen's spirit much more than the house in which he was born or the temple-like museum attached to it.

Before the war the house and the museum attracted a vast number of English visitors. Most of the English, I was told, disliked the frescoes which on the walls of the museum rotunda depict the life of Hans Andersen and are the work of Nils Larsen Stevens, the father of modern Danish painting. I admire them greatly. The most moving is the Torchlight Procession which portrays Andersen's return as his town's most famous man to receive the freedom of the city and to be acclaimed by its citizens. It was Andersen's greatest triumph. It was spoilt for him by a raging toothache, as of course it was bound to be, for almost everything went wrong for him. Perhaps that is why he created such beautiful myths and why he put on paper all that he had been unable to find in real life. Stevens, like Andersen, was the son of a poor cobbler. Success came to him late in life, and he has put into his frescoes much of the wistfulness of Andersen's gentle spirit. It was also a very sentimental spirit, for Andersen preserved with the greatest care such mementoes of his travels and frustrated romances as wild flowers pressed into books, a lock of Goethe's hair, and a flower from Dickens's garden at Gadshill. These and many others are on show in the Odense museum along with the paper figures for his miniature theatre. The Dickens flower now looks like a piece of straw.

Today psycho-analysts and ultra-modern educationists, who see nothing but harm in the old fairy-tales, are seeking to remove Andersen from his throne. They accuse him not only of terrorising children with his witches and giant dogs, but also of disturbing their minds dangerously with unnecessary sadness and distress. It will be a sad day for the world if ever these faddists get their way.

Since boyhood I have been an Andersen worshipper and I remain unrepentant. I have read his tales in several languages and, indeed, have used them constantly in order to improve my own knowledge of Czech, Croatian and Dutch. It is a method which I recommend to young linguists, for the language is simple and modern. Incidentally, the Danes never say Hans Andersen, for there are too many Hans Andersens in Denmark. They refer to him always by his initials of H.C. which are pronounced Ho Say.

On my last visit to Odense in April 1951, my wife and I travelled from Copenhagen in a first-class carriage with four American sergeants who had been on ten days' furlough in Denmark and were returning to their units in France and in the American zone of Germany. Two were airmen and the two others infantrymen. Their conversation was extraordinarily unrestrained. As for my wife and myself, we might not have been present. We remained silent, looked at our books, and listened. Apart from the usual "grouses" against the military police and a description of the methods by which bad and weak officers could be driven out of their jobs, their conversation revealed both pride and interest in their jobs. One of the air sergeants, a good-looking young man of twenty-one, was going back to France to help in the building of a large air-supply centre for General Eisenhower. He declared that the United States had in Europe spare-parts for every type of aeroplane now made. He also expressed complete confidence in the power of the United States to "knock hell out of Uncle Joe" if ever he started any trouble. American superiority they all took for granted. Europeans and, particularly, the Russians, who were slow-witted and unmethodical, were no good. No word was said about the British, presumably because we were present, but the

French were dismissed as lazy, inefficient, and desperately slow in building aerodromes.

There was also some stupid talk about drink and night passes. What was interesting and indeed astonishing to us was the attitude of all four men towards the cost of living in Copenhagen. We had found it expensive—as dear, in fact, as London. But these Yankee sergeants thought Denmark a fairy-land of cheapness. One sergeant, the nicest and smartest, recounted how he had spent his ten days in Copenhagen. He had found a girl-friend. He had hired a car and toured half Denmark with her. He had stayed at an hotel where he had had his uniform pressed every day. He had also given a great party for four people with cocktails, akvavit, champagne, cognac and beer. It had lasted until the early hours of the morning. His ten days, he said, had cost him *only* two hundred and fifty dollars, which were then worth about £100. "Copenhagen for me every furlough," he exclaimed, "it's the cheapest place I've struck." These sergeants were not men of private means. On the contrary, they were simple and rather countrified young men. All four had only one wish in the world: to get back home to "civilisation" and a progressive United States and away from an uncivilised and backward Europe.

I tried to envisage a British sergeant or, indeed, a British officer spending a hundred pounds in Copenhagen in ten days, and my wife had to give me smelling salts to bring me back to sanity.

Danish life does not run true to a single pattern. Both in the life of the land and in the character of the people there is as wide a difference between Zealand and Jutland as there is between England and Scotland. Jutland has hills and on the higher parts even heather. It has swift-running rivers which hold salmon, and lochs in which trout abound. Its two chief towns, Aarhus and Aalborg are growing rapidly, and Aalborg is not only the centre of the akvavit industry but also makes the Danish whisky which, because of the short supply of Scotch, is being sold in England and even in Scotland. The Jutes are sturdy, strong-minded men with a large streak of independence in their character. They are hard workers and great farmers who know how difficult it is to wrest a living from a harsh soil. They are also the Scots of Denmark in the sense that they despise the soft life of Copenhagen and chafe under the frustration of an over-centralised government.

If I were younger and had the necessary currency I should like to spend two years in the heart of Jutland and write a book and fish. But if I were back in our foreign service and were given my choice of a European post, I should choose Copenhagen which is as London might be if Hyde Park and St. James's Park were arms of the sea and ocean-going steamers sailed up to the gardens of Buckingham Palace. I might fall by the way, for Copenhagen has physical temptations as well as romantic beauty. As it is, I should be content to spend the rest of my days in painting Nyhavn which, with its tall brightly-coloured houses, some royal blue, orange, apple-green, terra cotta and mauve, and all with long windows and high gables, looks like Montmartre before the foreign tourists spoilt it.

But in the Nyhavn of today the mis-spelt house signs tell their own story, and "Wellcome all Sailors", "Musik and Dans", "Tatoo-Jack", "Ham and Eggs" and discreetly-coloured windows and screens betray the nature and the international character of the street. Here the purpose of the proprietors is to take the pants off the visiting sailor both metaphorically and literally. The side-streets, quiet enough by day, assume a sinister aspect at night when the sirens of Copenhagen's prostitution issue forth from the furnished lodging where hard-bitten landladies take the cream of the spoils which they receive from the sailors. Here the police never go singly, for drunken brawls and fights are not infrequent. In a row the Swedes and the Finns are dangerous, for they take to their knives at once. They are ugly weapons. Early one morning I saw a young sailor coming out of a Nyhavn store with a newly-bought knife which he was testing on his palm. The blade shone brightly in the sunlight. He smiled like a silly child. He was still drunk from the night's debauch. He reminded me of Ransome, the cabin-boy in *Kidnapped*.

Nyhavn has a compelling charm which makes one go back again and again. It can serve, too, all kinds and conditions of writers as, indeed, it has served and still serves Danish painters

Its moods change almost hourly. In the clear sunlight of the early morning it is a place of strange and silent beauty. As the sun begins to set and, at the end of the street, the sea-going steamers sound the first warning note of their departure, the bridge and the gabled houses provide the background for a Loti farewell. In the twilight, as the mists of the approaching darkness wreathe the roofs with grey garlands, the street assumes a fairyesque aspect, and the spirit of Hans Andersen emerges from the apple-green house in which he spent part of his Copenhagen life. Later, as the lights go up in the bars and the blare of radio and gramophone blends with the laughter of the sailors a budding Goncourt or a Maugham can gather all the material he needs for a scathing comment on our social system and note the details which will give him the realism to whet the appetite of his readers.

Nyhavn acts on me like a drug. It recalls the quicksands of my youth and memories of episodes which are better forgotten.

Copenhagen has great shipbuilding yards, fine toyshops, a famous porcelain industry, a comfortable opera-house and a ballet school second only to the Russian, and an ancient university whose students speak and understand English so well that you can talk to them at the same speed as to British students. The university has a very active Students' Union whose president in 1951 was M. Rusager, a composer whose works have been performed in Britain and the United States and who himself has been a judge at the Welsh Eisteddfod.

The Copenhagen students are eager to enter into closer relations with British students, and, if we are to have anything approaching European unity and a European army, it would be wise to begin with the young men and to facilitate exchanges of students, visits and inter-university debates. The main obstacles to this interchange are the financial difficulties of Britain and the lack of the necessary currency. All Western Europe wants us to be strong. A nation cannot even appear to be strong so long as its pound is worth only ten shillings in virtually every capital of Europe.

As a final and, to Scots, a magnetic, attraction, Copenhagen has the most flourishing St. Andrew's Society on the Continent. Its presiding genius is Mr. Duthie, who comes from Aberdeen, but has spent over twenty years of his life in Denmark. He is a keen Scot, is popular with everyone, and has put the Society on the map not only of Denmark but also of Scotland. Every year Scottish pipers and some Scottish celebrity are invited on such occasions as St. Andrew's Day or a Burns Nicht.

Mr. Duthie is almost the only Scot in the Society. The vast bulk of the members are Danes, and their enthusiasm has the true Scottish fire. The financial genius of the Society is M. Grantzow, a business man who organises the St. Andrew's Ball. It is one of the great social functions of Copenhagen and tickets for it are sought almost as eagerly and extravagantly as tickets for Wimbledon in England. Like several other Danish members of the Society, M. Grantzow wears a tartan dinner-jacket, and, although he has no Scottish blood in his veins, the tartan is of course the Grant.

Scottish reels and country dances like "Strip the Willow", "The Gay Gordons", and "The Dashing White Sergeant" have gripped the Danes like a fever. The dancing class, taught by a Danish lady who had studied in Edinburgh, is always full, and the keenest enthusiast is our ambassador, Sir Alec Randall, a hundred per cent Englishman.

On the last night of my last visit to Copenhagen he gave a dance at the Embassy, nominally in my honour, but in reality to enable him to have one final fling at Highland dancing before the season ended. It was an unforgettable evening. There was a galaxy of Danish and English beauty. The country dances were performed by all present, the Danes piloting their bewildered English partners with surprising skill. The great event of the evening was the eightsome reel, for which there were two teams, one led by Sir Alec Randall. With most of the guests I sat on the side-lines and watched. The first team, composed of one Scottish man, a Russian lady, and six Danes, danced very correctly though perhaps a trifle too sedately. But the ambassador's eightsome was a sight worth going a long way to see. There were mistakes and muddles. Dancing skill was lacking. But there was fire and a tramping of feet which made the heavily-framed pictures of the Royal Family quiver on the walls. The fire was kindled almost entirely by Alec Randall himself, and my heart warmed to him as, holding himself very erect, he advanced into the centre and leapt into the air with his eyes blazing, his fists clenched, and a long wisp of hair streaming from the top of his head like the feather of an Indian brave.

To wind up the evening or, to be accurate, to usher in the morning we danced a final eightsome and through the efforts of the indefatigable service attachés we formed a third, very scratch team in which I took part. Although performing with great zest, I was soon blown and retired to my seat. Alec, however, was indefatigable and his energy was maintained to the last bar of the music. As I watched him with envy, a local Scot who was sitting next to me whispered: "He's the most popular ambassador we've ever had here. The Danes love him, but, gosh, when he dances he reminds me of a hen on a hot girdle."

The next morning I was up early and, dreading always that it might be my last chance, I had arranged with the Chancery chauffeur to drive me round my favourite haunts for a final farewell. On our way back, we stopped before the Danish Parliament to look again at the four massive sculptured figures above the entrance. I had always supposed that these huge Grecian heads, each as ugly as Socrates, were symbolic of the burdens and responsibilities which lie heavily on the shoulders of politicians. The chauffeur interrupted my thoughts with a chuckle: Do you know how we Danes have christened these old gentlemen. We call them: "Headache, Earache, Stomachache and Toothache." I looked again and had to admit that the names fitted.

Then the chauffeur said proudly: "The Germans and Swedes like everything massive, irrespective of its beauty. We Danes like little things because they are beautiful."

Chapter IV

RETURN TO GERMANY

*"A Press campaign of four months will convince the
German people of the rightness of any idiocy you like to
suggest."*

KIDERLIN-WAECHTER, German Foreign Secretary, 1910-12.

GERMANY was the first foreign country that I ever visited.
I went by sea and rail from Leith to Berlin in May 1905,
when I was still under eighteen and had not yet seen London
or even crossed the Scottish border into England. Of all my
voyages this first journey stands out most vividly in my memory.
I can remember every incident from the emotional farewell of
my father at the pier of Leith to my own shy arrival at the Lehrter
Bahnhof in Berlin where, not knowing a single word of German,
I was met by Fräulein Tilley, conducted to the famous Institute
Tilley and forced to promise on my honour to remain silent until
I could splutter a few words of German. As the penalty for speaking or reading English was instant expulsion, I kept my promise
and learnt German with great speed and some accuracy. Although
in recent years I have had little occasion to speak it, it remains my
best foreign language.

I owe much to Germany. At school in Scotland, apart from
some minor successes in games, I had been a failure. In Germany
I learnt to work and I have never forgotten the lesson. It was
there, too, that I first acquired an abiding interest in music, pictures
and the theatre. So strong was my enthusiasm that, temporarily
at least, I abandoned the family passion for Rugby football. When
I came home in December 1906, for my first holiday, my parents
had moved to England, and my father welcomed me in London
with two tickets for the Oxford and Cambridge match in his
hand. Priggishly I replied: "I have put away childish things. I

N

should like you to take me to the National Gallery." Of course I went to the match and enjoyed myself thoroughly.

Since then I have returned to Germany many times and, apart from East Prussia, there can be few parts of the Reich that I have not visited.

The First World War was a harsh and cruel shock to my earlier enthusiasm for Germany and things German. I blamed the military caste, went back and made new friends. In those difficult years of the "'Twenties" there were two possible policies towards Germany: to give support and encouragement to the German Republic or to hold the country down by military force. On these two policies France and Britain were divided. The French went into the Ruhr. We stayed out. As the Americans had withdrawn from Europe, the breach between the Allies was wide open and the half-measures which had caused it created Hitler. In March 1938, I paid my last pre-war visit to Germany and came home with the uncomfortable feeling that it was pre-war.

The Second World War produced an entirely different effect on me. I had no wish to see Germany or Germans again. The only German friend who wrote to me during the war was Albrecht Bernstorff, a former Rhodes scholar who knew London and England better than many Englishmen and who believed and continued to believe until the advent of Hitler that a democratic and pacific Germany was possible. To this aim he devoted his life. Rather than serve the Nazis he sacrificed a brilliant diplomatic career. During the war he suffered imprisonment and torture and less than a month before its end was murdered by the Gestapo. I had another friend who was interned by us and released before the end of the war. He came to visit me at once and I refused to see him. He was a deeply religious man whose brother had been shot by the Nazis. He wrote me a long letter which pricked my conscience. I did not answer it. Today I feel ashamed. Like the Irish, we Scots have long memories. There was no hate in my heart, but I could not forget. It is the great virtue and perhaps the great weakness of the English that they not only forgive but also forget so quickly.

After the war I had several opportunities of re-visiting Germany.

They did not tempt even my curiosity. In the early summer of 1947, I passed through a large part of Western Germany on my way to and from Prague. On both occasions the weather was superb, and in the shimmering sunlight the contrast between the green, well-cultivated fields and the twisted devastation of the towns gripped me with its horror. I wanted to turn away, but could not keep my eyes from the window. Cologne was a shambles; nothing seemed to be left of the once beautiful Nuremberg. The Germans whom I saw were mostly old men or young boys. They were miserably dressed and looked underfed. At Nuremberg where I had to wait an hour I threw a cigarette end on to the platform, and at once five or six lads dived for it. The Germans were down, and I thought that years must pass before they could recover as a nation. The savagery and futility of war came back to me with renewed force, but I had still no desire to renew my associations with Germany and the Germans. That part of my life, I thought, was for ever dead.

Then in November 1951, I received a letter from a Dutch lady who had just revisited Munich and had met an old German friend of mine, a business man of most upright character, whose famous trout water on the river Sempt in Bavaria I had fished many times. He was now eighty-six, but in good health and still able to fish. He sent me his greetings and said how happy he would be to take me to the Sempt again.

I had supposed him long dead. The fact that he was alive woke a chord in my heart. I wrote for his address. By the time that I received it, I had been invited officially to visit Radio Free Europe, the station in Munich from which Poles, Czechoslovaks and Hungarians broadcast daily, under private American auspices, to their compatriots behind the Iron Curtain.

The coincidence of these two invitations decided me, and, although the end of January was no month for trout-fishing, off I went to Munich. The rococo Bavarian capital which I had known so well was vastly altered. Almost all that was most beautiful and, alas! of least military value in it had been destroyed. I put up at the Vierjahreszeiten, the only one of the big hotels to escape damage, and there were the two Walterspiels, older but otherwise

little changed, to welcome me. I went straight up to my room
to find on the table a letter marked "to await arrival". I opened
it carelessly, expecting some invitation. It was quite short:

"You cannot imagine how happy I am to know that you will
be in Munich tomorrow. I shall do my utmost to bring back
to your memory the many happy days which you have spent in
this town. But we cannot be together with my dear father any
more. He died just two weeks ago."

My old friend, who had never done a mean or a cruel act in
his life, had looked forward to the last to taking me to his river
in the spring. Now that he was no longer there to meet me, I
felt that a large slice of what was best in Germany had gone with
him.

Two days later his son came to drive me out to Ottenhoven,
the tiny village by the river Sempt, where in the little house next
to the smithy we used to have luncheon. It always began with
freshly-caught trout, grilled by Frau Geiser, wife of the owner
of the smithy and mother of a large family. The trout were followed by a colossal Schweinsbraten, and to wash it down there
was beer and a bottle of choice Moselle.

On our way out of the city we had to pull up for the traffic,
and my old friend's son pointed to a house on the right.

"In that building," he said, "is the flat in which Hitler first
lived when he came to Munich and which he kept to the end."

I was doubly surprised, first, because, although I had been
nearly three days in Munich, I had heard no mention of Hitler's
name and, secondly, because few landmarks of the Fuehrer remained
standing. I had already been to the Buergerbräu, the famous
beer cellar in which he had fired off his pistol in order to start his
first ill-fated Putsch. The place, now filled with middle-class
Bavarians eating sausages and drinking beer, was intact, but of the
Nazi Brown House, over which I had been piloted by Rosenberg
soon after it was opened, not a trace remained.

The flat before which we had stopped was now the office of
the commissioner in charge of the liquidation of Hitler's property for

the benefit of the victims of Nazi oppression. I discovered later that the commissioner was a Jew! Moreover, Goering was not the only Nazi who made a hobby of collecting art treasures. Hitler's personal booty was enormous and ranged from priceless pictures to millions of books. Nearly seven years after the war the task of finding the owners had not been completed and probably never will be.

As we proceeded on our way, my friend's son told me of his father's love of Ottenhoven and his passion for fishing. He had fished to the end and in the summer before his death had caught a trout of six pounds. I recalled my chance meeting with him in May, 1920, the friendship that followed, and the subsequent enchanting days in that peaceful Bavarian valley. Then it had always been spring or summer. Now the whole countryside was deep in snow, and when we approached Ottenhoven I had some difficulty in recognising it.

We drove first to the smithy by the bridge, and disenchantment followed at once. Old Geiser was dead. His wife had gone to live in another house some distance away. The smithy had been modernised and now had a power-station beside it. In order to provide water for it the banks of the river had been dug out to form a deep canal. Above the bridge there was a small reservoir which had been stocked with—carp. The famous Sempt trout were gone, or, at least, greatly diminished.

All this was told to us by one of Frau Geiser's nephews, and my friend's son who was no fisherman and who had not been to Ottenhoven for five years was as surprised as I was.

"Why have the trout disappeared?" I asked innocently.

The Bavarian peasant shrugged his shoulders. "The Americans," he said. "They are close by. At first they threw handgrenades. Now fifty or more fish the river all the time. No stream will stand that."

Everything had changed, and yet not quite everything.

"We must see Frau Geiser," said my friend's son, and rather against my depressed will I went with him. The house was on a hill, and, as the car would not mount the frozen road, we had to walk through the deep snow. When we reached the house in the middle of a well-stocked farm, it seemed to be deserted, for although we knocked loudly no one answered. We went round to a window and knocked again. This time a woman came to the sill, threw up her arms and shouted: "Da ist der Lockhart." It was Frau Geiser's daughter, now a woman of some fifty years. We were brought into the spotless kitchen. There was Frau Geiser, still flourishing and looking forward to her eighty-fourth birthday. There was another welcome, and then much talk of old times. Albums of fishing photographs were produced, while Frau Geiser's daughter bustled to and fro laying the table with new linen. We were to have a meal—and what a meal, everything home-made and home-brewed, with eggs straight from under the hens. Not for many years have I eaten so many at one sitting. Half-ashamed, I made the excuse that fresh eggs were rare in London. This led to questions about England. Did we still have food-rationing? Was it true that meat was scarce? I answered truthfully, and with innocent wonder in her eyes Frau Geiser's daughter exclaimed: "You won the war, and you have nothing. We lost it, and we have everything."

I was glad to have seen the Geisers. I have always liked people who live on the land. I had a deep affection for these Bavarian peasants who had always treated me so kindly and who now welcomed me back after so long an absence.

As we drove away, I looked back at the little village with its green and red window-shutters shimmering in the winter sunlight. Guessing what was in my heart, my friend's son said: "I am giving up the water, but I can always arrange for you to fish whenever you come." He guessed wrongly. I knew that never again should I fish the Sempt, that never again should I want to fish it.

If Ottenhoven left a permanent scar on my heart, I cannot say truthfully that I had time to indulge in regrets or in my once favourite pastime of searching for lost footsteps. I had been accompanied on my official visit by Gregory Macdonald, the head of the Central European Service of the B.B.C., and both of us were worked overtime. The Americans who ran Radio Free Europe were eager to show us what they had achieved. They kept us busy all day, and at night they entertained us with truly American hospitality.

In an incredibly short time they had accomplished a modern miracle. In five months they had built a brand-new radio station equipped with all the latest broadcasting machinery and had assembled teams of Czechoslovaks, Hungarians and Poles to broadcast to their countrymen behind the Iron Curtain. Already the Czechoslovaks were broadcasting twenty hours a day. The Hungarians were doing twelve hours, and the Poles were to start in the spring. German workmen built the broadcasting station, but only American drive and energy could have produced such speedy results and inspired the enthusiasm which infected everyone we met. Even more remarkable were the canteen and the new block of flats provided for the comfort of the *émigrés* who worked for Radio Free Europe. I spent an evening in one of the new flats which had just been occupied by the Polish director. It was furnished with American efficiency, private enterprise, and of course abundant dollars. Nothing had been forgotten. In the kitchen even aprons, brooms, mops and polishing wax had been provided. The flat would have made many young English people envious. Poor Gregory Macdonald, suffering from the Tory Government's "cuts" in the Overseas Services of the B.B.C., said nothing, but he must have felt that even in radio money counts.

Radio Free Europe is an independent organisation run by private subscriptions and free from government control. Its aim is to allow the *émigrés* to speak to their people at home with as little interference as possible, and at the end of my visit I was satisfied that, subject only to the necessary minimum of political guidance, they enjoyed great freedom in the preparation of their own programmes.

As for more than five years I have been broadcasting once a week to Czechoslovakia, I naturally saw most of the Czechs and Slovaks among whom I found several old friends. There were nearly two hundred of them and in age they ranged from elderly ex-ambassadors to young students who had recently made the perilous escape across the frontier. It was inspiring to see them working together. All felt that they were in the front line and some perhaps were anxious, for if war came all realised that the Russians could be in Munich in a few hours. The Americans, however, keep them fully occupied, and work is assuredly the best antidote to the despair which every exile has to fight. These Czechoslovaks of Radio Free Europe were, I felt, in a far happier position than their unfortunate compatriots who escaped from Communist Czechoslovakia and are now interned in the Valka camp near Nuremberg. This camp is now administered and guarded by Germans and in one sense is a danger to the West, for every refugee who escapes from an Iron Curtain country does so not only at great peril to his life, but also with the hope of a warm welcome from the free countries. On arrival at the frontier he is carefully "vetted" by the security officials, and this he accepts, for he knows that his Communist government sends agents abroad disguised as refugees. Then he finds that the West does not want him or cannot place him, and he is left for months in a camp administered by men of the race which during the war occupied and ruined his country. Virtually a prisoner of his former enemy, he tends to give way to despair and perhaps even to a change of heart.

There was one item of the Czechoslovak programme at Munich which made a lasting impression. It was a song included in a remarkable series composed by Josef Stelibsky, the Czech composer of numerous popular operettas. It is called "The Song of the Prague Bells". The music is hauntingly nostalgic and the words with their message of everlasting faith are attuned to it. The effect brings tears and the song, I am sure, wakes an echo in all Czech hearts whenever it is played.

Radio Free Europe has the same problem which confronts every Western radio, including the B.B.C., that broadcasts to the Iron Curtain countries, namely, how to keep the spark of faith alive without raising false hopes of speedy liberation.

Radio Free Europe has, I think, another problem. It chose Munich as the centre of its operations because of the benevolent attitude of the Bavarian Government. Bavaria, however, has absorbed the bulk of the Sudeten Germans from Czechoslovakia, and, as and when Western Germany acquires more independence and more freedom of action, it is perhaps wise to ask oneself how long the Bavarian Government will allow Czechoslovaks to broad-cast from Munich propaganda material which is and must be sub-

stantially anti-Sudeten, or Poles to advocate from the same station
the retention of the Oder-Neisse line.

The Americans in Munich are, I think, acutely aware of both
problems. They can solve the first. The second may be more
difficult.

In spite of hard work and hospitality I did find time to see
something of Munich and to meet some Germans. In the sixty-six
air raids which the city had to endure, the Residenz, the Odeon,
the Old and New Pinakothek, the Glyptothek, the National
Theatre, the Residenz Theatre, the Bavarian State Library, and
many old churches have been totally or partially destroyed. Art,
music, literature and architecture have suffered most. The Nazi
Brown House has gone, and that, I feel, was good, but the Fuehrer-
bau in the Arcisstrasse, where on September 30 the Munich Agreement was signed by Hitler, Mussolini, Chamberlain and Daladier,
remains. It has now become the Amerikahaus, and this, too,
seems to me just retribution.

I also found, in the Schonfeldstrasse, the house, probably not
the same building, in which Ibsen had lived ten years before I
was born. I had been an early Ibsen worshipper, and his *Ghosts,*
which I saw in Paris in 1906, the year of his death, was the first
serious disturbance of my hitherto carefree and youthful outlook
on life. Ibsen, I was reminded by a German friend, had spent two
summers in Berchtesgaden, but I had neither the wish nor the time
to make the long, cold motor-drive to the Fuehrer's mountain
eyrie which has now been demolished. My visit to the Schonfeldstrasse was my only pilgrimage.

If Munich of my youth and middle-age had gone, I was as-
tounded by the stupendous effort which the Bavarians had made
to re-build their capital. The work of reconstruction had been
amazingly rapid and in spite of the snow was still proceeding at
great speed. The shops were full of goods, and Herder's book-
store, almost opposite the hotel, was well-stocked with books of
every kind, better-printed and better-bound than our own and
cheap in marks and not very expensive even in our depreciated
currency. Incidentally, easily the two most popular books at

that time in all Western Germany were Guareschi's *The Little World of Don Camillo* and *That Was My Life*, by Sauerbruch who was Lenin's, Hitler's and Stalin's doctor. In the list of best-sellers *Kon-Tiki* was a very poor third. Food was plentiful and good; very expensive certainly in Walterspiel's famous restaurant, but reasonable cheap in the ordinary eating-houses where the helpings were enormous and the menu a yard long. The people were decently dressed and went about their work cheerfully. Doubtless, American aid had helped recovery. Doubtless, too, life was expensive to the German worker as well as to us poor British. But one thing was certain. Munich was now a going concern. Hope had take the place of despair, and a child could have read it in the faces of the hard-working Bavarian people. I was not surprised to find that most Americans, especially the young non-commissioned officers, regarded the Germans as the only European people who did an honest day's work. It was and always will be, I imagine, the admiration of technician for technician.

Clearly the German industrialists, especially the textile manufacturers in the Rhineland, were making big money. Many of them, too, were evading taxation and placing large sums abroad, perhaps not entirely for selfish reasons, for foreign trade was going ahead by leaps and bounds. Here, I felt, was one concrete argument in favour of the rearmament of Western Germany. An unarmed Germany would soon be underselling Britain and the United States, both heavily burdened by their own rearmament programmes, in every part of the globe. Indeed, the underselling had already begun.

Closer contact with some German friends showed that the picture was not quite so rosy as it seemed. Behind the gloss of prosperity there was a dark shadow. The contrast between high profits and low wages was apparent and seemed to me dangerous. The factories were well-equipped, but the workers were badly housed and, in relation to the cost of living, badly paid. So long as they remained disciplined, I was assured that all would be well. "What will happen if they don't?" I asked my best German friend. "Our workers have always been disciplined", was his stolid but not very reassuring answer.

The young people, I was told, had great difficulties in making a start in life. Among the professional classes the lawyers were doing well because there were big transfers of property and big legal fees in connection with them. On the other hand, medical students were in real distress, and I was introduced to a young doctor who, after passing all his examinations brilliantly, was receiving eighty marks a month (approximately £7 in our weak currency) as a hospital assistant.

Among my few German acquaintances, none of whom belonged to the officer class, I found no sense of guilt with regard to the last war. I did not expect to find it. I consider it unreasonable that a whole people should confess their guilt for events over which they had little or no control. There are few people who at all times can resist the mass-suggestion engendered not only by dictators but also by demagogues. What did astonish me was to find that, when my German friends mentioned Hitler, they blamed him, not for plunging his country into war, but for the foolish mistakes which he made in conducting it and thereby turning certain victory into defeat. The mistakes were many, and every German seemed to have his own pet Hitlerian blunder.

I must admit that I heard no talk of a war of revenge, nor did I find much enthusiasm for German rearmament for the defence of Western Europe. Those Germans who were in favour of it disliked what they called a position of inferiority. But, as far as I could discover, there were, in Bavaria at least, many Germans who disliked the whole idea of rearmament. In point of fact, I found as much fear of Russia among the Bavarians as among the *émigrés* in Radio Free Europe. The fear arose partly from apprehensions lest one day the Americans would grow tired of Europe and leave her to her own fate. No occupying force can be popular for long in a defeated country, and this axiom applies to all the armies of occupation in Germany today. But no non-Communist German wanted the Americans to quit at this moment, and because of their anxiety on this score one or two Munich businessmen of my acquaintance had qualms before accepting profitable American agencies.

There was also fear of the Russians because of the disparity,

obvious to every German, between the military strength of the
Soviet Union and the tardy rearmament of the West. Moreover,
the Soviet forces were on the German doorstep. The real strength
of the United States was far away. One German in whose honesty
I had confidence said to me: "If war comes, I have no doubt that
you will win in the end, but we shall be over-run at once; it will
take you perhaps two years to liberate us, and what good will
liberation be to me when I am dead." Another said bluntly:
"You let the Russians come so close. It is for you to push them
back."

There were other features of the new Germany which were more
disturbing. Duelling, although forbidden, had started again
among the Munich students in much the same way that it had
begun after the First World War. The Munich newspapers were
respectful and restrained in their attitude towards the West, but
contained vigorous attacks on the Czechoslovaks for the brutality
with which they had expelled the Sudeten Germans after the war.
These attacks are a clear proof that the Sudeten question is far
from dead. Although I met no avowed Nazis, I heard something
of their activities, and what I learnt was not reassuring. Once again
the open split between the Allies who had defeated Germany with
such difficulty had given to the Germans the golden opportunity of
playing off East and West against one another, of blackmailing the
one by pretending to embrace the other and of coming to terms
with neither except at the time of their own choosing. At this
game the Nazis are past masters, and no one who has any knowledge
of Soviet-German relations can be foolish enough to believe that
any Communist repugnance to shake hands with Nazis or Nazi
reluctance to sit down with Communists would deter either the
one or the other from making a devil's bargain if both believed it
to be opportunistically profitable. Both Nazis and Communists
are extremists, and extreme understands extreme and shares a
common dislike of all liberal ideas.

I did not doubt that there were Germans who desired peace
because it was the only hope of recovery and who believed sincerely that German unity could come only from the West and
through the West. They were to be found among the older

men who because they were old were wiser and milder. I saw, however, no clear sign of any admiration for Western institutions, nor did I find any burning enthusiasm for the democratic way of life. In particular, German youth seemed to be more interested in survival than in democracy and to be swayed by a vague belief that, in some way yet to be revealed, hope would triumph over unhappy experience. Politically the country seemed hopelessly divided and had not found its way. I had the unpleasant feeling that if a new leader were to arise, German youth would again follow him. In this respect the Germany of 1952 bore an uncomfortable resemblance to the Germany of 1929.

To me there seemed to be only two hopes for the future: first, that sufficient Germans would realise the necessity of a permanent Franco-German understanding, which, indeed, is the key to the settlement of *every* European problem, and, secondly, that Gremany would produce sufficient young men of the type of Albrecht Bernstorff to devote their lives to the work of reconciliation and peace. Of the first hope I found some signs which justified a cautious optimism. I did not know the new Germany well enough to form any satisfactory conclusion regarding the second hope.

I noted one remarkable change in the Munich of today. During my stay I did not see a single British man or woman apart from the British Consul-General and his staff. Between the wars Munich had been a finishing school for young English girls, a magnet for music-lovers, and a centre of attraction for British tourists of all classes. Now currency restrictions had barred our way and austerity had cramped the valuable activities of such institutions as the British Council and the European Services of the B.B.C. The effect on the Continental mind, in particular, the German mind, is much greater than most British people imagine. Indeed, a most intelligent American diplomat told me frankly that he feared we should suffer one day for our neglect of Germany. With the prospect of recovery now bright, the Germans, he said, were studying again with their customary zeal and thoroughness the problems of the future of Central and South-Eastern Europe. In that German future Czechoslovakia and Poland had no place as independent states. If war came, the United States would win and would probably leave Europe. Germany, and not Britain, would then fill the vacuum created by the American withdrawal. If there were no war, Germany would still come to the top by her industry, her determination, and her capacity for hard work.

The picture may be exaggerated, but for a long time I have felt uneasy about the manner in which we frequently deride American diplomacy and assume complacently that the long experience of our own diplomatists gives them a vast superiority over their American colleagues. American diplomacy suffers from one serious defect: the appointment as a political reward of non-professional ambassadors. But the career American diplomats are a remarkable body of men thoroughly trained for their job, eager, receptive, more alive to the social convulsions of a changing world and less conservative in their attitude than many of their British colleagues. I think that ever since 1918 they have been more often right in regard to Europe than we have and that man for man they are fully our equals. Inevitably they have many advantages of which dollars are not the least. Diplomacy is devitalised when it is not supported by real strength and money, and Britain of today is short of both.

On my final day in Munich—almost certainly the last that I shall ever spend there—the sun shone brilliantly, melting the snow, but also exposing more vividly the material ruins of the city. Here far more than in London I realised the fragile impermanence of European capitals, and in spite of the sunshine I felt sad until Gregory Macdonald swept me off to shop or rather to help him to shop. It was a rare experience and a real pleasure for me to watch how carefully this hard-worked and highly intelligent man chose his presents for his wife, his children, his secretary and other B.B.C. colleagues. His store of marks being strictly limited, selection had to be adjusted to price. I took him first to the Oberammergau Wood-Carving Shop. It was full of exquisitely-carved wooden animals: deer and fauns predominating, but too fragile for children and far too expensive for our purse. Gregory, who has imagination, bought a small head of an angel in wood and said to me: "I can easily get this turned into a lapel brooch for next to nothing".

We then went to a fascinating toy-shop near the station. It was
laid out with wonderful toys including motor-cars, bicycles,
whole farmsteads, Noah's Arks, and dolls that looked alive. All
were beautifully designed. But Gregory was unhappy. There
were no European tin soldiers, and these were what Gregory
wanted. "What," he said, "no tin soldiers in Germany? Is this
an order from the Allies?" I came to his rescue. I had spotted
a corner in which was laid out a whole array of tin cowboys complete with chaps, rifles and revolvers and Red Indians with head-
dresses, bows and arrows, tomahawks and wigwams; in fact, all
the accoutrements which psychiatrists say make the young bloody-
minded. Gregory spent his last mark on them.

The rest of the day was spent in packing, in saying farewell
to the hospitable Americans of Radio Free Europe, and in receiving
Czech and Polish visitors. Then at half-past seven we drove to
the Hauptbahnhof to catch the 8.15 p.m. train to Ostend. The
night was bitterly cold, and an icy wind blew across the open
platforms. Arriving half an hour too early, we learnt to our horror
that the train was ninety minutes late. With so much time on
our hands, we decided to dine in the station restaurant or rather in
one of the three station restaurants which are side by side and
correspond roughly to what we should call first-class, second-
class, and third-class. Selection was difficult, for all were full.
Finally we found a table in the centre of the best restaurant. It
was the first time that we had dined alone and we determined to
do ourselves as well as we could afford.

The room was full of solid, well-behaved Bavarian bourgeois,
few of whom, I imagine, were travellers. We were given an
excellent dinner: the best smoked salmon I have ever tasted, a
perfect Wiener-Schnitzel with the usual trimmings of capers,
sauté potatoes, little gherkins and salad, and a bottle of exquisite
Piesporter. The service was efficient, and as everywhere else in
Munich the friendliness of the staff was delightful and seemed
unforced.

While we were finishing our wine, a young American G.I.
came into the room. Although he was not reeling, I saw at once
that he was very drunk, for he walked with the slow, desperately

deliberate gait of a man who is determined to get somewhere and is not sure of his next footstep. A quarter way down the large room he found an empty seat at the end of a table occupied by an elderly German and, without asking by your leave, sat down clumsily. Tall, dark, and lightly built, he did not look more than twenty. As he was the only American soldier in the room, we watched possible developments with interest.

Presently Gregory said to me: "Ho-ho, you were wrong, he's not so drunk after all; just see what a fine strategic position he's taken up." I looked and saw that at the table, which he had previously passed, and face to face to him sat a rather pretty German girl who, although not an obvious tart, was alone. The G.I., half-sprawling over his table-end, was staring hard at her.

I pointed out to Gregory that the girl did not look like an "Amizone", as the Germans call the girls who go with the American soldiers. But Gregory would not have it.

Presently the G.I. rose, walked over to the girl and, pointing to his own table, asked her to join him. Gregory smiled. But to my joy the girl went scarlet in the face, said something which I could not hear, and the G.I. slouched back to his place. It was now my turn to smile, but Gregory was not convinced. "You'll see," he said, "in a few minutes they'll both get up, leave separately, and join up outside. That will be the technique. The Yank knows it. Otherwise, he would not be here."

I was not sure, but I still put my money on the girl. Meanwhile, the whole room was furtively watching the cat and mouse drama. It was soon ended when the young German, husband or boy-friend, for whom the girl had been waiting, came in, and the two started their meal after an animated conversation during which, I imagine, she had been scolding him for being late.

The G.I., now thwarted, subsided on the table with his face buried in his outstretched hands. From time to time he would raise his head wearily to look for a "sexy" second at his lost light o' love. Finally he collapsed completely, and as he bent farther over the table a wider and wider gap opened between the top of his trousers and his Eisenhower tunic until a large expanse of crumpled shirt showed between the hiatus. A few minutes later, in came two

American military policemen, one a white and the other a husky well-turned-out negro. They were looking for drunk and disorderly G.I.'s. There was only one to engage their attention, and, as he was not disorderly, they ignored him. The Germans, who had watched the scene without a sign of emotion, returned to their beer-mugs and their newspapers, but both Gregory and I knew, as if we had been listening in, that in their hearts they were saying proudly: "Thank goodness no German soldier would ever make such a sight of himself in a public restaurant".

The thought was apposite, for no German or for that matter no British soldier could have afforded the expense. Had I not known from personal experience that there is more idealism in the schools, universities, and among young people generally in the United States than in the whole of Europe, my comment would have been: "Thank God money is *not* enough", for, although it is often untrue, I like to think that sometimes virtue triumphs over the dollar.

This little drama nearly made me miss a train for the first time in my life. We caught it just as it was leaving the platform. Moreover, we had been lucky in deciding to dine in the station restaurant, for in the wagon-lit the lights passed out at the start and never recovered. On our journey to Munich the heating had failed. These were the only mishaps during our whole visit. For the sake of Britain's reputation I hope that the Wagon-Lit Company is no longer British-owned.

o

Chapter V

THE NETHERLANDS IN TRAVAIL

"The children in Holland take pleasure in making
What children in England take pleasure in breaking."

EVER since I went to Malaya as a young man, I have known Dutch men and women. I have not only liked them; I have admired them. After the First World War I was appointed to Prague where the Dutch Minister was Edgar Michiels who afterwards until his death in 1952 was the much-loved and greatly respected Dutch ambassador in London. Prague was, I think, his first diplomatic post abroad. He was then still in his thirties and was as attractive and as cheerful a man as one could find in the whole diplomatic corps of Europe. He spoke English almost like an Englishman; he could do everything well. We had great tussles at golf, for he was a fine player who had been amateur champion of his own country and had competed at least once in our amateur championship. As a diplomatist he had a compelling courage which was the more irresistible because it was supported by tact and disarming charm of manner. Above all, he was a man to whom you could say anything with the absolute certainty that it would remain a life-long secret between you and him. Prague was a wild place in those days, and he pulled me out of one scrape and helped me to save others from more serious disasters including blackmail. I kept in touch with him up to and during the last war, and without him Holland will never be the same place to me.

Between the two wars I was a fairly frequent visitor to the Netherlands and was on friendly terms with Dr. van Karnebeck, the former Dutch Foreign Minister, and with Hendrijk Colijn, the most famous and most resolute of all modern Dutch Prime Ministers.

Both were pro-English, and Colijn was a close friend and ardent admirer of Winston Churchill, but after Hitler's rise to power the two Dutchmen were critical of British policy. "I marvel," Colijn said to me in November 1937, "how England can go on lecturing Europe when she herself does nothing to forestall the danger; in plain words her policy is an invitation to all the robbers to take what they can."

As their great dykes against the sea prove, the Dutch are a constructive people, thorough, efficient, highly educated and always planning ahead, and Colijn himself was a man of action with a deep-rooted mistrust of rule by committees and a rude contempt for what Sir Ivone Kirkpatrick, our present High Commissioner in Germany and my colleague during the war, calls "waffling".

Today both Colijn and Karnebeck are dead. Many of my other ties with Holland have been broken, and since the last war I have felt a reluctance to return, not through any indifference to its fate, but because to me it is a land haunted by the ghosts of a happier past. I had a deep affection for the peaceful Dutch countryside, for the neat and quiet little Dutch towns like Breukelen which gives its name to Brooklyn, in America, and for the rich polder-land reclaimed with such patient effort from the sea. I remembered the advice of my friend, Negley Farson: "Where you have been happy, never go back."

Above all, my conscience twinged me when I reflected that, while we had remained in Malaya after the war, we had done little or nothing to prevent the Dutch from being pushed out of Indonesia. In 1935 I had visited the Dutch East Indies and had been deeply impressed by the miraculous job which the Dutch had done there. Some of the businessmen had been too greedy, but I thought the Dutch administrators superior to our own in Malaya. With few exceptions they were highly educated men of sterling character and integrity who took their duties very seriously indeed. Indonesia was to them what India was to us. They had made it, and to their work alone Indonesia today owes its education, its rubber and sugar plantations, its rice fields which are a monument to Dutch agricultural engineering, and, above all, its teeming population composed of many races who but for the Dutch, would have spent their lives in internecine warfare and today would number thousands instead of millions. Admittedly, the Dutch took much wealth from Indonesia. But they created the wealth and they spent much of it in and on the country itself.

Indeed, they had brought the Indonesian peoples to a much higher state of civilisation and, therefore, of independence than we had done in Malaya. This fact is an argument in favour of our remaining in Malaya, but I could not expect the Dutch to see it in this light. They themselves may have made mistakes, but my sympathies were with them.

Moreover, the Dutch had suffered more horrors during the war than any of the occupied countries of Western Europe. They had been heavily blitzed in 1940. Throughout the Nazi occupation their resistance was tough and resolute. Just before their liberation they were on the verge of starvation. Disaster lay heavily upon them and, with their greatest assets gone, they were faced with an appallingly difficult task of recovery and reconstruction. I did not wish to indulge my insatiable curiosity in their difficulties.

Then in December 1948, I received an invitation from Mr. Croll of Rotterdam to lecture to the Netherlands–England Societies in Holland. I hesitated, and at the New Year the invitation was followed by a long Hogmanay telegram, for Mr. Croll has good Scottish blood in his veins. The wording appealed to me, and in the middle of March 1949, I made the journey back. It was a miserable day when I left England. The sky was mournful and misty, and, as we flew low towards the coast the inlets and the islands to the south as far as Walcheren (where our Army and Marine Commandos had won imperishable fame in helping to free the entrance to the port of Antwerp) looked like oily patches in the leaden grey sea and not at all like the poet's "green emerald flats, where, in proud rivalry, land strives with water, water strives with sky."

But at Schipol the sun was shining, and on the aerodrome March hares were performing ridiculous antics and providing to tired travellers the object-lesson that even hares are not afraid of aeroplanes. I drove to our Embassy at The Hague where my

host was Sir Philip Nichols, an old friend whom I had met first
just after the Kaiser war when he was a young secretary in Vienna.
Before coming to The Hague he had been ambassador in Prague
and both Lady Nichols and he had been close friends of President
and Madame Beneš and of Jan Masaryk.

Once again I slept in the Churchill room, for the ubiquitous
Vin-stone had already paid his post-war visit to The Hague. He
has long been a hero to the Dutch, and I recalled my last visit to
The Hague when a fortnight before the war I had lunched with
Colijn, then Prime Minister, and he had said to me very earnestly:
"There will be no war provided you do one thing. You have
only to show a stiff front, put Winston in the Cabinet, and the
Nazis will climb down."

Since the war Mr. Churchill has become an idol to the Dutch.
When he came to The Hague, even the time and place of his
arrival were supposed to be a secret. He landed at a private aerodrome, but for seven miles from the capital to the doors of the
Embassy the Dutch people lined the streets and waited to give him
as rousing a welcome as even he has ever received.

Two years after the war three English intellectuals were travel-
ling in a Dutch train and were tearing Mr. Churchill to pieces.
The only other occupant of their compartment was a tall and
hefty Dutchman. At last he could stand the denigration of his hero
no longer and, rising to his full height, he said politely but very
firmly: "In England you have free speech and you can say what
you like. We Dutch also believe in free speech but in Holland
we allow no one to insult Winston Churchill." The Englishmen
were silenced.

I did all my lectures from The Hague. The Dutch were
hospitable, dignified, earnest and stolid. They remained as I
had always found them: the hardest-working and best-educated
race in Europe. They had already done a marvellous work of
reconstruction. The centre of Rotterdam had been heavily
bombed, but by 1949 much of it had been splendidly restored.
In Amsterdam I was shown one of the neatest pieces of bombing
by the R.A.F. during the whole war: a street in which the headquarters of the Gestapo had been totally demolished without any

damage, apart from a few broken windows, to a single Dutch house. This raid, carried out on special intelligence supplied by a Dutch resistance group in order to punish and stop cruelty and torture even more outrageous than the customary Gestapo sample, has put the R.A.F. high above all other air forces in the estimation of the citizens of Amsterdam.

The Dutch have their own domestic political difficulties, mainly because the population is divided almost equally into Catholics and Protestants, and also because there are too many political parties. But in foreign affairs the Dutch are the most co-operative of all the nations of Western Europe. They accept the North Atlantic Treaty Organisation. They have played their part willingly and beneficially in all the committees and organisations for the recovery of Europe and they are, I think, ready to accept almost any form of co-operation which will strengthen European unity and security of defence. More serious than the Danes, less volatile than the Latin races, they are realists with a good foundation of common-sense and a clear understanding that small nations, in order to survive, must be more efficient and industrious than Great Powers. They stimulate my conviction that Europe has not changed so much as many people believe and that, but for the menace of Soviet Eurasia and the burden of armaments which it entails, it would recover quickly.

I had an interesting experience in Amsterdam when I went with the Ambassador to see the Bureau of War Documentation in that city. The director is a former member of the Dutch section of our Political Warfare Executive, and the Bureau contains an almost complete collection of the P.W.E. leaflets and miniature magazines dropped by air or distributed by agents over Holland during the war. I was photographed holding in my hand a copy of *Werfelwind*, the miniature magazine edited by Terry Harman, the head of our Dutch region during the war, and beautifully printed by Harold Keeble, a wizard of his craft and now editor of the *Sunday Express*.

The Bureau also contains many valuable exhibits of the German occupation including the diary of Mussert, the Dutch Nazi leader, a large signed photograph of Goering presented to the same Dutch "gentleman" with the name Mussert characteristically mis-spelt, and a monster example of *Mein Kampf* printed on the most expensive parchment. There is, too, a German hand-book for England showing exactly how the country was to be divided up and administered after the invasion which never came off. We were also shown a German film of the prison trains carrying off Dutch Jews to the horrors of Belsen and to the cremation incinerators of other camps of death. The Bureau is open to the public and attracts many visitors. I felt ashamed, because we have nothing of the same kind in England. When the war was over, P.W.E. was disbanded as quickly as possible, and I do not know where our archives are deposited or even if they exist.

With my lectures and talks with Dutch officials and journalists, I was kept busy, but I found time almost every morning to seek lost footsteps in The Hague which has always been one of my favourite capitals. The weather, too, was remarkably good for March, and I was wakened early by bird-song from the Embassy garden and by the chimes of the Jacobus Church. My favourite walk was the round which takes in the Lange Vorhout, the Vijver Lake, the Binnenhof and the Mauritshuis, the world-famous picture gallery in which Marlborough had once stayed when it was used as an hotel for ambassadors and V.I.Ps. Fortunately there had been no bombing in this attractive quarter, and I spent happy hours looking at the pictures, watching the duck on the lake, inspecting the book-shops, and finishing up at the Vieux Doelen, the restaurant where Colijn used to give his famous luncheons. Its glory had vanished. It had been taken over by the Government. There were other changes which increased my nostalgia for the ineluctable past. The owner of my favourite book-shop remembered me from pre-war days. He looked old and mournful, but his shelves carried a magnificent stock of international literature. I asked him how the Dutch translation of my latest book had gone. "Not very well," he replied tactfully. I pointed to a table stacked with English books and asked how they had sold. "Not at all," he replied. "Books here are too expensive and there is a buying slump." The Dutch are great readers. They had been very prosperous. Now they could not afford to buy books. Indeed, I discovered that in every respect they were much worse off than the Belgians or even ourselves. Yet in their stolid, sturdy way they did not whine.

One morning I took a taxi and drove to the Peace Palace. It is not beautiful, but I never fail to visit it, mainly, I think, because its tragedy numbs at once my incurable romanticism and brings my feet down to the damp earth of reality. The building was the creation of the first Peace Conference held on the initiative of the unfortunate Tsar Nicholas in 1899. It was not begun until 1907 and was finished in 1913, just in time for the First World War which cost over 10,000,000 lives.

The foundation was laid by Nelidov, the Russian ambassador, and the money, a million and a half dollars, was provided by Andrew Carnegie. All the nations supplied contributions in kind to the building. Britain's was coloured glass for the windows in the Great Hall of Justice. The glass represents the four successive epochs that lead to universal peace: Innocence; Might; Science, Philosophy and Art; and Triumphant Peace and Arbitration. Innocence! Might! We have long passed the first epoch. Shall we ever emerge from the second?

My last lecture was in The Hague and I gave it in the ball-room of a restaurant called "The House of Lords". After it was over, the members of the Committee took me into the café for drinks. I sat down beside a pretty Dutch woman. She was the daughter of a former Dutch civil servant in Java and had spent the whole of the war in Indonesia. She knew that I had been in Malaya, and, expecting understanding, she told me her story. While she talked, the orchestra played Viennese music of pre-war days: "Wien, Wien" and "Im Prater blühen die Bäume". I listened as in a dream and then I heard her say: "What was hardest of all was to see people who had been so friendly before, turn against us Dutch who had done so much for them." I looked at her and saw the tears well in her eyes.

I knew that she spoke the truth, but none of us can tell more than a part of it. The Dutch had given peace to the different races of Indonesia. The only discontent—and I had found it myself—was among some of the sultans, the intellectuals, the lawyers, the large half-caste population, and, above all, the professional politicians. The Dutch were experiencing to the full the bitter truth of the maxim that the progress of all colonial development is achieved in the long run at the expense and ultimate withdrawal of the colonising power.

Before the First World War the British Legation, as it then was, at The Hague was the pleasantest of posts. The staff was small. The work was light, and the minister had ample time to cultivate intimate relations not only with the Dutch Foreign Minister, but also with all the members of the Government and the whole society of officialdom. Today diplomatic life has changed. The personnel has increased greatly, and service attachés and departmental heads have now staffs nearly as large as the whole Legation staff of old days. As each head of department desires to see the ambassador several times weekly, the demands on his time are exacting. In The Hague the Indonesian question, let alone O.E.E.C. and other European Committees, were enough to keep Phil Nichols busy by themselves. He worked long hours at his desk and had to fit in his official visits to the Dutch Foreign Office as best he could. The system may be more efficient, but the heaviest strain falls on the ambassador.

For my last night Sir Philip and Lady Nichols gave a dinner-party for me. They explained that they had to go to say good-bye to a departing diplomatic colleague, but would be back on the stroke of eight. As the Dutch were very punctual, an Embassy secretary would receive them. Some might be expected a little earlier. Drinks would be in the small drawing-room at seven. I could come down whenever I liked and had only to press the bell.

I was down soon after seven and duly pressed the bell and was given what I wanted. The minutes passed, and no secretary appeared. I pressed the bell again and felt more cheerful. Still no secretary. At a quarter to eight the first Dutch guest arrived. I introduced myself. He introduced himself. In the course of the next ten minutes several more guests arrived and I repeated the same procedure. I was now in my best form and enjoying myself. At five minutes to eight Sir Philip and Lady Nichols arrived. As soon as he had a chance, he whispered to me: "Where is X?" I shook my head in ignorance. He arrived some minutes later.

The next morning I took my leave, and the tardy private secretary accompanied me to Schipol to see me off. He was a cheerful young man who looked on the world as a ripe fruit which was ready to hand for the plucking and who was quite incapable of bearing malice. He opened the conversation quite unabashed. "Whew!" he said. "I received a terrific rocket from the Ambassador this morning for being late last night."

On the drive he kept me amused with a bright account of his experiences, and then he told me an obviously made up Churchill story based, like so many others, on the great man's supposed penchant for speaking "pidgin" French. I did not tell the young man, but of course Mr. Churchill can speak French much better than he does. He puts on a British accent in all foreign languages out of bull-dog patriotism.

During the war General Sikorski went to No. 10 Downing Street to ask Mr. Churchill for a loan for the Polish Government in London. As General Sikorski spoke no English, the conversation was in French. The General was a prime favourite of Mr. Churchill's, but, as the Polish Government had already received a substantial loan, Mr. Churchill hesitated. "I'll do my best for you," he said, "but this is a matter on which I must have a word with the Bank of England. Come back in a week."

General Sikorski returned at the appointed hour.

"Mon Général," said Mr. Churchill, shaking his head mournfully, "je regrette beaucoup. Mais je suis impotent. La vieille dame de Threadneedle Street ne veut pas."

In this manner the secretary regaled me until I stepped into the aeroplane. He was perhaps not exactly the right man for the punctual and rather formal Dutch, but I think and hope that he will go far. And for that bright half-hour I shall always be grateful to him.

I am also full of gratitude to the Dutch, and early in 1953 I am going back to visit them, confident that I shall find fresh signs of progress and recovery. One adjective fits them like a cap. They are reliable.

Chapter VI

BELGIUM AT WORK

Slender leaves of virgin green and a cloudless sky of blue
Old men with pipes and stolid women in sombre Sunday hue
Stay-at-homes taking their rest when the day's work is done
After the blizzard—spring and the miracle of a midsummer
*   sun*
Mothers and nurses with children in low-wheeled chromium
*   prams*
Shaded lanes and the harsh clang of distant yellow trams
Boys chasing butterflies on the gritty sanded path
Impudent sparrows splattering their wings in a dusty bath
Here in this Belgian park with the shy King's palace beyond
Grotesque Greek statues around me—and a tiled, octagonal
*   pond*
No soldiers, no sailors, no scientists from their secret atomic
*   laboratory*
No Reds, no Fascists, no Nazis, no Hyde Park soap-box
*   oratory*
Only leaves of lilies, somnolent carp, and fresh-water mussels
And peace for an hour at Easter in silent, deserted Brussels.
                                        Easter Sunday, 1952.

MORE than a quarter of a century ago I spent a month in
Belgium. It was one of those rare occasions in my life
when I was free from all preoccupations, and for this
reason the holiday remains one of my pleasantest memories. I
knew no one and had very little money to spend, but the weather
was perfect, living was cheap, and I explored all Belgium with the
zest of a hungry schoolboy. Since then, apart from a night or two
in Brussels, I had never re-visited the country, although I had passed
through it often on my journeys to and from Central Europe.

In the spring of 1952 I received an invitation to deliver a series of lectures in Belgium under the auspices of our Foreign Office. I was to stay at our Embassy where the Ambassador, Sir Christopher Warner, was a friend of many years' standing. I could "do" all my lectures by car.

As a Scot I prefer Edinburgh to London and small capitals to vast metropolitan cities which need a life-time to explore. If my taste seems shamefully provincial, I glory in my shame. Brussels has grown, but is still provincial. Like Edinburgh, it relies for its theatrical talent on actors from a larger capital—in its case, Paris. I saw in my Belgian paper that during my proposed visit M. Weber of the Comédie Française was to play the title rôles in *Cyrano de Bergerac* and *L'Aiglon*. It would be pleasant, I thought, to see in a Brussels theatre two plays in which nearly fifty years ago I had beheld the two Coquelins and Sarah Bernhardt at the height of their glory.

Brussels has a long-standing reputation for tolerance. Here in 1845 had come Karl Marx to prepare his Communist Manifesto after he had been hounded out of Paris. Here, too, in 1906 had come Lenin to attend the Russian Social-Democratic Conference which ended in the final split between the Mensheviks and the Bolsheviks. True, both Marx and Lenin were too much for Belgian tolerance, and both men had to go to the more tolerant London to finish their work.

Belgium and Brussels seemed a pleasant prospect, and I accepted without hesitation the attractive invitation of the Foreign Office. After all, in what other way can the British student of foreign affairs travel today except by singing for his supper?

Everything seemed in my favour. The Ambassador's residence, overlooking the park, was a haven of peace and comfort, and no one could have been kinder and more considerate than Christopher Warner and his charming and most efficient sister who had done a wonderful job in caring for the needs, and fighting for the better treatment, of British prisoners during the war. Moreover, I had my wife with me, and in the opinion of all my friends my second marriage has been the wisest course that I have ever taken in my life. I do not dispute the verdict. A general's daughter, she served me faithfully for five strenuous years in the war, arriving early and staying late, keeping all my top secret documents and covering my backslidings and unpunctuality with ingenious excuses. I was an irritable and trying master. I married her after the war, and now I am a tamed and obedient servant, deferring to her better judgment on all, or almost all, occasions.

She was a great stand-by during our Belgian visit, for I had under-estimated my physical strength and under-rated the danger of the table temptations to which I was to be subjected. I have always maintained that only a fully-trained Rugby football internationalist can undertake an American lecture tour without risk to his constitution. But it would have needed a giant of vast digestive power to survive the splendour of the hospitality which the Belgians spread before me.

So long as my health lasted it was fun. But the going was hard. On lecture days we would set off in the Embassy car with Jetta and Christopher Warner and my wife in the back and myself in the front beside Hogarth, the chauffeur, who had taken part as an airman in the liberation of Belgium and had married a Belgian girl. No matter to what town we went the routine was virtually the same. In the car I talked to Hogarth, an excellent guide and a cynic who summarised for me the faults of the British and the Belgians with the strictest impartiality. A Middlesbrough man, he had only two enthusiasms: his car and Association football. The Belgians were the worst drivers in the world and had the best food. His estimate of the British was exactly the reverse. As the Middlesbrough team was then in some danger of relegation from the First League, I surmised that Hogarth's cynicism had reached a low point. I was correct, for, when Middlesbrough climbed to safety, he became a new man.

When we reached our destination, there were introductions and drinks followed by a sumptuous dinner which lasted from six to eight. Then I climbed on to the platform and delivered my address. It did not lend itself to much humour. I had to follow my brief and try to explain to the Belgians why Britain could not join a European federation or integrate its forces in a European army, and at that moment nearly every Belgian was depressed by what they considered our withdrawal into isolationism. The audience, however, was invariably kind and long-suffering. After the lecture there was a reception with more food and drink and an opportunity to talk more freely than I could on the platform. Then I would crawl into the car, gossip with Hogarth, and drive back to Brussels and bed.

I enjoyed most my visit to the great Catholic university of Louvain where after my address I had a lively discussion with a group of students. Both mentally and physically they struck me as a very sound and healthy group of young men who, with no illusions about the difficulties of European life, were determined to make the best of it. Nearly every one of them knew what he was going to do, and for over an hour they plied me with eager questions about English youth, about Scotland, about the effect of Munich on the Communist coup in Czechoslovakia, and about what they called the defeatism of the French. They were strongly opposed to Sartre and Anouilh and declared in no uncertain terms that they preferred modern English literature to mournful French plays and novels. Later I discovered that their views were shared by most of the Belgians I met. I was surprised. Modern English literature, as represented by T. S. Eliot and Graham Greene may have more to say, but it does not strike me as replete with joy.

Louvain University, which was heavily damaged by the Germans in the First World War, suffered again in the Second War both from German bombardments and, unavoidably but unfortunately, from our bombing. The university had a noble record in the resistance, and about three hundred and fifty of its students lost their lives in the common cause.

The great moment of my evening was my talk with the Rector Magnificus, Monsignor Honoré van Waeyrenberg, a warm-hearted and courteous old man who radiates charm, modesty, and abiding faith. His name is a byword for courage throughout Belgium, for during the war he defied the Nazis by his dogged persistence in refusing to deliver to them the addresses of the Louvain students whom the German authorities had called up for mobilisation as labour battalions. He was of course imprisoned.

My most emotional experience was at the Free University of

Brussels when, after my address, M. Frérichs, the President, mounted the platform and made a most impressive speech in praise of England which had liberated Belgium twice from the German oppressors. His eloquence was so moving that I could hardly answer him for the sob in my throat. I had a long talk with him afterwards. He was a fine old gentleman without fear and without reproach, and his admiration for England was unstinted. France, he told me, was an idea and Germany a barracks, but England was a nation. His hero was Winston Churchill, and the proudest day of his life was when he conferred on the Englishman the degree of Doctor honoris causa of the University of Brussels. In introducing the great man M. Frérichs said: "He lives most who serves most".

Mr. Churchill wished to know where M. Frérichs had found the quotation and asked his daughter, Mary, to find out. M. Frérichs replied: "In a cab". Two years previously, he had been in Paris and had found a valuable ring in a taxi. Inside the ring was engraved the quotation from Emerson. M. Frérichs took the ring to the police. A year elapsed, and, as no one had claimed it, the French police returned it to him and he presented it to Mr. Churchill's daughter with the request that, if she found the owner, she should return it, but, if not, she was to keep it.

Apart from my lectures there were luncheons and dinners at which I met Belgians of all the political parties. The ordeal which I feared most was a Press Conference at which some thirty journalists were present. Being a journalist myself, I expected a grilling and, to give myself courage, took a full measure of the "glass of friendship" which was given me. Then, after a halting speech in French, I offered to answer questions. For a moment there was complete silence and I looked sheepish, feeling that I had failed to make myself understood. I was mistaken. The President of the Belgian Press Association filled my glass again and said: "You are one of us". Then he added a polite French equivalent of "Dog does not eat dog." It was a unique experience and a gesture for which I was truly grateful.

During all my official encounters I was briefed and shepherded

most efficiently and tactfully by Christopher Warner who came to
my rescue on all occasions. It was easy for me to understand why
he is the most popular British ambassador we have had in Belgium
for half a century. In addition to a keen sense of humour and an
acute political mind he has the happy knack, by no means common
to all British diplomats, of making everyone to whom he talks,
from a minister to a mannequin, feel that he or she is the one
person in the world that matters. It is a natural and enviable
gift, for his interest is genuine.

His wise counsel was the more valuable to me because Belgium
is full of traps for the ignorant and the unwary. The country
is divided linguistically and racially between Walloons and Flemish,
and a Fleming has only to know that you are a Scot and he will
ask you at once about Scottish Home Rule and Scotland's desire
for devolution. There are also class distinctions starting with a
proud and much inter-married nobility which keeps largely to
itself and only under financial duress mixes with big business.
The industrialists and bankers are rich and efficient, and today you
see more large and expensive American cars in Brussels than there
are in all Britain, apart from those owned by Americans. Then
comes the lower middle-class which works hard, finds life expensive,
but is thrifty and knows how to make ends meet. Thrift and hard
work are the Belgian virtues. In the towns the shops are open
from early morning until late in the evening. In the country the
land is excellently farmed up to the last available inch.

Finally come the workers who again are divided between the
non-clerical Socialist and the Catholic trade unions. The Socialists
are Marxists: the Catholics of course are not. Both, however,
combine in disputes concerning wages. Above all, the country is
divided almost equally between pro-monarchists and anti-mon-
archists or, perhaps I should say, between pro-Leopoldists and
anti-Leopoldists, for it is the deep difference of opinion over the
attitude and personality of ex-King Leopold which has split and,
indeed, still splits the country. In this connection the ex-King's
second marriage is held against him more seriously than his behaviour during the war when he was placed in an admittedly difficult
situation.

The monarchy is a delicate subject for any foreigner to discuss with Belgians. The pro-Leopoldists will not listen to any criticism, and even Mr. Churchill, outstandingly the most popular statesman in all Western European countries, comes under their fire for not removing from his memoirs his strictures on the ex-King. Every unbiased person, I think, must feel deep sympathy with King Baudouin on whom lies a heavy responsibility. Only twenty-one, he came to manhood in exile during the most trying years of his father's life. He is shy and is said to have a usurper's complex. He still lives with his father at Laaken and comes daily to Brussels to his large palace to conduct his royal business. It is not a happy nor an easy situation, and perhaps his greatest handicap is the fact that he is still surrounded by the aged members of his father's household. In this respect I agree with the verdict of M. Léautaud, the eighty-year-old French cynic who after years of neglect is now enjoying an immense popularity: "Rare are the men who after sixty know how to adapt themselves to new situations." And that goes for generals and statesmen as well as for court officials.

At times there seemed to be so many divisions that I wondered how Belgium could exist at all. Then I would go out by myself, talk to the people in the shops and in the art galleries and reassure myself from the happy faces and general well-being that there was, indeed, a Belgium, and a very good Belgium at that. It had a provincial aspect and a provincial patriotism, but there was a unifying influence in the Roman Catholic Church to which both Walloons and Flemish belonged.

Like all the other nations in Western Europe the Belgians wanted Britain to be strong, and not infrequently the desire was expressed with some criticism of her present and some doubts about her future. One important magnate was pessimistic enough to compare Britain's prospects unfavourably with those of France. French politics were rotten to the core, but economically the country was sound. The gold, too, was there if it could be extorted from the hoarders. Britain had, or used to have, the best-behaved Parliament in the world, but two world wars had dealt a mortal blow to her recovery, and her people did not work. Belgium's recovery had been accomplished, partly by a policy of

P

high wages and a multiplicity of consumer goods, but mainly by hard work.

This was an extreme view, although it came from a good source. But I heard frequent references to the alleged idleness of the British worker and I formed the opinion that this widely spread impression had been created by disgruntled British tourists who, chafing under the meagreness of their foreign travel allowance and the low purchasing value of sterling abroad and finding themselves unable to buy the rich food and luxury goods which filled the shops, vented their chagrin on the British worker. Both privately and publicly I did all I could to correct this commonly held but false impression and fortunately, with the help of the Embassy, I was able to quote some remarkable figures.

Belgian recovery was there for all to see, although the workers were not so enthusiastic about its blessings as the big business men. In the large industrial areas like Charleroi and Liège there was no unemployment. I was also told that almost no Belgians now went down coal mines. Their place was taken by imported Italian and Polish labour. New building was going on everywhere with great vigour, and, compared with the Belgium which I had known twenty-five years before, the countryside, except in the Ardennes, had almost disappeared. The people seemed contented. The children were well-dressed. The newspapers devoted even more space to sport than our own. Littlewood's had an office in Brussels and ran football pools on the results of the matches of the English and Scottish Leagues. Nor in the field of sport are the Belgians merely spectators and cautious gamblers; they are expert cross-country runners and cyclists. They excel in both forms of hockey and in rowing, and in association football their international side, the famous "Red Devils", can hold its own with the best English professional teams. Golf, too, has its devotees, and Victor Hugo's *morne plaine* of Waterloo is now enlivened by an eighteen-hole course which, if not on the actual battlefield, runs alongside it.

Belgium is fortunate to be in this comparatively happy and healthy state, and I give full credit to the Belgian people for the efforts which they have made to create it. Nevertheless, she enjoyed at the end of the war many advantages which were denied

to Britain. Without depreciating in any way the horrors of the
Nazi occupation I must point out that Belgian industry suffered comparatively little from the Germans who were eager to extract the
maximum benefit from the Belgian economy. Indeed, in some
instances the economy benefited. Moreover, the Congo, which
with its deposits of uranium is today an immensely valuable asset,
remained free throughout the war, thanks to Britain and the
British Navy. Many Belgians realise these advantages, but some
do not. And that is the real trouble about European unity.
Europe may indeed be one body, as M. de Madariaga maintains,
but in every limb self-interest is still stronger than self-denial.
As the country of M. Spaak, Belgium is a strong advocate of almost
any form of European unity and has a European college at Bruges
to train Belgian and foreign students to its way of thinking. But
when its Government is asked to enter into a full economic union
with Holland and Luxembourg, it refuses because its finances and
international trade are in a much stronger position than those of
Holland.

During my month's visit I met some of the Socialists: excellent
and highly intelligent men who, assuming, quite incorrectly, that
I must be a Tory, gave me full credit in their newspapers for
"Fair-Play Britannique" because in my lectures I praised certain
achievements of the British Labour Government.

At that time the Belgian Socialists were mainly interested in
three problems: European unity, the attitude of the Soviet Government, and rearmament. In the sense that they consider that the
cost of rearmament should not fall unfairly on the workers, they
have a Bevanite wing, but dislike the ascription of Bevanism,
mainly, I think, because they had advocated a similar policy long
before Mr. Bevan had raised his voice on the same subject.

While I was in Brussels, General Gruenther gave high praise
to the Belgians for their contribution to the North Atlantic Treaty
Organisation. The American General's commendation was more
than mere encouragement, for the Belgian Government had voted
large credits for rearmament and had introduced two years military
service. Nevertheless, the Belgians are a jealous and businesslike

race, and their own contribution is limited by the condition that all other members of NATO must do as much as they do.

The Belgian Socialists realise the necessity for rearmament, but want a reduction of the two-year period for military service. They have also no liking for the methods of the Soviet Government and are highly intelligent in seeing through and exposing Soviet propaganda. Under the leadership of M. Spaak they are strongly in favour of an eventual United States of Europe. They have, too, the greatest respect for Mr. Attlee and the late Ernest Bevin, and more than one Belgian Socialist told me that every country in Western Europe owed a debt of gratitude to the British Labour Party for the firm stand which it took against Communism at the end of the war. Communism was then a real danger in all Western Europe, and but for the strong line taken by the Labour Party the Continental Socialists would have been forced into dangerous coalitions with the Communists.

Today there is little Communism in Belgium, and if the cost of living, at that time high for the workers, can be kept in line with wages, the Communists are unlikely to make any headway. They run a newspaper called *The Red Flag*, and on April Fool's Day the Belgian National Front of Independence printed and circulated a "rag" edition which had a huge success. All Belgium, including the Socialists, enjoyed the joke, more especially because the Communists, instead of ignoring the incident, showed that they had been hit on the raw by trying to answer the clever insinuations of the "rag" edition and thereby giving it additional publicity.

In Brussels I heard from the lips of Prince Reginald de Croy a piece of hitherto unwritten history which throws some light on the methods of Soviet diplomacy. During the last war the Prince, for many years Belgian Counsellor in London, was Belgian Minister in Stockholm. The Soviet Minister was Madame Kollontai who, as is well-known, played an important rôle in ending the Finnish-Russian war. Prince de Croy was on good terms with Madame Kollontai who for all her Communist convictions never forgot that she was a Tsarist general's daughter. In 1940 she came twice to see the Prince alone. He told her on both occasions that

Germany had evil intentions against the Soviet Union and that it was foolish of the Soviet Government to help a country which intended to destroy it. Madame Kollontai listened, but said nothing. Then she fell ill, but sent M. Semenov, her Counsellor, to see the Prince. The Soviet Counsellor talked for a long time about the weather, the Swedish winter and, in fact, everything except the one subject which mattered. The Prince listened politely. At last the Counsellor said: "The Finns must make peace." The Prince listened. The Counsellor again changed the subject. Then he said abruptly: "It is important that the Finns should know." Still the Prince said nothing until finally the Counsellor blurted out: "Won't you tell them?"

The Prince went straight to the Swedish Foreign Office. The Finnish Minister was informed, and two days later he called on his Belgian colleague. He brought the Finnish terms. He refused to sign them, but left them with the Prince who then gave them to M. Semenov. Six days later Semenov again asked to see the Prince, and again he talked about the weather. On this occasion the Prince cut the proceedings short by saying: "What has happened about the Finnish peace terms?" "Oh!" replied Semenov, "it was no use sending them to Moscow. The Finns must be serious." Later, Madame Kollontai, now better, called on the Prince who told her about his encounter with Semenov. Madame Kollontai, who of course was fully informed, laughed. "All your messages, including the warning about Germany, went straight to Moscow, but Semenov was instructed not to tell you so."

This was the beginning of the successful peace talks with the Finns. Prince de Croy had a White Russian servant who, as he was helping on Madame Kollontai's long felt snow-boots, said politely: "Just like St. Petersburg, Your Excellency." "Leningrad," replied Madame Kollontai at once.

"For you perhaps, madame, but for me, a former Tsarist officer, St. Petersburg."

During the month I spent in Belgium the weather played pranks which the English climate has never equalled even in its most freakish mood. For the first week we had a mild and muggy

Manchester drizzle. Then March went out with a blizzard, and the thermometer dropped to its lowest point of the whole winter. A week later it shot up to over seventy in the shade, and we had blue skies and midsummer heat until we left.

My wretched skin broke down under the strain, and I had to take to my bed for a week. I was sad because hitherto my whole time had been occupied in meeting people, and on the whole I prefer places to persons. Now when my lectures were nearly over and there was an opportunity of seeing the country at its best, I was tied to my room.

Fortunately Christopher Warner had an ample supply of books dealing with every aspect of Belgian life, and I did my best to refresh my rusty knowledge of Belgian literature. The newspapers were full of M. Georges Simenon who was born at Liège and was then re-visiting his native country for the first time for several years. He was received by the Belgian Academy and must be, I think, the first writer of thrillers to achieve this distinction. The Belgians resent his being always labelled a *French* writer, but M. Simenon himself wishes no fuss and remains wholly unspoilt by success. What he enjoyed most during his Belgian visit was his call on the Liège police headquarters from which as a young crime reporter on the *Gazette de Liège* he received the material for the first article that he ever wrote. I made, too, a minor addition to my knowledge of a poet whom I have always admired and whom, to my eternal regret, I neglected an opportunity of meeting before the First World War. This was Guillaume Apollinaire, whose mother was a Pole and a Polish adventuress at that. To this day it is, I think, unknown whether Guillaume's father was an Italian nobleman or a Monagasque bishop.

As a youth Guillaume spent some weeks in the Ardennes with his younger brother, until his mother, short of funds, sent him a message to join her at Ostend. With no money to pay the bill, the two brothers crept out of the hotel at Stavelot with the first streak of dawn. Today his Belgian admirers have set a plaque to his memory on the hotel building. Guillaume, then nineteen, had a splendid fighting record in the First World War, was severely wounded in 1916 and died two days before the Armistice.

During my incarceration my wife, who has no illusions about her husband's deficiencies as a speaker, reported to me faithfully the comments of my Belgian critics. I soon realised that I had not succeeded in convincing the Belgians that Great Britain could not possibly join a European federation. Here is a fragment of her conversation with a Belgian professor. It is typical of the attitude of many Belgians at that time.

Belgian professor: "Your husband is an optimist, but he must feel sad about losing your Empire."

My wife: "But, professor, we haven't lost it. Britain is now the centre of a great community of nations."

Belgian professor: "Well, have it your own way. But I still don't see why you shouldn't sacrifice your selfish interests and come into a European federation. After all, France is coming in with her Empire, and we've come in with our Congo."

At this point the London-born wife of the Rector came to the rescue. "Congo! My dear professor, Congo! Are you comparing the Congo with Canada, with Australia? You are the cleverest man in the university, but when you get on to politics, you don't know what you're talking about."

Thanks to an excellent Belgian doctor I made a quick recovery and before I left the hospitable Embassy I was able to go out and enjoy the sunshine in the Park just opposite. At Easter the conservative *Nation Belge* announced that Brussels was empty. *Le Peuple,* the Socialist newspaper, declared that the city was full for the Easter processions and meetings of the Young Belgian Socialists. Both newspapers told the truth. The Embassy end of Brussels was, in one sense, empty. The Rue Ducale was silent and deserted. The Park had none of its habitués. Instead, it was sparsely filled with house-porters dressed in their Sunday best, and nursemaids in charge of children too young to be taken on the motor exodus to the coast. Their behaviour was decorous beyond belief. I found a small octagonal pond alive with large carp, floating in the hot sun like submarines half-submerged, golden orfe, and goldfish in profusion, and a few tench. The carp were giants of four or five pounds. A pair of mallard swam peacefully among them.

Sparrows, poising themselves on a large water-lily leaf, slaked their thirst.

In Scotland—I cannot speak for England—boys would have chased the duck and thrown stones at the fish. Even my own mind, with a jump of fifty years, played with the idea of creeping out at dawn and tempting the biggest carp with a small hook concealed in a well-kneaded ball of bread. I estimated that the deed could be done with impunity. But, although there were no park-keepers to protect the pond, no such thought seemed to enter the Belgian mind. The old men sat on the park seats and smoked their pipes. The nannies kept their charges away from the edge. The largest boys threw an occasional crumb to the fish. The carp took no notice. The mallard remained fearless.

I was fascinated and returned to the Park every day until I left. I never saw even a tiny pebble break the stillness of the surface.

My happiest outing in Belgium was my drive to the Abbaye de Villers which by the direct route via Waterloo lies about twenty-five miles south-west of Brussels. To see more of the countryside we took the long way round through the Forest of Soignes. A fortnight previously I had driven through part of this country. It was then under snow, and the great beeches, dark and sinister in their winter bareness, looked like mutes at the funeral of nature. Now all was green, and the ground was a carpet of wild flowers. Through undulating country we drove along the valley of the Thyle by roads hardly wide enough to hold the Embassy Rolls. Then, descending a steep hill we came suddenly on the Abbaye itself, a magnificent ruin extending from the bottom of the valley up the side of a steep hill. A Cistercian foundation, established by St. Bernard in 1147, it had been for over six hundred years a self-supporting institution with its own farms, fish-ponds, mill, bakery, gardens, and leper-house. Then it was sacked and suppressed during the French Revolution, and for many years afterwards the local peasants carried off the stones at their own will. Now the State has turned a wilderness into order. The rich grass is neatly cut; the paths are trimmed, and pious care has created beauty out of chaos.

The fish-ponds remain, and the stream which runs through them and used to work the mill contains splendid trout. The mill itself is a restaurant, and in the unwonted warmth the tables were set out in the open air. We sat down and, hot from my exploration of the abbey, I studied with zeal a menu with a long list of drinks. Suddenly my eye caught the magic word of "Scotch". I looked at the price. It was only three francs fifty a glass, and even in expensive Belgium I calculated that this was the cheapest "Scotch" in the world. I gave my order. Then my face fell. Belgium is a beer-drinking country, and on every Belgian menu "Scotch" means, not whisky, but Scotch ale.

As we sat and talked of the curious restaurants which we knew, Christopher Warner capped all my exotic experiences with a story of the late Ernest Bevin whom he admired greatly. Not long after the war the Swedish Minister in London gave a luncheon in honour of the Crown Prince (now the King) of Sweden. The chief British guest was Mr. Bevin, then Foreign Secretary, and Christopher Warner, as the Under-Secretary in charge of Northern affairs, accompanied him. The luncheon was held in a small private room in the Écu de France in Jermyn Street, and the guests sat on narrow benches. One bench accommodated the Crown Prince, Mr. Bevin (in the middle), and a large and heavily-built senior Treasury official. It was a tight fit, but the food and wines were excellent.

Over coffee Ernest Bevin began to tell his famous story of the Fascist, the Communist and the Trade Unionist who are wrecked in a small boat in a stormy sea in the Channel. The Fascist pushes off first and with no thought for his companions strikes out for the shore. But, as he insists on keeping one hand for the Fascist salute, he soon tires and is drowned. The Communist follows him, but as he keeps shouting Marxist slogans he swallows so much water that he, too, goes to the bottom. Then the solid British Trade Unionist plunges into the water and, swimming a steady breast-stroke, makes good progress towards the shore. This was one of Mr. Bevin's favourite stories, and normally it finished up with the Englishman hearing the sound of the factory siren just when he is almost ashore. Being a good Trade Unionist, he, of course, stops swimming and he, too, is drowned. On this occasion, however, the story had a different ending, for Mr. Bevin, who liked to illustrate his stories, gave such a lively imitation of the breast-stroke that with one arm he caught the Crown Prince in the chest and nearly doubled him up and with the other sent the Treasury official sprawling off the bench.

My visit to the Abbaye de Villers was my one day off duty. For the rest of my time I talked, dreamt and lived politics and met all kinds and conditions of politicians from the elderly M. Pierlot, formerly Prime Minister of the Belgian Government and now fearful lest man in his blind folly should destroy himself, to brilliant younger men like M. André de Staerke, a favourite of Mr. Churchill and now the Belgian representative on the North Atlantic Council.

In the end I found it hard to come to a clear conclusion. Official life in Brussels was like a return to the Edwardian decade in England, and such was the politeness of the Belgians that I had great difficulty in distinguishing what was sincere from what was merely an accomplished art of paying compliments. There were Belgians who felt that unless there was general acceptance of some form of world government the world itself was doomed. In the main, however, the politicians, baffled by the perplexities of the world situation, were preoccupied with internal affairs and party politics. There was no one in Belgium who did not want peace and who did not discuss seriously even the most ingenuous ways of preserving it.

While I was in Brussels, considerable prominence was given in the local Press to a statement by Erwin Stransky, the Professor of Psychiatry in the University of Vienna. After examining and discarding the various peace proposals of governments and other institutions the professor concluded that the only way to stop war was to allow the psychiatrists to examine dictators like Hitler and Stalin who were in one sense geniuses and in another madmen! Oh wise and most excellent professor! But who is to bring the genial Stalin beneath your gaze and who is to certify the sanity of the psychiatrists?

What I admired most in the Belgians was their diligence and

their energy. Their country had been occupied twice within twenty-five years and was today in almost the most exposed position that one could imagine. They were, of course, sensible of the dangers, yet they showed none of that lack of confidence which is prevalent in some other Western countries, and all sections of the population went about their daily work with exemplary zeal, very possibly because a full belly and good wages are the best antidotes to too vivid imaginings. If they had an occupation complex, it was in the sense that they knew how to handle their occupiers—an illusion fraught with alarming dangers if ever their country has the misfortune to be over-run again by different occupiers.

I had, too, great confidence in the Belgian youth who struck me as first-class in every respect, but on reflection no better than our own.

On taking leave of my Belgian friends, I noted one comparison with the past which saddened me. In this little country which has been so long the cockpit of Europe and in which so many British soldiers lie buried, I saw virtually no English. Between the two wars, when the British people first began to travel, Belgium had been one of the most popular countries with the British tourist. Now the stringency of our financial situation has reduced the tourist traffic to a trickle. Economies, I know, are necessary, but do we always choose the wisest? If we are ever to progress towards a better understanding between peoples, let alone towards anything even remotely approaching world government, peoples must meet peoples. The trouble is the Foreign Offices of the world do not believe that peoples count. In war—yes. Then we have money for the European Services of the B.B.C., foreign information services, and the foreign work of the British Council. During the war the peoples of Western Europe learnt English by radio lessons from London in a truly remarkable manner. But when so-called peace returns, there is a tendency to revert to traditional diplomacy, and foreign travel and these foreign services are cut just when they might be powerful for good.

One of the great paradoxes and evils of today is that, while the increased speed of transport has made the world smaller, travel has become much more difficult for the individual. Because of the cut in the foreign travel allowance, the average British traveller is limited to a bus tour of a few days during which he meets nobody. As for the Iron Curtain countries, it takes three months to get a visa, and for every visa granted a hundred are refused. Peace suffers.

Chapter VII

SALUTE TO FRANCE

"Warm summer sun, shine friendly here;
Warm western wind, blow kindly here."

THE two countries which are the most difficult for British people to understand are the United States and France. In both instances our misconceptions arise from the fact that we believe we know them better than other nations. The United States is a young Continent with little worlds of difference between North and South and between the Atlantic and Pacific sea-boards. France is old and more or less homogeneous and therefore complicated, and while Paris is the most attractive of all international cities it is infinitely less France than London is England.

As a young man I went from Scotland to study in Germany and then straight from Germany to France. It was, I think today, a mistake. One's first visit to a foreign country, especially if it is a long visit and not merely a short pleasure trip, makes a deep and often lasting impression. With the young, externals count for too much, and on my youthful mind German punctuality and German plumbing exercised an exaggerated influence. If I was not anti-French, Germany came first in my estimation. I must admit, too, that after the First World War I was very critical of French policy in relation to both Germany and the Soviet Union, for it seemed to be dictated not only by the instinct of self-preservation but also by financial greed.

I have repented long ago of my rash judgment. Although I have been a frequent visitor to France, I still find the French hard to understand, but culturally and intellectually I rank them far ahead of all other nations. Their way of life is the most stimulating and today, when they are divided and in difficulties, my affection for them and for their country has increased. I cannot visualise a Europe without France in the intellectual and cultural van, or a European recovery in which the French will not have a leading part. In spite of their political weakness I am confident that they will rise again. Today it is still an essential function of my active life to study Slav Communist literature, and it is dreary and repetitive stuff, but for pleasure and mental stimulation I read French. In post-war Britain it has been found almost impossible to run a serious monthly review, and the few that exist maintain a precarious life. France has almost too many, and nearly all are written with verve and literary talent. This contrast may not be wholly to the advantage of the French who tend to indulge themselves in an orgy of introspection and self-analysis, but it marks a fundamental difference between the French and British character.

Although I have not revisited Anjou, with which I associate the happiest memories of my life, I have been back to France several times since the war. Indeed, in 1949 and 1950 I made two long trips and saw more of the country in six weeks than in all the years that I had spent there.

In contrast with the period after the First World War when a pound was still a pound, bought far more in France than it did in England, and made even the poor tourist feel rich, British currency difficulties now put us among the very poorest of France's visitors. We have to count the cost of every dish, of every drink, and of every theatre, especially if we have to make each visit last a month or three weeks as I have to do. We can only look at the shops; we cannot buy. The Americans have the money and where they go prices rise. In Paris, which always takes the tourist's money gladly, the shopkeepers and the waiters show little interest in the British. They know that we have no money; they reserve their salesmanship and their tip-extracting genius for the Americans. For the first few days I found this a little galling, but now I have no envy in my heart. Our poverty is a not unwholesome reminder that we are today in much the same position in which France found herself after the First World War when, until we were ready, she held the brunt of the German offensive, lost the flower of her population, and saved Europe.

During my lecture tours I fed in the cheapest places and recalled my student days in Paris when I used to lunch in a little restaurant close to the Sorbonne for ninety-five centimes and a five centime tip to the waiter. The meal comprised a choice of soup or hors-d'œuvres, a meat dish and vegetables, a sweet or cheese, unlimited bread and a small carafe of white or red wine. Even when one allows for the comparative depreciation of the pound and the franc, the cheapest meal in France is immensely more expensive today. Nevertheless, I shall always remember a dinner at Toulon in January 1950. The war had created considerable damage: the naval town was not what it was. Moreover, the state of my purse demanded stringent economy. So off I went to a tiny restaurant in the Rue des Trombades, a narrow street in what used to be the sailors' quarter. Flanked as it was by low *bordels*, and full of queer-looking aesthetes of doubtful sex, tougher bourgeois of swarthy countenance and suspicious aspect, and workmen, the restaurant was not inviting. But we had a wonderful meal including a rich variety of hors-d'œuvres, red mullet, escalope de veau, a banana sweet, heavy with real clotted cream, and a superb cup of coffee. With tip and a litre of excellent vin rosé the bill came to eight shillings.

While we were eating, two mechanics in dungarees came in, sat down close to me at what was obviously their usual table, and summoned the *patron*. For twenty minutes they examined the menu and discussed it with the same careful attention with which a Foreign Office official studies a draft. Their conversation fascinated me. France has good cooking, because the French working-man demands good food and sees that he gets it. The English working-man, and, indeed, most Englishmen put up with what they are given. All my experience of Europe convinces me that the chief obstacle to a flourishing continental tourist traffic to England is neither the lack of hotels nor the cost of living but the poor quality of English food offered to the Continental tourist of moderate means.

The French pride themselves on being logical. They are also paradoxical, and one of their paradoxes is that, while much of non-Communist France is politically and even sentimentally pro-British, Britain is nearly always the whipping-boy whenever public opinion in France is dissatisfied with some aspect of international affairs. During my lecture tours I spoke for the most part on Scotland of yesterday and today, and inevitably the Scotland of today requires some reference to the Scottish desire for some form, moderate or extreme, of devolution. In no other country does the Scot enjoy a greater advantage over the Englishman and the American than in France. The ancient alliance still makes a sentimental appeal. Much more so does devolution, for France suffers more than Scotland from over-centralisation. Almost everywhere I went in the French provinces I heard the same complaint from the local authorities: "Everything you say about centralisation in Britain applies even more forcibly to every big region in France. Here in —— we have to refer even the smallest detail to Paris for approval, and the delays are interminable. The weakness of France is in and around Paris; its strength is in the provinces."

The warmest pro-British sentiment which I found in any region of France was in Normandy in 1949. Normandy has a bad record for rain and on that account is called the *pot de chambre* of France. On this occasion, however, I was lucky, for it was May and the weather could not have been kinder. The Normans themselves have a reputation for toughness, and today it is an admirable virtue. Much of their country suffered severe damage during the war, both from the Anglo-American invasion and from the preliminary bombing which served as the softening process for the landings. But the Normans bore no grudge. On the contrary they are proud of Normandy's scars. My visit to Caen, where I lectured to the University, was an exhilarating experience. The devastation was appalling. Whole quarters of this ancient town, once full of historic monuments, had disappeared. The University, founded in 1436 by the Duke of Bedford, had vanished—it was somewhere in the wilderness of rubble that blocked many of the streets—and the Rector, Pierre Daure, was living in a small wing of the Ecole Normale. I wondered how the town could ever spring to life again and whether it would not be wiser to build a new city some miles away. But the Normans were not downhearted. They had already started on an ambitious programme of reconstruction. "In twenty years we shall have a modern new city far ahead of any other city in France or, for that matter, in Europe." If one person said this to me, the whole town echoed it. The spirit of the inhabitants was superb in its confidence, and later I found the same buoyant optimist at Rouen where the Assistant Prefect took me over the vast ramifications of the new port, then in course of construction, and explained to me how, with the deepening of the Seine and the natural advantages created by the wide stretches of flat land situated on the left bank of the river and eminently suitable for the construction of factories, docks, roads and railways, ships of 20,000 tons and more would be able to come up to Rouen without unloading at Le Havre. The scheme, the Assistant Prefect said, will take ten to fifteen years to complete. "Then," he added proudly, "we shall have the most modern and the biggest port in Western Europe." The dreams may very well come true. The French Government may be on the verge of financial bankruptcy. But, in contrast with our own policy, it has put many millions, including American aid, into capital investment.

The Rector of Caen University was an ardent Gaullist and his brother had served with the General in London during the war. Mr. Churchill is greatly admired in Normandy, but he hurt the feelings of more than one Norman when he visited the front soon after D-day and took with him Field-Marshal Smuts and not General de Gaulle. The Rector, a man of great administrative ability, defended the General strongly and gave me his view of the political situation in succinct terms. If the French Communists ever tried to seize power by violence, every Frenchman, who was not a Communist, would look to General de Gaulle. If there was no such Communist attempt, the General would never seize power. He was not a professional accountant, and accountants were all that was necessary to keep in power the kind of government which France now had. I imagine that this estimate of de Gaulle still holds good today.

Incidentally, French professors are poorly rewarded. I travelled to Caen with the late Professor Ifor Evans, then vice-Chancellor of the University of Wales and a brilliant linguist and most entertaining

Q

companion. He was preparing a comparative study of the universities of Western Europe and told me that, in comparison with 1938, British professors were better paid today, Dutch rather worse and French worst of all.

As I left Caen towards sunset, the twin towers of the magnificent Church of St. Etienne, fortunately spared from the almost general destruction, stood out clear-cut against the luminous skyline. They seemed to me like giant sentinels watching over the birth of the new city. The church was built by William the Conqueror as a penance for breaking the laws of Holy Church by marrying his cousin. The Bishop who inspired the design was Lanfranc who went from Bayeux to Canterbury. The citizens of Caen like to tell the visitor that by the agency of Lanfranc Canterbury Cathedral was modelled from St. Etienne.

On my way to Trouville I made a détour to Arromanches-les-Bains which lies in a cove between cliffs and is protected on the land side by grassy and sparsely-wooded hills. Before the war it was a tiny and very cheap *plage* with one moderate-sized hotel and a few small villas. Though V. E. Day anniversary was near the place was deserted. My wife and I had the beach to ourselves, and, in spite of the remains of the *Mulberry* and the hulks of several cargo ships sunk inside it, I found it hard to realise that five years previously Arromanches was a living hell and that, as one of the locals said to me, "You could not see the sky for aeroplanes or the sea for ships."

For years to come Arromanches would be a pious pilgrimage for British people, and already the local paper shop had prepared a large stock of maps and photographs for the anniversary of D-day. Although there were still signs of destruction, there were also new things: a Quai Admiral Sir Bertram Ramsay, a Cale Maréchal Montgomery, a Café du 6 Juin, a Hotel Mulberry with walls of a rich orange and windows with green shutters, and on the beach itself in solitary grandeur a massive stone engraved with the words Port Winston.

The Normans, not very pro-American because of the bombing of Le Havre on the eve of its liberation, have the deepest respect for anything connected with the British landings. On a beautiful spring afternoon I paid a visit to the little lonely cemetery

on a high wooded hill above Deauville. Just below it is a lovely
Norman orchard, and from the cemetery itself there is a wide
view over the Channel and the beaches of Normandy. Here lie
German, French, Belgian and British soldiers of the First World
War and British heroes of the liberation of Normandy. The
women of Trouville not only have each adopted a British grave
but have also established contact with the relatives of the dead.

I dislike all fashionable resorts, but I have a passion for them
when they are out of season or in decay. In Trouville I found a
place after my own heart. Once the summer resort of famous
French writers and painters and still remembered as the scene of
Flaubert's romance with the daughter of the local chemist, it has
long suffered from the rivalry of its luxurious neighbour, Deauville.
In that sunny May of 1949 it was deserted, and, having a free week-
end, I spent happy hours in exploring La Poissonerie, with its rich
variety of fish which range from sole and lobsters, langoustes and
shrimps to less familiar varieties like monk fish, gurnards and
congers.

On Sunday, May 8, Trouville celebrated the anniversaries of
both V.E. Day and St. Joan's Day. It seemed to me curious that on
the same day the French should be commemorating Joan of Arc
whom we had burnt at the stake and the ending of another holocaust
in which Britons played such a different rôle. But the Normans
saw nothing incongrous in this twin remembrance. British and
French flags were flying everywhere. The front was gay with
the brightly-coloured awnings of the shops and the long line
of booths on the quay. As I stood amidst the throng, there was
a blare of military music, and like one man the crowd turned
to the main street and was silent. With a catch in my throat I
watched the procession pass with flags flying and band playing.
It was composed of soldiers of the two world wars and for a small
town it was large. Old and young marched bravely and solemnly
as they made their way to church. The whole character of the
commemoration was religious.

In Trouville I met three outstanding personalities. The first
was Madame Sauvia, formerly the hostess of the once famous

Cheval Blanc at Honfleur, and in 1949 the proprietress of the Hotel Flaubert in Trouville. In the past she had met and entertained many of the poets and Bohemian writers of France, and her Livre d'Or was full of famous names. Now much older than her blonded hair, she was still a vigorous and efficient exponent of private enterprise, firmly convinced that the first duty of a democrat is to oppose the central government. Four-fifths of her was cynicism and the rest generosity. France, she told me, was composed of twenty per cent brave people; the others were "crapules". Presumably the twenty per cent contained a generous proportion of Normans.

Then there was the aged Mayor, who had made a fortune out of an aperitif called "Suze". Although then over eighty, he was still the big man of Trouville and its greatest benefactor.

Finally, there was the Duc de Fitz-James, a relation of the Duke of Alba and a descendant of King James II and his mistress, Arabella Churchill. Of medium height, with scanty light brown hair, and a clean-shaven face which showed signs of hard living, the Duc looked unmistakably English. His English was perfect, and when he spoke it he assumed the calm, gestureless attitude of an English aristocrat. His French was also perfect, and when he spoke it he became a Frenchman, alive, alert and making full use of his hands and arms as auxiliary interpreters. Although I am no judge, he was apparently also a master of Spanish.

Before the war he was rich, had a large motor-car, and was a well-known figure in Deauville. In 1949 he had fallen on hard times. I guessed that gambling at the Casino had cost him dear, for he talked much of great coups and great losses and still believed in systems. In May, of course, the Casino was closed, but the Duc had it opened for me, and, as we went through the empty theatre, cinema and concert hall, with seats and tables draped with dustcloth, I felt as if I were at a funeral. Only the *salle privée* roused a flickering interest. More than twenty years before, I had stood in the same room and had watched the Greek Syndicate holding the bank at baccarat against all-comers. In my ignorance I supposed that the Casino had lost its glory and its profits since the war, but M. André's secretary—the great man himself was in Paris—

assured me that on the contrary the Casino was flourishing and that it was already too small for the post-war crowds. I asked him who came to it. To my astonishment he replied: "We have many Americans both North and South and many Belgians, but the leaders and the big gamblers are still the English." My eyebrows went up. I expressed my doubts, but he stuck to his story, and Fitz-James corroborated it.

The Duc, in fact, was the friend of all the English who came to Deauville or Trouville, and, although too poor to gamble himself, he was ready to act as cicerone to Englishmen who wished to visit the Casino. He could not have been kinder to me. He introduced me to his friends in the whole district, and he had many. He still did everything in the grand style and, although he tired easily, his innate politeness never left him. His clothes, a little the worse for wear, came from Savile Row. His manners were charming.

After a long and tiring walk he took me one afternoon to have tea with some aristocratic friends of his, the Villersmonts. After I had been introduced, I sat down beside him at the end of a long room. He looked very tired and I realised that he was much older than I had first thought. Suddenly he turned to me and whispered: "If you will have a cognac, I can have one too." Only very rarely do I drink brandy, and I certainly did not want to at five in the afternoon, but to please him I said that, if he wanted a cognac, I would have one to keep him company. At once he cried down the room to our host: "Henri, Henri! Lockhart needs fortifying." Henri came forward. What would I like? He had gin. I told a white lie and said I never drank gin. Henri regretted that he had no whisky. He made no mention of brandy, and I felt and looked a fool. But the Duc came to the rescue. "Lockhart," he said firmly, "needs a cognac." Henri produced it. I took a glass. He gave another to his brother-in-law and then offered one to the Duc who, to my amazement, refused it. Then, just as Henri was about to take the bottle away, the Duc, with an air of consummate indifference, said, as if by an afterthought: "Well, perhaps I'll have one too."

What a diplomat he would have made but for that wretched

Casino. He reminded me of Mr. Eden conducting a delicate negotiation with M. Gusef.

The story has a sequel. From Trouville I went to lecture at Honfleur where my sponsor was M. de Brèvedent. On the night of my arrival my wife and I dined alone with him. M. de Brèvedent, a pioneer of aircraft construction and a staunch friend of Britain, is a teetotaller, but at the end of our meal he said eagerly:

"And now of course you'll have a cognac!"

I refused politely.

"But you had one at five p.m. at the Villersmonts."

I told him the story of the Duc's alcoholic diplomacy, and he laughed. He was a great friend of the Villersmonts and on the afternoon of the cognac-drinking had come to dine with them after the Duc and I had left. Our host had been perturbed by the state of my health and had said to M. de Brèvedent: "Poor Lockhart is in a terible state of exhaustion. He had to have a cognac here today at five in the afternoon. I do hope he'll be able to get through his Honfleur programme."

My Honfleur programme was certainly a heavy one. It began with a tour of the town. Honfleur lives on its great past. From here sailed Champlain to Canada. Here, too, was born Pierre Berthelot, the pilot and cosmographer of Henri the Navigator. It still produces sailors, but owing to the vast stretch of mud and sand between Honfleur and Le Havre, its glory as a port has long departed. The town itself, built on a steep hill, is full of fascinating old houses which, in the warm sunshine, made me feel that I was in some ancient settlement by the waters of the Mediterranean.

After the tour of the town came a luncheon given by Madame Gaunel, a generous supporter of the local Société France-Grande Bretagne and a talented and most charming hostess. The food and wine were super-excellent, and every menu, with a separate design for each guest, was done by hand and illustrated with some incident commemorating Anglo-Norman friendship. There was much talk of politics and much hero-worship of Mr. Churchill, and, although there were no speeches, I rose at the end and thanked Madame Gaunel who must have worked for days to prepare so wonderful a welcome.

She spoke only two lines in reply, but I shall remember them always: "It is our debt to Winston Churchill, and we cannot pay it often enough."

Sometimes the foreign observer sees more of our British scene then we do ourselves. He or she sees the peaks while we are bogged in detail, and many foreigners see Winston Churchill even bigger than we do. When he passes, we shall extol him, but Western Europeans will feel that with him has gone a large piece of what in their eyes was England.

After the luncheon there was more sight-seeing and before the lecture a formal reception by the Mayor and his councillors in session. There were speeches and champagne, and the mayor, a butcher by trade but in appearance and dignity an aristocratic-looking barrister, read a formal speech in which he paid grateful compliments to England and to Scotland.

It was, as you see, a heavy programme, but in spite of that 5 p.m. cognac I came through it safely. I remember one compliment paid to Britain by M. de Brèvedent. "In Britain, you have at all times only a very few men who are ever likely to become Prime Minister. Here in France we have about thirty men who not only can but do, in fact, become Prime Minister and, in order to enable them to do so, the Government changes every six months."

Nor shall I forget Mademoiselle Turgie, a formidable old lady who smoked a pipe and kept a bull-dog. During the war she sheltered for over a year an officer and eight men of the Seaforths. In 1949 she was the heroine of Honfleur though by some strange omission she was never decorated by us.

That spring of 1949 has a niche in my memory as the date of my first visit to Paris after the war. My impressions were a hotch-potch of regrets and transient pleasures. I arrived in superb weather forty-eight hours before May Day when Parisians were discussing the preparations for the Gaullist and Communist demonstrations and the date of the next meeting of the Four Ministers. Few active diplomatists could say off-hand how many such meetings there have been before and since. As for the May Day demonstrations, they were the quietest since the war, for the two rivals held their manifestations at opposite ends of the city, the Communists in the Place de la Bastille and the Gaullists in the Bois de Boulogne. For the rest of Paris it was a joyous *fête* with thousands of families enjoying the sunshine and buying small bunches of lily-of-the-valley which were on sale in every street. With great recklessness I hired a car and in the afternoon drove to Montmartre expecting to be disappointed, for even in my student days it had already become a bogus attraction maintained for the seduction of gullible foreigners. We were fortunate, for on May Day there were no tourists, and the Free Commune of Montmartre was celebrating the day in its own fashion. The Place du Tertre was *en fête*, and a family *fête* at that. Every table with its orange or chocolate-brown umbrella-shaped awning was occupied, and Bohemian-clad artists, feeble shadows of braver lights like Utrillo, Suzanne Valedon and others known and unknown, stood or sat at their easels. But they were only playing. Everyone was watching the Republican procession to mark the radicalism and independence of the Commune. A band headed it. Boys and girls with Republican hats followed, and the main body, composed of men in white trousers and blue tunics, marched behind.

The terraces below Sacré Cœur were packed with people admiring the view over Paris, and automatically my thoughts went back to 1871 when Montmartre was a key point in the first Communist revolution that the world had ever seen. Sacré Cœur itself was the monument erected as thanksgiving for the liberation of Montmartre from the Communards.

The sunshine, however, was more pleasant than history, and, retracing the footsteps of my youth I went to look at the Lapin Agile, passing on my way the tiny vineyard of Montmartre which I was glad to see is still carefully tended and still produces wine. The Lapin Agile was of course not open at that hour, and, apart from the picture of the famous rabbit, gay, debonair and upright in his collar and red tie, and balancing a bottle of wine in his right fore-paw, the place looked derelict. A small board conveyed the information that it opened at 11 p.m.

Doubtless, a different world now frequented it. What made

Montmartre in my student days was its countrified atmosphere, its distance from Paris and the cheapness of its life.   Now it is *in* Paris and can be reached by car in fifteen minutes or less from the centre of the city.

I felt sad, but Montmartre was an infinitely more satisfying experience than my attempt to discover my old haunts around the Sorbonne.   The old university landmarks were recognisable enough, but everything was strange, because more than two generations had passed since my time.   There were different shops and cafés and different names on those that had remained.   Only the book-stalls round the corridors of the Odeon Theatre, now called the Salle Luxembourg, were the same.

Our taxi-driver, a Russian of sixty-five, was understanding. "Looking for the past?" he said.   "It is undiscoverable, and better so."   He had been an officer and a member of the Tsarist mission to Paris during the First World War.   He told me that there are now approximately a million Russians in France.   Seven hundred thousand of them are the exiles and their offspring who settled in France after the Russian revolution of 1917.   The remainder, he said, were "politicos" and refugees of the Second World War and wanted watching.   With some pride he told me: "We of the First World War have remained taxi-drivers and commissionaires, but our sons and daughters have become French, have passed their examinations, and have taken root in France as civil servants, engineers, chemists and scientists.   Many do not even speak Russian.   The next generation will hardly know that they are Russian."

I asked him how the Russian taxi-drivers fared in Paris.   "Not so badly," he said, "the French have been very good.   We have our own club.   In the evening I play bridge."

He was a philosopher and a kindly old man on whom the tragedy of his life seemed to sit lightly.

That same evening Captain Howell, R.N., then the energetic and successful director of the British Council in Paris, took my wife and me to the Salle Luxembourg to see Yonnel in *Le Lever du Soleil,* a modern historical play the theme of which is the love of the young Louis XIV for Marie de Mancini, the niece of Mazarin.   In the part of Mazarin, Yonnel, one of the great actors of the world, was magnificent. But the play itself was uneven, and soon I found my mind straying back to the various plays that I had seen as a young man. As the Odeon the Salle Luxembourg had been the first theatre to which I had ever gone by myself. I was barely nineteen and during the next year I saw from the gallery of Paris theatres many of the best French plays and the most famous French actors and actresses: the Coquelins, Sarah Bernhardt, Réjane, and Mounet-Sully. Then I had time and enthusiasm, but no money. Now when I have a little more to spend on the theatre, I seem to have no time. From this I deduce that the early enthusiasm has gone. It is the gift of youth and is worth more than the knowledge of all the old men in the world.

In 1949 anti-American sentiment, although not so strong as it is today, was already manifest among the Parisians. One did not have to look for it. The evil thing was thrust on one. It was fomented by the presence of over 7000 American officials in Paris, all with cars and money to burn, but it began, I think, from the first days of the liberation. In the full flush of their success the American troops expected a victors' triumph with free champagne and French girls throwing themselves into the arms of the liberators. The American conception was perhaps foolish. With their acute sense of currency values the French made the Americans pay extravagantly for what they wanted, and inevitably the Americans thought the French not only ungrateful but also stingy.

There were also cultural differences, for, like most of the European races, the French adopt an arrogant attitude towards the American way of life which most Americans regard as the height of culture. Soon after the liberation, half Paris, still very emotional and eager to cement the Franco-American friendship, went to the first concert given by an American military band in the open air at the Eiffel Tower. The bandmaster, young, bespectacled and very serious, announced that his first number would be selections from *Manon*. The band was good and the number was well enough received. Then the French, the men wearing their war medals and the women in their best and all keyed to a high pitch of emotional intensity, waited for the *Mar-seillaise* or some other patriotic motif. The bandmaster came forward and announced solemnly:

"We will now play 'It must be Jelly; Jam wouldn't shake that much'."

French emotion and French enthusiasm for Franco-American culture collapsed like a pricked balloon.

Of course there are many Parisians who are pro-American, but opinion is divided in all classes and even in families. My wife and I dined alone with a husband and wife. The husband was very critical of the Americans. The wife pulled him up sharply and said very properly: "We French should be more grateful than we are for the most disinterested help ever given to any nation by another."

I have an ardent admiration for the French, but I must admit that they are a most critical race with even more prejudices against foreigners than we have, and an obstinate refusal to learn any language but their own.

In this connection I had one trying ordeal. I had been invited to lecture to a combined audience of the Caledonian Society and the Association France-Ecosse. I knew that the Caledonian Society was composed of Scots resident in Paris. My knowledge of the Association France-Ecosse was non-existent, but I assumed that I should be able to deliver my lecture in English or, if necessary, in broad Scots. I discovered just in time that the members of the Association were Frenchmen of Scottish descent dating back to the famous Scottish Guard of the earlier French kings and that many spoke neither English nor Scots. In 1550 a Scottish Montgomery, the Captain of the Guard, had the unfortunate distinction of acci-dentally killing King Henri II in a jousting tournament in Paris. Now I had to face the ordeal of talking in French to an audience of which nearly half were my own compatriots.

On this first post-war tour my happiest night in Paris was my last. We had saved money from our currency allowance, and my wife and I dined alone at the Café de la Paix. Wiser now to the mysteries of French menu prices, we had an excellent dinner. The evening was as warm as a perfect midsummer's night in

England. When we came out of the restaurant, there were no taxis, but only a line of cabs with rather good horses. "Let's take a cab," I said, and up I went to the driver, gave my address and asked how much. He named a price about five times higher than the fare of a taxi. For a moment I hesitated. But I have never been strong in resisting temptation. I saw a vision of the famous lady driver, red-coated, top-hatted and very smart, who made headlines in the French and British newspapers when she drove her cab from Paris to London and whom we had seen almost daily during our stay driving Americans up or down the Champs-Elysées. So in we jumped.

To my surprise our Jehu not only was a skilful driver, but also had a genuine love for his horse which went at a spanking trot the whole way and kept its place quite easily in the tangled mass of motor-traffic in the Champs-Elysées. It was an exhilarating experience, and the lights and the scent of the trees were more intoxicating than wine.

When we reached our hotel I had a long talk with our driver, mostly about horses and racing. Did I realise why the French racehorses had done so well in England that year? I confessed my ignorance. It was the oats that did it. France had a good harvest the previous year and the oats had been magnificent. Did I believe his horse could run last year like he ran tonight? I could bet my shirt that he couldn't. This year he had had the good oats. With that the driver said good night and drove off merrily for another fare.

Chapter VIII

TWILIGHT OR DAWN

"For love of domination we must substitute equality; for love of victory we must substitute justice; for brutality we must substitute intelligence; for competition we must substitute co-operation."

BERTRAND RUSSELL.

WESTERN EUROPE of today is dominated by two fears: fear of the Soviet Union and fear of Germany. Among the smaller nations fear of Soviet aggression predominates. In France fear of Germany is as strong as fear of the Soviet Union. I must admit also that in varying degrees the smaller nations share a common lack of confidence in the stability of post-war France. For myself I make a difference between the France of Paris and provincial France.

In my post-war visits to Paris I have felt myself immediately enveloped in an atmosphere of inertia and lack of faith. Politically France seemed hopelessly divided. The Gaullists wanted and want the military leadership of Europe as the reward for rearmament, and the project of a European Army, which is a French concept, is devised as much for this object as for the prevention of a military revival in Germany. There are many Frenchmen who believe that France is no longer strong enough to perform this rôle. They include the advocates of peace at almost any price. These escapists tried and are still trying to comfort themselves with uneasy hopes of remaining neutral in the event of a clash between the Soviet Union and the United States. Inevitably this conception fosters anti-Americanism. Those who believe in it maintain that France cannot afford a third liberation. Before the French Revolution France with twenty-five millions as compared with Austria's twenty-two, Russia's eighteen and Britain's nine had the largest population of any European country. Now France has fallen to fifth place.

In Paris I also found healthy elements. They included numerous champions of European federalisation who in their enthusiasm criticised the British Government for standing out. British approval of the project was not enough. She must be a federal partner. Failure to federalise, said these French champions, had ruined Greece. If Western Europe made the same error, Great Britain would be not only the culprit, but also one of the victims.

The Communists, still the largest political Party in voting power, followed the lead of Moscow.

In this confused atmosphere I accepted with more hope than conviction the official view that the majority of Frenchmen realised the necessity of an understanding with Germany and, sooner or later, would agree to any reasonable project which, backed by the United States and Britain, would unite France and Germany in the common defence of Western Europe.

In the provinces I found less preoccupation with politics, almost no pessimism, and an altogether better spirit, especially among the young people and the university students. They had their anxieties about their own future, and what European youth has not? They lacked the same respect for their elders that the French youth of my generation had always shown. They were, in fact, highly critical of both the politicians and the writers whom they blamed for decadence and for lack of ideas and ideals. In their criticism there was little or no cynicism. It was a challenging criticism which expressed itself in an attitude of mistrust towards complacency and compliance, an attitude of questioning before accepting blindly which is the right attitude and the prerogative of youth. I regarded it as a healthy criticism. In my view the university youth of provincial France is healthier, more curious-minded, and mentally and physically better equipped for what is admittedly a harder life than was the French youth of my own student days. In spite of the political disorder which he sees around him, I am convinced that the average French student refuses resolutely to accept the theory of the permanent decline of France.

During my tours of the provincial departments and universities I found much to strengthen my faith in France's future. I also had the opportunity of meeting several Prefects, members of that admirable body of men to whom France owes so much.

At Valence I lunched with the Prefect and his wife and, as usual, had more to eat and drink than the shrunken British digestion can stand. Like most French Prefects, our host was very able, very hard-working, and decisive. He was then engaged in super-intending the construction of a vast hydro-electric scheme. He was an admirer of Mr. Eden whom he described as the only English-man of his acquaintance who understood Europe, meaning of course that Mr. Eden was a friend of France. He had, in fact, met Mr. Eden at some pre-war conference at which Mr. Eden had advocated the sharing of French and British aerodromes.

On the future of France and Western Europe the Prefect spoke frankly and without any heat. Western Europe, he said, could not defend itself alone. It needed the help of the United States. But if Western Europe did not put its house in order, American aid would dry up. The key to the whole problem was Anglo-French solidarity and not, as many Americans and some English seemed to prefer, Anglo-American wooing of Germany at the expense of France. That would be fatal. I agreed with him and agree still.

At Nancy, too, I had long talks with the local Prefect who struck me as a particularly able man. He made no concealment of the weaknesses of France : the political discords, the selfishness of the rich bourgeois, and the tendency of the young peasants to leave the land in order to seek the regular hours and fixed wages of the industrial cities. He was not afraid of Communism which was on the decline. There were, he said, many Communists who now realised that they had nothing to expect from the Soviet Union. "I know," he added. "It is my business to know." From this I guessed that, if the Communists had their spies and fellow-travellers in Government offices and other high places, the Prefect himself had his informants inside the Communist Party. He ended on an optimistic note: "French Governments may come and go, but France will recover. She is rich and self-sufficient."

If we British were to have as frequent changes of Government as there are in France or to be so long without a government as France often is, we should almost certainly have a revolution. Thanks to her Prefects whose functions combine those of a lord-lieutenant, chief constable, and chairman of a county council, France carries on with little or no disturbance to the daily life of the people. Although they are subordinate to the Minister of the Interior, the Prefects have wide powers and are accustomed to take decisions far beyond the competence of our senior civil servants. I doubt if as good a system or as efficient and highly trained officials exist in any other country.

On my way to Nancy in the early train from Paris, the weather had turned wet and stormy, and the countryside, mostly farm-land with little villages on rising ground and meadows and canals lined with weeping willows and poplars, was deep in water. The rivers were in heavy flood. Bird-life seemed to have disappeared. Just before reaching Nancy I saw a single magpie.

At the station I was met by Mr. Arnould, the Nancy director of the British Council. He looked lugubrious and almost at once he told me that the British Council's services in France were being cut down drastically and that his own directorate was being closed. He had received the blow only that morning and it lay fresh and heavy upon him. The hard work of four years, he said, was being thrown away.

As more than forty years had passed since I had been last in Nancy, I was eager to see something of the town which, in the Stanislaus Place, has one of the finest squares in Europe. Arnould, however, was eager to show me all the work that the British Council had done, and I had not the heart to resist him. I spent a busy afternoon inspecting the Council's offices and library and recording at the Nancy Radio an unrehearsed interview in French on my impressions. I might have saved my energy for I soon discovered that without any support from me Arnould stood high in the estimation of everyone in Nancy from the Prefect and the General commanding the district downwards and that all regarded the closing of the Council's directorate as a disaster. Indeed, the Prefect begged me insistently to explain to our ambassador that

Nancy was far from Paris and Germany very near and that in this part of France Anglo-French relations were not so good that they could stand such a drastic proof of British poverty or British indifference.

I promised to do what I could, but I knew that my task would be in vain, although personally I thought the withdrawal a mistake. France is always a difficult country to know and today more so than ever when wounded pride makes Frenchmen of all ages sensitive. Doubtless, the British Council has not always used its funds wisely. There is in its charter almost no limit to what it may do, and obviously policy must be related to finance. But in France the Council had done a very good job, and in my opinion France is the one country in which it is wholly unsatisfactory to leave the conduct of Anglo-French relations entirely in the hands of the Paris Embassy. Between Paris and the provinces there are fundamental differences of attitude and character, and the gulf between the British and French ways of life is not easy to span. In this connexion the British Council can provide a far better bridge than can Embassy officials who today are immersed to the neck in an endless spate of politics and paper, or the Ambassador himself with his social obligations.

A much more stimulating experience was my visit to Grenoble, the capital of the Dauphiné. I went by car and was driven by Mr. Ruffer, director of the British Council for the Rhône district. He has every virtue including a fine war record, a perfect knowledge of French, and admirable administrative ability. His only defect in my eyes is a passion for fast driving. At first I was frightened by the speed, but, as we climbed higher and higher into mountain country, my heart rejoiced. Like Ruskin I believe that mountains are the beginning and the end of all natural scenery. It was my first visit to Grenoble which, built at the confluence of the Isère and Drac rivers, lies in the noblest surroundings, and even the most patriotic Scot must admit that the Scottish Highlands have nothing to compare with them.

My spirits were a little damped when, on arriving at our hotel, I found that my big suitcase had fallen off the top of the car during Ruffer's frenetic attempt to beat the Valence-Grenoble record.

R

All, however, was soon well. Within two minutes of what seemed a tragedy, the telephone rang in my room. The police had found the suitcase some nineteen kilometres away. It had fallen off very conveniently near the police station.

My lecture at the University went better than usual. The students were not particularly interested in Scotland, but were hot on the subject of decentralisation, and the presence of two or three Scottish students helped to stimulate enthusiasm. Afterwards Ruffer and I drove back to rescue my suitcase, and with the full moon shedding a ghostly light on the snow-capped mountains we made an unforgettable re-entry into the town.

The Dauphiné is quite unlike any other part of France. Food is scarcer. The wine is not so good, but like all mountaineers the people are hardy and independent. The big men of Grenoble are Bayard, the *chevalier sans peur et sans reproche,* Stendhal and Fantin-Latour, each of whom is honoured with a museum. The University, renowned for its summer course for foreign students, has a superb situation. In the opinion of the professors the best French-speaking Englishman is Harold Nicolson who is a Doctor *honoris causa* of the University and who, the Dean told me, gave the best address in French ever delivered by a foreigner.

I spent three busy days in Grenoble, had private talks with students, and was entertained by the Rector and the Dean. The students were full of heart and agreed with the Prefect of Nancy that Communism in France was on the decline both among the workers and among the intellectuals, and Ruffer, a shrewd and even cynical observer, shared this opinion. The professors, however, were less confident, and the Rector told me that the Communists were still gaining at the expense of the Socialists. Generalisations about any country are always dangerous and about France particularly so. But, although all Frenchmen want peace, I had the feeling that the older men desired it at almost any price, whereas youth was more resolute and by no means defeatist.

One day I was taken by car in glorious weather up the steep road to the Vercors, a natural fortress, which today bears the proud name of "Citadel of the French Resistance." It is a formidable mountain stronghold, heavily wooded and almost impenetrable.

The last bear was killed in 1898 and wolves, still existent, used to be numerous. Here, throughout the last war, the men of the maquis, supplied with arms by the special British organisation concerned with these subversive operations, harried the Germans and organised raids and sabotage.

Our route led through the wild Gorges d'Engins and the valley of the Furon, a small mountain stream in which, to my surprise, I saw several French anglers fishing for trout from banks deep in snow. From different points there were magnificent views of the mountains: La Grande Chartreuse, the Swiss Alps, and, above all, the Belledonne—the finest panorama of a range that I have ever seen. On my way home we made a détour in order to show me St. Nizier-de-Moucherotte where on June 15, 1944 the Germans, in a big attack on the maquisards, burnt the village to the ground. The Dauphinois are proud of the maquis. Brave Frenchmen of all faiths made their way there, and, although there were some bandit elements among them, I do not doubt that their example still fires the heart of their compatriots.

I have a passion for running water, and the Isère and the Drac of the Dauphiné have their place among my favourite streams. But the *supreme* river of France and perhaps of all Europe is the Rhône. I have caught trout in its gin-clear waters before it enters Lake Geneva from its source. My first view of the splendour of its lower reaches was at the end of an unforgettable motor-trip from Aix-en-Provence.

We made our way across country via Salon, whither Nostradamus, the sixteenth-century Jewish doctor, retired when his skill in dealing with the plague provoked the jealousy of his colleagues. In Salon he devoted himself to astrology, and his Almanach, a collection of remarkable predictions, had an astounding success both with prince and peasant.

From Salon we climbed to Les Baux with its ruined castle perched like an eagle's nest on the summit of a high, jagged peak. The view is one of the finest in the world and, although the historical glory of Les Baux is long past, it has its place in modern history, for it gives its name to bauxite which, discovered here in 1822, has produced the vast aluminiun industry of today.

Turning due north in superb spring weather we crossed the fine range of the Alpilles and, descending into the plain, were soon in Avignon.   And there before me in its sunlit glory was the Rhône.
No other river has had so profound a civilising influence on Europe.   Its course has seen the flow and ebb of barbaric invasions from the North, and thousands of Teutons have been drowned in its waters.   Along its banks the Romans advanced, paving the way for that Mediterranean civilisation which is the origin of European culture.   To the summer tourist it seems a stream of eternal sunshine, but its moods range from serenity to savagery and its hues from silvery blue to a despondent ochre.   It recalls to me the lines of John Buchan:

> "And by the lipping river path
> Where in the fog the Rhône runs grey,
> I see the heather in the strath
> And watch the salmon leap in Spey."

No two peoples have so many deep-rooted prejudices about each other as the French and the English, but to those English men and women who love France the French give their hospitality and their confidence.   These British lovers of France are numerous, but two, I think, are in their own way outstanding for the affection in which they are held by the French.   The first is a new acquaintance whom I met in Lyons where he was known to all as "Sir Parr".   He was then Mr. Robert Parr and had come to Lyons as British Consul-General in 1944 after a long record of service in the Middle East and in the French African colonies.
With his monocle, his old-fashioned, but well-fitting clothes, his beaver hat, his face clean-shaven but for the neatly trimmed side-whiskers, and his rotund figure, he belonged to a diplomatic school which I thought had long ceased to exist.   He spoke slowly in well-rounded sentences which rarely failed to impress.   His erudition covered a wide field.   He had written lyrical poetry. He knew his Dickens thoroughly and looked as if he himself had stepped out of a Dickens novel.   His knowledge of the history of the Rhône and of its wine district was profound and scholarly.

To know any aspect of French life better than a Frenchman is the straightest road to the French heart and the Lyonnais loved him, respected his judgment, and consulted him freely not only on Anglo-French matters but also on their own affairs.

He was also the king of hosts and no mean connoisseur of French food. The luncheon which he gave for us could not have been bettered in its choice excellence by Brillat-Savarin himself, and my wife who sat next to him enjoyed herself. Here is a sample of their conversation:

"How did you find Paris?"

My wife explained that she found the traffic so rapid and bewildering that she was afraid to cross the streets.

"Why cross the street?" Then after a pause: "What, pray, are taxis for? In Paris I consider it as essential to take a taxi in order to cross a street as it is to take a gondola to cross a canal in Venice."

I guessed that behind this slightly artificial façade of English phlegm there was an acute and active mind and that his knowledge of France and of the French must be of great value to our Embassy. Nor was I mistaken, for in the next birthday honours he received a well-earned Knighthood. The Lyonnais, I felt sure, would continue to call him "Sir Parr".

My other Francophile is Millicent, Duchess of Sutherland, who has spent her life among the French ever since the First World War. At her house at Juigny and at St. Vincent-sur-Jard I had written parts at least of my first books and with her had explored all the corners of Anjou and the Vendée. When I last saw her in the early summer of 1949, she was living in the famous No. 2 Rue de l'Ile St. Louis, once the home of Voltaire. She was, in fact, about to leave, but the packers were not coming until the next day. As she showed me her treasures, her pictures, her books, her writing-room with her signed photograph of Baudelaire, and her garden on the first floor with its fascinating view over the Seine, she talked of the past. She had known all the famous French men and women of the last fifty years, understood them, and liked most of them.

She was now old, but her face bore witness to her famous beauty.

Always utterly fearless and outspoken, she told me of her encounter with M. Thorez, the leader of the French Communist Party.

A year or two after the war there had been some trouble about her house, part of which was occupied by Polish refugees. They were suspected of hoarding arms, and the Communists, who were then in the Government, threatened to search the building. Her servants were frightened. Without hesitation she took up the telephone and rang up M. Thorez. "Who wants him?" said a gruff voice. "Millicent, Duchess of Sutherland." M. Thorez came, and, when she explained what had happened, he asked her to send a letter with all the details and he would look into the matter. The letter was sent. It included an invitation to tea. M. Thorez declined the invitation politely, but obviously took action, for the house was never again molested. Had the same contretemps occurred in Moscow, she would have got through to Stalin somehow or other, and my bet is that she would have gained her point.

Our farewell was emotional, for, although she was tired and therefore really wanted me to go, she kept holding me back as though eager to cling to the past.

Today there are two Frances. The first is epitomised in the words which Marshal Pétain spoke after the collapse of 1940. Going back to the heroism of the First World War, he said:

"Victory won, self-sacrifice yielded place to self-indulgence. Our deserts fell short of our demands, and being thrifty only in energy we encountered disaster."

This France radiates from Paris, and to my mind its worst and most dangerous feature is the selfishness of the wealthy bourgeois who, with no confidence in their own country, gamble against the franc and put personal before national security. French Communism gains its strength not so much from Stalin's propaganda as from the misuse of riches. As it has so often done at different periods in its history the Catholic Church today denounces this misuse of wealth, and, in particular, Father Riquet, the great Paris preacher and writer, has more than once reminded his listeners and his readers that a Christian is not rich for himself alone, but for the common good of human society. Judged by this standard, many rich Frenchmen are below par. To them apply the words of St. Jerome: "Every rich man is unjust himself or the inheritor of the injustice and iniquity of others." Today big money corrupts French politics and, consciously or unconsciously, works for the detriment of the whole country.

France is the most intellectual country in the world. Where we British can hardly maintain a single intellectual review, France counts them by the score. Is this, I often ask myself, a sign of French strength or of French weakness? Before the last war French writers were very serious about what they wrote. Now it seems to me that they are more concerned with how they write. They still do it better than the writers of any other nation, but the substance lacks any joy of living and loses itself in the quicksands of sterile criticism and of the sickness of decay. Much of the criticism, too, is querulous and ultra-introspective. Like Britain and, indeed, all Europe on both sides of the Iron Curtain, France has produced no great writer since the war. Is this a sign of permanent decline? According to M. Pierre Reverdy, the dice have long been thrown when an epoch begins to discuss its own decadence.

Again there is the French genius for oratory. Is it an asset or a liability today? In France it is learnt. I remember how as a young man I attended the senior class of the Lycée at Douai for philosophy and elocution. The senior boys could make a better speech than the average British politician. Their command of language was remarkable. Since then I have heard many of the great orators of Europe. For invective and passion Trotsky was outstanding. With hysterical emotion Kerensky could compel the wives of the rich Moscow merchants to throw their jewels on the platform when he was appealing for comforts for the unarmed, half-starving Russian soldiers in the trenches. I have seen Hitler lash a vast German crowd, intoxicated with nationalism, into a frenzy. But for classical oratory the French stand alone, and the greatest of modern French orators was Viviani, once a magician of words who swayed multitudes and today only a shadowy memory.

His method defeated him and in the end destroyed him. Every

speech which he made as Prime Minister put him out of action for three days: one in which to prepare his speech, the second to deliver it, and the third to recover from nervous exhaustion. He died in a home. A former anti-clerical, he became a prey to religious mania and spent his time in making little altars and in playing at being a priest.

In a world of violent changes words are not enough, and, as M. Maxime du Camp has left on record in his memoirs, there is a book to be written under the title of "The Influence of Rhetoric on the Misfortunes of France."

Much as I love Paris, I feel today that it oozes pessimism and that it contains too many clever men who talk seriously of the end of the world in an epoch which in the space of fifty years has seen the greatest changes in history. True it is that man's power to destroy himself has increased in a terrifying manner. But in every crisis of man's existence similar disasters have been predicted repeatedly. During the French Revolution and the Napoleonic Wars rumours of the end of the world were widespread and well-informed English writers described the changes of the period as the greatest since the beginning of time. Shrewder observers, however, realised that the French Revolution was burning out and saw already the revival of the Great Monarch myth although the title was then only First Consul. In the Soviet Union of today it is Generalissimo. Communist dogma teaches insistently: "Those who are not with us are against us." But in Paris—and in London too—there are men who are afraid to say: "Those who are not with us are with them."

Fortunately, there is another France, the France of the provinces, a France of sturdy, hard-working men, steeped in tradition, yet progressive, a France which produces great engineers, doctors, professors, scientists, and administrators; men who, unperturbed by political turmoils, go about their daily tasks with conscientious devotion. It is the France of which M. Clemenceau spoke in February 1912, when, referring to the Franco-German Treaty, he said: "we have been defeated, but we have not submitted. The living will be faithful to the dead. We have still something to say and to do in the world."

This France still exists. It lives in the new generation of French youth whose healthy outlook impresses me so deeply and whose actions, I feel sure, will confound the prophets of disaster. In this France I see determination to resist and to survive and a refreshing absence of that apathy which more than any other cause brings great and small nations to decay and ruin. Small nations like Norway, Holland and Denmark have suffered cruel blows, but they have never lost the traditions and characteristics of their race. To many their survival may seem miraculous, but, in point of fact it is the survival of quality as distinct from mere numbers.

Is there not then greater hope for France, the cradle of modern European culture and civilisation? I am sure there is. Just as there are Frenchmen who mistrust Britain, so, too, there are Englishmen who have no confidence in France. But the fate of the two nations is intertwined, and we have much to learn from each other.

In this connexion I agree with Harold Nicolson's dictum that for an Englishman "frequent visits to France are a necessary jog not only to the liver but to the heart and to the mind."

Most of all, however, when I think of France, I like to remember the words of another English Francophile who has so often suffered in his career from being right too soon for the leisurely pace of his countrymen and who has the power beyond all other orators to rouse to action the heart and mind of resolute men.

In a broadcast exhortation to France during the last war, Winston Churchill ended his message with these words:

"Good night, then sleep to gather strength for the morning. For the morning will come. Brightly it will shine on the brave and true, kindly on all who suffer for the cause, and gloriously upon the tombs of heroes. Thus shall shine the dawn. *Vive la France.*"

Today the Europe in which I spent the best years of my life is gone for ever, and it would be as easy to paint the present in gloomy colours as to predict that the future will be hard for Europeans and hardest of all for European youth. The dangers and puzzling perplexities of the atomic age cast a dark shadow over a shrinking world. They arise from fundamental weaknesses in man himself who has a formidable list of evil characteristics including envy, hate, fear, cruelty, racial prejudice and lust for dominion over his fellows. There will be no end to wars so long as mass emotion continues to express itself in admiration of dictators and conquerors, and today there are probably more people who worship Stalin than Jesus.

It is, too, a disturbing thought that, biologically at least, man has not altered since his first appearance on earth and that, if a child of primitive man were to come into the world today and to be brought up with children of intellectual parents, he would learn their habits, their thoughts and their cultured speech and might even acquire them more quickly.

This, however, is only one facet of the many-sided truth. The quality that has enabled man, the weakling, to survive is his intelligence which has made him master over all other animals. Through the increase of scientific knowledge this precious gift has brought him immense material benefits and, if used rightly, can give him peace and plenty.

I therefore end this book on a note of optimism, partly because although both hope and fear are irrational, a reasonable optimism nurtures hope and helps to drive out the fear which strangles our present existence, but mainly because I consider that a reasonable optimism is justified.

Although the military power of the world has now passed to Eurasia and to the New World, I believe that, sooner or later, both will undergo much the same social convulsions which Europe has experienced and survived. I have no faith in the permanence of Stalinism, and social changes in the New World are taking place more rapidly than many Europeans realise.

Europe, therefore, has altered less and perhaps lost less than the pessimists and revolutionaries believe. It still produces the best thought. Its inventive power is undiminished, and with a long acquaintance with the habits of various European nations I have great confidence in the fortitude, physical energy and mental vigour of European youth.

Although it is as foolish to ignore the past as to cling to it with nostalgic regret, it is right that youth should look to the future not only with hope but also with an open mind. It is among the youth of Europe that one finds the strongest support for European federation and eventually for some form of world government. It is a healthy sign. Today the world is already unified economically in a higher degree than ever before. Its hope for the future is that, stimulated by the instinct of self-preservation, it will have the intelligence to unify itself politically.

INDEX

INDEX

Manchester Public Library, 18
Marchand, René, 53
Marconi, Marchese Guglielmo, 47
Margaret, Princess of Denmark, 155, 156
Marshall, Gen., 124, 126
Marx, Carl, 75, 81, 210
Masaryk, Jan, 87–103, 106, 107, 110–118, 120–127, 129, 131–9, 203
Masaryk, Thomas, 87, 89, 101, 102, 111–12, 115, 131, 134, 137, 139
Maude, Aylmer, 13
Mayakovsky, 36, 65
Medhurst, Arthur, 9
Mein Kampf, 164, 205
Memoirs of a British Agent, 29, 36, 42, 45, 48, 68
Merriman, Seton, 4, 5
Mexico City, 42
Michelsen, André, 68–9
Michels, Edgar. *See* Baron Michels van Verduynen
Moeller, Mme. Christmas, 174
Moeller, Gustav, 147, 152
Molotov, M., 72, 75, 83, 88, 89
Montgomery, Field-Marshal Viscount, 167, 169, 173
Mounet-Sully, 240
Moura, 48, 54, 55–6
Munch, 166
Munich Agreement, 92, 100, 102, 106, 122, 123, 131, 132, 135, 136, 191, 212
Mussert, 204
Mussolini, Benito, 71, 191

Nelidov, 206

Netherlands, The, 200–8, 217, 255
Amsterdam, 203, 204
Breuklen, 201
Netherlands-England Society, 202
Rotterdam, 203
The Hague, 202, 203, 205
The Hague—British Embassy, 129, 202–3
Walcheren, 202
Werfelwind, 204
New York, 51–52
Century Club, 52
Waldorf-Astoria Hotel, 51
New York Herald Tribune, 129
Nicholas, Grand Duke, 22, 23
Nicholas, Tsar, 206
Nicholas II, Tsar of Russia, 12, 20, 23–5, 55, 72
Nichols, Sir Philip, K.C.M.G., M.C., 90, 98, 100, 114, 127, 129, 203, 207
Nicolson, Harold, 248, 255
Nobel Prize, 57, 155, 166
North Atlantic Council, 224
North Atlantic Treaty Organisation, 149, 165, 172, 173, 204, 217, 218
Norway, 42, 143, 157–167, 175, 255
Bergen, 157
Christiania, 157. *See also* Oslo
Communists in, 161
Eckeberg, 161
Frederichstat, 159
Frijheid, 161
German Occupation, 158, 159, 163, 165
Holmenkollen, 158